Gathering Those Driven Away

Also by Wendy Farley from Westminster John Knox Press

Tragic Vision and Divine Compassion: A Contemporary Theodicy
The Wounding and Healing of Desire: Weaving Heaven and Earth

GATHERING THOSE DRIVEN AWAY

A Theology of Incarnation

Wendy Farley

WESTMINSTER
JOHN KNOX PRESS
LOUISVILLE · KENTUCKY

First edition
Published by Westminster John Knox Press
Louisville, Kentucky

11 12 13 14 15 16 17 18 19 20—10 9 8 7 6 5 4 3 2 1

Scripture quotations from the New Revised Standard Version of the Bible are copyright © 1989 by the Division of Christian Education of the National Council of the Churches of Christ in the U.S.A. and are used by permission.

Quotations of lyrics from the song "Soldier Laddie" by Dervish are used by permission of Michael Holmes/Dervish.

The Quotation from Nan Merrill's *Lumen Christi—Holy Wisdom: Journey to Awakening* (Continuum 2002), copyright © Nan C. Merrill, is used with the permission of Continuum.

Excerpts from *Hadewijch: The Complete Works*. Translated by Mother Columba Hart, OSB. Copyright © 1980 by The Missionary Society of St. Paul the Apostle in the State of New York. Paulist Press, Inc., New York/Mahwah, NJ. Reprinted by permission of Paulist Press, Inc. www.paulistpress.com.

Book design by Sharon Adams
Cover design by Night & Day Design

Library of Congress Cataloging-in-Publication Data
Farley, Wendy, 1958–
    Gathering those driven away : a theology of Incarnation / Wendy Farley.—1st ed.
      p. cm.
    Includes bibliographical references.
    ISBN 978-0-664-23321-1 (alk. paper)
    1. Incarnation. 2. Marginality, Social—Religious aspects—Christianity. I. Title.
BT220.F37 2011
232'.1—dc23
                                       2011023556

To Maggie

Contents

Acknowledgments

The older I get the more I realize how deeply my thoughts are largely embedded in communities that shape me and give me my particular point of view. This book draws attention to the marginal voices of Christianity, those despised and turned away by many mainstream institutions. But at this moment I feel gratitude for the institutions that have nourished me, which have not turned me away.

I am grateful to the Department of Religion and the Graduate Division of Religion at Emory. They have remained equally committed to diversity and congeniality, holding on to these with great discipline and integrity. In the process, I believe all of our scholarship has been invigorated and become more creative. It is easy to lose sight of the significance of this accomplishment in the preoccupation with daily academic chores. But it is also in these daily chores that these commitments are sustained.

Another setting is that of the Constructive Theological Workgroup, whose energy, ethical commitments, and collegiality remain continually inspiring. The range of writing produced by members of this group weaves in and out of this book, sometimes acknowledged in footnotes. But more than particular books, it is simply the existence of this group that helps to make possible work like my own.

Looking further back, I am grateful that I did my own graduate training at Vanderbilt Divinity School, where the ethical passions of my professors reinforced the rigor of their analysis and the creativity to which they called us. I would like to give a particular shout-out to Jack Forstman, former dean of the Divinity School. His support of my work from the very beginning, notwithstanding the complexities of attending a school where my dad taught, made my entrance into graduate work possible. He was a wonderful teacher, as gracious with the figures we studied as with us. His gigantic laugh will haunt my ears (I hope) all my days. In particular, I want to acknowledge his astonishing moral compass. When my partner and I talked with him over a glass of wine one December, she recalled the painful reception she received as an M.Div. student at Candler School of Theology when she tried to create a space for the LGBT community: Sacred Worth. Jack was sympathetic to the pressures a dean might feel but in his nonjudgmental way recalled the opposite response that occurred under his watch at Vanderbilt. We wish that people who write inspiring works like *Christian Faith in Dark Times* are as inspirational in real life, but it is not always the case. His deep goodness is evident in his spontaneous recognition of the moral high ground, even at those moments when it is not at all clear in which direction history is moving. I loved him all the more when he told the story of his own coming to graduate work. He finished college at a somewhat conservative Christian school and sold insurance. This path to fortune if not fame was rerouted when a small church in Alabama asked him to be their preacher. He said he did not know what—or that—he believed. They accepted him on these terms. They would explore questions of doubt and faith together. It is perhaps because he entered ministry and then graduate education on the basis of his doubt that his moral compass has stayed so clear these many years.

I cherish these things but I think I cherish even more Jack's long, deep laughter. I hear it wafting on the air like pipe smoke. I cherish the sound of my father's piano, the gentle riffs of jazz that I have heard almost every evening I have been home. I can see in my mind's eye Jack and my father's radiant smiles, so happy to see each other, to see their wives, children, grandchildren, friends. They are both old men now but they have the large hearts that are the gift to them for their ruthless honesty and enduring kindness. They have taught me about the vocation of a scholar, but mostly they have shown me by simply being who they are. Their capacity for ordinary joy and clear-eyed embrace of the inevitabilities of aging is poignant testimony to their own "courage to be."

I am also grateful to my dad, who has read drafts of this work and saved me from some of my worst impulses. He is, as always, a generous and incisive reader, somehow combining unqualified support with searing questions that take my understanding through doors I did not even know existed. It is a great gift to have a smart and learned person willing to read one's work. But it is even more wonderful to have a father who so thoroughly supports my work, even—perhaps especially—when it moves in directions different from his own. And it is only fair to acknowledge, too, the unflagging love and support of my mother, whose own work among abused teenagers, homeless men and women, young women ministers (still, at seventy-nine) remains a witness to the deep ethical and activist roots of faith.

My professors taught me theology and philosophy but mostly they embodied for me something of the ethical vigor of a scholar's life: Sally McFague, who directed my dissertation and showed us that women could be theologians and continues to inspire us to remember the fragility of the body of God; Peter Hodgson, who taught me Hegel and the joys of sailing, who read with such tenderness Coleridge's poem, "To a Young Ass," and who taught liberation theology when there were not many to do so; John Compton, who, smiling his spritely smile, threw Husserl's *Logical Investigations* across the room when I demurred adding it to my exam list; Walter Harrelson, who always welcomed me like Santa Claus when I was discouraged; Mary Ann Tolbert, whose generosity to a disoriented first-year student I still cherish; Gene TeSelle, who protested Reagan's wars in Central America in between classes on Augustine and Athanasius. They donned their black robes to march against apartheid and cancelled classes the week of the presidential election so we could drive people from the inner city to the polls. They wrote skits poking fun at the students (as we did in return) and danced and drank with us at parties.

These scholars prove that the invisible church can be found in the most unlikely places. When I am tempted to throw up my hands in despair of "the church," I remember them. They are the church; they live a faith that is deep and wide, generous and compassionate, courageous and skeptical. I am inspired by their long dedication to learning, their ever-deepening ethical passions, and their generosity to the next generation—especially to women and other marginal identities.

I am unspeakably grateful to this community of scholars for everything they have done for me, and for the study of religion, and in defense of theology's prophetic vision.

Gratitude for another aspect of my work is due to Daniel Braden and Don McKim. Don has shepherded two of my books through the publishing process, and I am grateful for his care and kindness. Daniel is the kind of relentless editor that writers like me desperately need in the transition from ideas to readable text. I offer many thanks to both for making this book possible.

Preface

A few friends gather on Christmas Eve, sharing the joy of the season. At one point the women each tell a story that captures the meaning of Christmas for them. One woman chooses to accompany the stories with improvised piano music. In this theology of incarnation narrative and music are equally essential to its meaning. The first woman recalls her boredom at a Christmas Eve service. She is about to depart but sees a woman sitting alone, "holding a child to her bosom," oblivious to the service. "There, at that moment, I came upon the sanctuary, the holy place, I had been seeking so long in vain." The woman is simply dressed but her "grand and *gentil* bearing made of the open bench an enclosed chapel." Her face displayed gladness and dejection, "Yet what was communicated through it all was a sense of affable serenity, of loving devotion—radiating gloriously from her dark, downcast eyes. . . . The child also seemed to me uncommonly lovely. It stirred energetically and yet quietly, and seemed absorbed in a half-unconscious dialogue of love and yearning with its mother."[1] The woman became a "glorious tragic figure, who has influenced my life and my inner being more than anyone in this world. . . . Although I have had nothing but sorrows to share with her, yet I count my association with her among the loveliest, weightiest of my life." The beautiful baby grows up to be killed in a war: "he died so heroically, and so sense-less, for the cause of freedom."[2] The three women tell stories which are ordinary moments of life: a chance encounter in a church, a spontaneous baptism, the near-death of an infant. Each vignette traverses the tenderness of love and the anguish of death. Each of these ordinary mothers' stories becomes the story of the incarnation. In their memories of Christmas, of serenity, death, love, they see

---

1. Schleiermacher, *Christmas Eve: A Dialogue on the Incarnation*, 58.
2. Ibid.

that every mother is Mary and every child is Christ. "Only the mother also sees the heavenly rays already streaming out from him."[3] Joseph enters at the end of the dialogue, putting an end to the theological pontificating of the men.

> For me, all forms are too rigid, all speech-making too tedious and cold. Itself unbounded by speech, the subject of Christmas claims, indeed creates, in me a speechless joy, and I cannot but laugh and exult like a child. Today all men are children to me, and are all the dearer on that account. The solemn wrinkles are for once smoothed away, the years and cares do not stand written on the brow. Eyes sparkle and dance again, the sign of a beautiful and serene existence within. . . . The long, deep, irrepressible pain in my life is soothed as never before. . . . I look upon all things with a gladsome eye, even what has most deeply wounded me. . . . And so I have roamed about the whole evening, everywhere taking part most heartily in every little happening and amusement I have come across. I have laughed, and I have loved it all. It was one long affectionate kiss which I have given to the world. . . . Come, then, and above all bring the child if she is not yet asleep, and let me see your glories, and let us be glad and sing something religious and joyful![4]

3. Ibid., 63.
4. Ibid., 85, 86.

Introduction

And in that day, says the Beloved, I will assemble the lame and gather those who have been driven away.

Paraphrased from Micah 4:6

If my sister or brother is not at the table, we are not the flesh of Christ. If my sister's mark of sexuality must be obscured, if my brother's mark of race must be disguised, if my sister's mark of culture must be repressed, then we are not the flesh of Christ. It is through and in Christ's own flesh that the "other" is my sister, is my brother; indeed, the "other" is me. . . . "The establishment of the Church is re-creation of the world. But it is only in the union of all the particular members that the beauty of Christ's body is complete" [Gregory of Nyssa].[1]

For me, the genesis of theology is pain. When my heart is broken, I expect theology to walk with me. It is, naturally, not my only companion in pain, but it is the one that erupts in writing. Theology is an academic discipline, a handmaid of the church, a doctrinal tradition. But it is also *sapientia*. It is longing for wisdom: pain seeking understanding. I do not find theology consoling because it provides me with correct answers. This is impossible and not even to be desired. Correct answers, even imagining there were such things, could help only the thinnest strand of mind. It might satisfy certain aspects of discursive reasoning, but that is neither bread nor roses for the suffering heart. Theology is a practice

---

1. M. Shawn Copeland, *Enfleshing Freedom*, 82.

that uses words and ideas, books and concepts to throw one's mind and heart toward the eternally Erotic Abyss that is our heart's desire. Theology lingers at the margin of concepts, passing back and forth between the womb of Divinity and the discipline of thought. Its language is shaped by the tradition in which it finds itself, the voices past and present who have written their longing and pain in the language of doctrine. Like poetry, its truth is evocative rather than literal. Its universality is the power of a particular voice to convey its pain and consolation.

The wound that moves in this particular piece of writing is the fight over sexual minorities in the Christian churches. It pierces me like a knife to know that some Christians insist that desire obscures the divine image: it renders lovers of Christ unable to minister, unable to parent, unable to share Communion, unable to be people of faith. The heart that is led to love and desire outside heterosexual marriage is understood to be uniquely unsuited to love and desire Christ.

The wound of this is not limited to the situation of gay, lesbian, and queer Christians: a small group of dispensable persons. The conflict over sexuality that troubles the "weaker brethren" tears the veil off Christianity's more general betrayals of the gospel. Recently the Vatican was quoted as saying, in an eerie echo of the chief priests, that it was better to hide the abuse by priests than to expose the honor of the church to criticism. Better a few suffer than the whole church be dishonored. Along with the irrelevance of children, the secondary humanity of women is so naturalized that it becomes laborious to cite examples. These moments when vulnerable members of the body of Christ are shown to be dispensable reveals something about the core identity of the church.

This might become clearer by a contrast. During World War II the people of La Chambon-Sur-Lignon spontaneously made a complex and dangerous underground that created schools to hide Jewish children and that helped thousands of refugees over the border. They were mostly Protestants scratching out a living in the French mountains near the border with Switzerland. But in the moment of historical crisis, they knew exactly where they stood and what their faith required. In interviews they became uncomfortable, not understanding the fuss: what else could they have done?[2] Such a stark contrast with the casual cruelty of homophobia, the acceptance of child abuse, the denigration of women!

The situation of queer Christians reveals the wound in so much of Christianity: it cannot perceive in its own members the beauty of Christ's body. Christians disagree about many things, as we always have. The author of the Johannine Letters gives us clues how to navigate disagreements. "Beloved, do not believe every spirit, but test the spirits to see whether they are from God. . . . Beloved, let us love one another, because love is from God; everyone who loves is born of God and knows God. Whoever does not love does not know God, for God

---

2. This story is told in Philip P. Hallie, *Lest Innocent Blood Be Shed*, and also in the wonderful documentary by Pierre Sauvage, *Weapons of the Spirit* (2007).

is love. . . . By this we know that we abide in him and he in us, because he has given us of his Spirit. . . . There is no fear in love, but perfect love casts out fear; for fear has to do with punishment, and whoever fears has not reached perfection in love. We love because he first loved us. Those who say, 'I love God,' and hate their brothers or sisters, are liars; for those who do not love a brother or sister whom they have seen, cannot love God whom they have not seen" (1 John 4:1, 7–8, 13, 18–20). First Peter makes a similar point: "Above all, maintain constant love for one another, for love covers a multitude of sins. Be hospitable to one another without complaining" (1 Peter 4:8–9). The way we treat one another is the sign of how we dwell in the divine presence. It is not a political or social issue; it is the most visible fruit of faith. If we fail here, we fail everywhere. If we revile any person, we defile the roots of our faith. Hard-heartedness toward sexual minorities is like finding a dead canary in the coal mine. Invisible poison has killed a tiny, insignificant bird but it will kill us too. But this is true of every person we are tempted to think of as dispensable: illegal immigrants, people without health care, the destitute of other lands, desperate people whose minds have been seduced by violence. It is true of the land itself, which cries out against our ravages.

There is no power that can resist that of the Divine Eros, who created humanity in its own image. To imagine that we humans could overthrow the power of ultimate reality is to imagine a Manichean world in which good and evil hang in the balance; in some ultimate and fundamental sense evil can contest the goodness of creation. We humans are free only to be what we are: bearers of the divine image. Everything else is bondage, and it is this bondage from which incarnate Wisdom seeks to free us. We human beings certainly share the solidarity of suffering that comes from this bondage. We are cruel and ignorant; we mar our beauty with self-loathing or consumer obsessions. We harm one another and ourselves by unskillful use of our sexuality. Adultery, sexual abuse, callous sex between spouses, betrayal, and objectification are all ways in which we harm one another. Domination of a partner, psychic cruelty, the implacable deadening of a loveless marriage can work catastrophic spiritual harm. Joyless promiscuity that honors neither ourselves nor our partners can forge chains that conceal the divine image from us. But of all the things that hold us in bondage, desire for our lover is the least likely to work us lasting harm. It is a form of love and as such is healing, lovely—a particularly potent sacrament of the eternal lovemaking between God and creation. Gay men and lesbians can use their sexuality in trivial or harmful ways, like everyone else. But how many girls and women have been abused by fathers, uncles, dates, pastors, strangers? How many wives or girlfriends must endure the casual cruelty of a dominating lover? This continent of normalized heterosexual suffering seems very large compared to the relatively small scale of homosexual violence. That sexual violence is a particular vice of too many heterosexual men is well known. Yet there is no call for heterosexual men to deny their sexuality altogether because some of them use it badly. They are not in principle excluded from ministry or community.

The other side of same-sex desire is the healthy, stable, and loving relationships and families it sustains. It does not seem to be a variable in whether a person is a good partner or parent or pastor. The existence of particularly wise, talented, compassionate, and creative gay and lesbian pastors and priests means that the calling to ministry by the Holy Spirit does not respect the boundaries of gender or sexuality. The existence of happy, stable families parented by same-sex couples means that being heterosexual is neither a necessary nor a sufficient requirement for a healthy family. That gays and lesbians generate healthy relationships, families, and ministries is simply a fact. They exist and so it must be possible. If healthy faith, committed relationships, and stable families are signs of blessing, then it does not seem God hates sexual minorities.[3]

The life-giving possibilities of queer desire and the harmfulness of many heterosexual relationships are not hidden, not secret. *People* magazine often has stories about both forms of desire, as does Oprah or Dr. Phil. They are no more difficult to see than other obvious truths: Jews were not vermin infecting an otherwise healthy Europe. Neither the Irish nor the Africans were subhuman beings without culture, worthy only of death or servitude. If you deprive women or black people or factory workers of education, they will be less educated than white, well-educated men. Native American children did not require salvation through incarceration in demeaning and abusive schools. Early Christians were not atheists and they did not eat babies. These are examples of outsized, outrageous, obvious lies, but ones that not only structured society and shaped history but in most cases were manufactured with the help of Christian theology and Scripture. The ease with which lies and deception become common sense is intrinsic to the way in which the power of domination works in history and in the church. Simple facts, the events of history, the teachings embedded in tradition and Scripture, the meaning of our identities are all vulnerable to ruthless prevarication. Lies hide obvious truths.

Every one of the groups singled out for mistreatment has an interesting culture and bears a distinctive, irreplaceable wisdom. Every socially and theologically manufactured degradation defaces individual persons whose unique beauty is lost to themselves and their community and to the family of humanity. If "sin" means anything at all it is this: to violate the goodness created and bestowed by a generous Divinity and to do so in "his" name. This is a general point. More specifically, to accept demeaning lies about sexual minorities and same-sex desire is to defraud precious human beings of their power to recognize themselves and others as bearers of the divine image. To use Scripture to do so is a particularly repellent abuse of what should be medicine and food from our Beloved. To imagine that same-sex desire so uniquely disqualifies someone from the human

---

3. For a particularly appalling example of religious hatred, one can look up the Godhatesfags Web site or read the book that exposes this group: Michael Cobb, *God Hates Fags*.

race that we are required to break communion with those who tolerate it seems the grossest violation of almost everything characteristic of gospel faith.

The world is full to overflowing with pain. It is a relentless source of dismay for a person of faith to struggle with the omnipresence of radical, destructive suffering. But for the source of suffering to come from the church and be justified by its Scripture and traditions is a kind of toxic, crushing pain that is hard to endure. It is particularly wounding for abuse to come from one's own home. Where does one turn to discover that one is beautiful, cherished, smart, interesting, important, if one's parents deny this every day? How can we be formed for love and respect if those most intimate to us withhold these? When the church itself speaks outsized lies about us, where do we go for truth? When the church withholds divine love, where can we go to learn our true name? We can run away from home. We can create a new family and identity. But we will be forever defrauded of the intimate nurture of our original family. Our first language will always be lies and danger.

The genesis of this book is pain. But it is mostly a long love letter to the Beloved, incarnate in the world, in Scripture, in Jesus, in every human being—even those that one might find irritating. I find in my tradition enormous nurture. Wisdom refracts herself in every culture and for every need. She is "vindicated by all her children" (Luke 7:35). The institutional church may have needs for exclusion and hostility, for purity and moral righteousness, for stability and the illusion of continuity. But the gospel also presents other faces of Wisdom, other aspects of faith. The gospel is an odd interjection of some other reality into the midst of the powers and principalities that dominate history, and the outcast has a particular wisdom about the shadow side of power. The gospel's countersign to might never gains the upper hand. It never displaces the main engines of power that govern world events. It tells the story of a kingdom always within and around us, but it is not a kingdom of this world. It speaks the truth about this world. The gospel does not remove us from the violence of the world or neutralize the lies it tells about us. But it listens to our pain and believes our stories. It tells us we are beloved and that we are essential to the story of the Divine Eros. Without our particular, unique, unrepeatable beauty, the beauty of creation would be incomplete. Without mothers, the motherhood of God would be invisible. Without queer lovers, the full range of the Divine Eros would be unfulfilled. Without the outcasts, Wisdom's joyous indifference to social norms would be unknown. The witness of Christianity's rejected and despised is essential to the gospel.

The witness of the great diversity of Christ's lovers is of an entirely different order than some tepid obligation to be inclusive. The church requires the voices of those driven away because these are ones that Wisdom herself uses: lovers of Christ who were declared heretics or were burned or consigned to silence, those who are difficult to find in seminary curriculum, womanist, feminist, queer, activist. They may not make up the structure of the institutional church, but without them the body of Christ is hopelessly maimed and dismembered.

We can be grateful that the institutional churches have what is required to carry Christianity forward through history. But the institution, ingenious in its mimicking of regimes of domination, is not what makes the church the body of Christ. Christ's own body was poor, brutalized, murdered. He describes the bodies of prisoners, of sick people, of the naked and hungry as his own body. Without those driven away, Christianity cannot be the body of Christ. A paradox lies at the heart of this body: Christianity moves through history carried by the impulses of domination and exclusion. It despises uppity women, no-hellers, contemplatives, queers, and thinks even less of those people outside Christianity altogether. But without their witness to the nearness and tender mercies of Emmanuel the memory of Christ is impossibly distorted.

The story of how women, slaves, queers, foreigners, and contemplatives were cast out of the *ecclesia* or kept on in humiliating servitude testifies, in a paradoxical way, to truths prefigured in the Gospels. In the gospel, incarnate Divinity is mercilessly destroyed by the completely predictable and commonplace superiority of might. But the good news of the gospel is that this victory is not the only reality. Through this story we are invited into the tender, fragile, adamantine kingdom of God. This odd metaphor initiates us into the strange world of incarnation because it is a kingdom that is nothing at all like kingdoms of this world: it is more like a hand grenade than an analogue. Feminists and others have been uncomfortable with this metaphor of empire and hierarchy. It did prove an imperfect strategy to subvert the meaning of *baseleia* by countering the law of empire with the law of love. A kingdom like the one Jesus preached and enacted counters the lies and violence of kings and their laws. But the subversion was too easily reabsorbed into regimes of power, and kings became, again, the upholders of divine right. Their hierarchical and violent justice testified to a divine sovereign that mirrors heaven on earth.

But the metaphors of the kingdom retain their subversive potential. In them we recover a way to interpret and inhabit our own stories. Rome and their lackeys in Jerusalem had no trouble arresting and killing an annoying prophet, incarnate Divinity or not. We should not quickly pass over the fact that whatever kind of power the Divine Eros possesses it did not seem to get much of a foothold against the power of Rome. Christians have turned this story into a theology of sacrificial atonement that keeps the Trinity in total control of the whole narrative, but we might linger over the raw historical fact that Jesus was impotent when the Roman Empire decided to take him down. We might remember this when we are caught in the maw of history, helpless in the hands of violent persons or wanton nature. When an unjust legal system steals our children or executes our sons we can remember that our Savior received no better. The gospel is not about a power that dissolves the efficacy of might.

On the other hand, neither is the gospel a bowed head, a hope that this will all get sorted out "farther along, Lord, farther along." Rome ended Jesus' life but became impotent when it came to ending his story. Something remains: something with no analogue in the kingdom of might. It is conjured through laws of contradiction that use Augustus Caesar's titles (Son of God, Savior, Prince of Peace) to describe the significance of a tortured criminal. Crazy, amoral stories linger in the air about sheep and seeds and widows and fathers and kings who behave in ways no patriarchal authority would ever behave. A meal gathers strangers and abolishes their social standing. When they slip out they are slaves again, women subject to the paterfamilias. But for a moment, like slaves in American hush arbors, they bore the full luminosity of their divine image. The incarnation of Wisdom in Jesus of Nazareth is announced in an impenetrable interplay of success and failure, victory and defeat. If we use it as a lens—perhaps a kaleidoscopic one—for understanding the displacement of Christ's lovers by their own church, our situation may take on a different meaning and our proximity to the Beloved might be witnessed anew.

Jesus suffered defeat at the hands of Rome, but the news of some other kingdom was not silenced. The defeat was predictable; the persistence of this whisper is not. The victory of patriarchy for control of the church is likewise perfectly predictable. Privilege and power are not easily renounced. The rule of love is exceedingly dangerous in a totality that maintains its political power through terror, privilege, and theologies of sovereignty. The failure of the kingdom to create nonpatriarchal institutions is foreshadowed in the gospel itself. Christ befriended women, as he did outcasts, lepers, soldiers, and sexual deviants. He entrusted a small group of women with the story of the Messiah's love and his victory over death. But their words "seemed to them [the apostles] an idle tale, and they did not believe them" (Luke 24:11). Many male disciples did not believe them, and much of the church they created in Jesus' name still does not believe them. The one, true apostolic church is built on the testimony of those who rejected the apostles chosen by Jesus. Incarnate Wisdom is merciful and does not reject those who reject her. The church has survived through two thousand years in many alien and difficult lands. But the story it tells about itself in history books is the story of those who betrayed the gospel and retold it to serve their own needs. It is like the story of Ireland told by the British or the story of the American West told by the U.S. cavalry.

For all of its brilliance and variety, mainstream theology has rarely extended its full reach. It has not been able to stretch fully into the awareness of the Divine Eros as the foundation of all reality, within which Christians are only the tiniest drop. It cannot embrace the random, chaotic, amoral beauty of the cosmos, irreducible to our needs or our ordering.[4] It violates the universal implications of the commandment to love by envisioning humanity split into sinners and saved. It cannot translate divine mystery into humility about our small efforts toward understanding. These constraints on spiritual practice and theology are like the mutilations the Greeks used to inflict on their slaves: cutting a tendon

---

4. Sally McFague's *New Climate for Theology: God, the World, and Global Warming*, Catherine Keller's *Face of the Deep: A Theology of Becoming*, and Daniel Spencer's *Gay and Gaia: Ethics, Ecology, and the Erotic* are examples of theologians attempting to dislodge our anthropocentric prejudices.

in their leg so they could hobble around in service of the master but could not escape. The condemnations of Christianity's great theologians—Origen, John Scotus Eriugena, Marguerite Porete, Meister Eckhart—are not because these betrayed the gospel. They did not enslave anyone or conflate the Divine with something merely human or reject the healing power of Christ. They reject the idea of hell. They identify the deepest nature of the Divine as abysmal love. They embody compassion in the pursuit of wisdom. This is not to say that canonical theologians do not offer brilliant insight into the human spirit in its search for the Divine. But by shackling our theology to the relentless assertion of authority, we have destroyed books and bodies that moved boldly beyond what institutions could tolerate. We have silenced some of our best spirits, transforming their devotion into a capital crime.

Marcella Althaus-Reid proposes another way: "The queer nation of the world represents in this way the second coming of God the Stranger. Curiously, it seems that we can know God better through a radical negation of the way of closeted knowing found in the tradition of the church and theology. This is the queer, stranger God who in our time and age is showing God's face amongst people who are God's lovers—and queer lovers at that."[5] Attention to the underside of Christian history and practice is an ethical obligation, an attempt at reconciliation after our long violence. It is a spiritual practice as well. Restoring the witness of the underside for Christian theology allows tradition to breathe into its own wounds and dead spaces, integrating what it has attempted to destroy and enlivening its wisdom with the wisdom it rejected.

For many on the underside there is only one word of gospel: love. "Know it well, love was his meaning. Who reveals it to you? Love. What did he reveal to you? Love. Why does he reveal it to you? For love. Remain in this, and you will know more of the same. But you will never know different, without end."[6] This love includes a call for justice, because it is through justice that the preciousness of the divine image is preserved in community. But this is justice as one of the faces of love, not justice hooded by authority and deformed into just desert. Because those on the underside know so viciously the betrayal of love, it is their witness that draws us back to the Beloved. The witness of love to the despised and by the despised is witness to the fundamental truth of the gospel. Monica Coleman tells the story of Kathi Martin, who founded the GSN (God, Self, and Neighbor) Ministries in Atlanta, "to teach this theology to all people but especially the black gays and lesbians who desperately need to believe that they are made in the image of God." Through this kind of ministry "they 'make a way of out no way.' They 'walk a way out of no way.' They 'love a way out of no way.' In so doing, they help to create the community of God here on earth."[7] The institutional church teaches that love is central to the Christian message,

5. *The Queer God*, 171.
6. Julian of Norwich, *Showings*, 342.
7. Monica Coleman, *Making a Way Out of No Way*, 165, 166.

but radical, nonjudgmental, universal love tends to cut against the impulses that preserve institutional authority. Because those on the margins of the church have less invested in the defense of authority, the intensity of divine love is sometimes better remembered there.

The perspective of the margins may or may not be privileged, but it reconnects with the witness of Jesus' first apostles. We see the Christ who is outside all structures of power, including those of the church. Noel Erskine, a liberation theologian from Jamaica, pointed out in a conversation that the Rastas and other poor Jamaicans believe that the church is "in bed with the government." The church is perceived to have thrown its lot in with the powers that produce but do not alleviate the anguish of poverty; it is not capable of hearing in the cry of mothers with no food for their children an echo of Christ's cry: Why have you forsaken me? Dr. Erskine, who trains ministers for a living, nonetheless emphasized that if we cannot look to the church to decry poverty, neither can we look to it to witness to Christ. Christ is not in that church. Christ is in the streets. The crucifixion of Christ is not only two thousand years ago, it is every day. It is the thorn and scandal of racism, of violence, of hunger, of homophobia, of patriarchy as these mutilate and murder souls who were created to be kingdoms where Christ could dwell. Nancy Lynn Westfield points out that Christianity was in many ways simply another system "intentionally designed to silence and render us docile and obedient . . . to strip us [black women] of our humanity, to strip us of our capacity to love and be loved, to strip us of our will to know and be known. . . . These systems of domination told Black women that we will not and cannot determine what is 'good' for our selves. 'Breaking' us meant that African-American women should only want to know what the 'master wants us to know. . . . What is 'good' for us is told to us by the oppressor—all we need to do is comply."[8] Ada María Isasi-Díaz criticizes theology "because it does not take seriously the religion of the people but seems to prefer the doctrines and dogmas of the church, and because traditional theologies seem to be content with seeing themselves as accountable only, or at least mainly, to the institutional churches."[9]

Accountability to queer or female or black or Asian bearers of the divine image would challenge certain aspects of traditional teaching. But surely doctrines are made for humans and not the other way around. Theology that holds itself accountable to institutions rather than persons too often reinforces behaviors that support institutional—patriarchal, racist, homophobic—power. Rosetta Ross points out that the behaviors that made post-Emancipation African Americans more acceptable to white people came to dominate the meaning of Christianity. Actions and ideas that benefited white racial superiority made one a good

8. Nancy Lynne Westfield, "Mama Why . . . ?" in *Deeper Shades of Purple: Womanism in Religion and Society*, ed. Stacey M. Floyd-Thomas, 132–33.

9. Ada María Isasi-Díaz, *Mujerista Theology*, 76. This point is echoed in many other writings, for example, Kelly Brown Douglas, "Twenty Years a Womanist: An Affirming Challenge," in *Deeper Shades of Purple*, 148.

Christian; those that might have benefited their own flourishing were "bad."[10] What benefits institutional power too often become the criteria of faith. The situation of African American women in our culture has been particularly acute. Their witness highlights another feature of the church's logic of domination. It perpetuates a lie in which oppression and degradation are somehow good for us. Womanist writers call out this lie and insist that obedience and docility are not marks of faith. They separate us from our true selves and therefore from the divine image in us. For women, for subjects of violence, for gay and lesbian and transgendered people, it is necessary to counter the supposed virtues professed by the church if we are to rediscover our faith. We are in the disorienting situation of being embedded in a religious community that trains us to despise the very things that our Beloved created us to be.

It is religious communities themselves and the scholars and theologians who support them that provide the justifications for treating Christ's lovers as sub-human. The church no doubt does many wonderful, healing things. But it is also the place where Christians go to flee the great revelation of the gospel. It is where we look for tidied-up bodies, "bodies better conformed to institutional needs."[11] For many people the institutional church is more than this, of course. But its virtues and ideals look more suspect from the perspective of those who have been harmed by it.

The reflections in this volume work on the hypothesis that the institutional churches and their canonical theologians do not represent the only lineage of apostolic witness from whom we know something about the mystery of incarnation. African American, white, Hispanic, Asian women, women battered or silenced, queers, the afflicted, the poor, the imprisoned can trace their own witness to the idle tale of women who were dismissed by male disciples. Mother Christ no doubt vivifies the institutional church but she also wanders outside the church, no more constrained by it than by the body that Rome crucified. When the voices that have been driven away are gathered back together, we do not get the one true, apostolic faith. But we are reminded of those traumatized women whom Jesus thought would be the most fitting witnesses to survival within the predations of might. We fold our story in with theirs; our witness is rooted in theirs.

The subject matter of this book is the incarnation: God from God, Light from Light. I stand in the ancient tradition that understands self-disclosure as an essential quality of ultimate reality and that in Jesus of Nazareth we find a particularly potent example of this disclosure. Ultimate reality cannot be or be like

---

10. Rosetta Ross, "Lessons and Treasures in Our Mothers' Witness," in *Deeper Shades of Purple*, 119.

11. Mark Jordan, "God's Body," in *Queer Theology: Rethinking the Western Body*, 283; Marcia Mount Shoop's *Let the Bones Dance* revisions theology and ecclesiology on the basis of women's very messy and vulnerable bodies.

anything in creation. If it were, it would simply be another piece of the furniture of the cosmos—Zeus or gravity but not YHWH. When we fall in love with the incarnation, we do so because we yearn for the unbegotten Good and we see this unnamable Abyss refracted in Christ. Because we really do experience salvation in Christ and we conceive of Christ as the full manifestation of the Godhead, it has been easy for us to reduce God to a local deity, concerned only with our corner of the cosmos and only the patch of history that relates to Jesus of Nazareth. If we begin by remembering that it is the transcendent Good, the one who refuses Moses a name because there is no name for this reality, we may enter more joyously into the incarnation without requiring that it exhaust the Divine Eros and her relation to creation. The structure of the book reflects this sense that meditation on incarnation rests in meditation on the nondual ground of reality. An outline may help orient the reader.

Chapter 1—"He Feeds on Ashes": Christology and the Logic of Domination. This chapter is a purgation. It sets out a logic of domination that has given shape to much traditional Christology. It presupposes but does not rehearse the criticisms of feminists, womanists, and others who find the atonement to be offensive and the exclusivism of Christianity to violate its gospel of love. Uncovering the logic at work in the rhetoric and theology by which certain strands of Christology came to dominate Christian consciousness is intended to deprive them of their obviousness and open the way to a more generous understanding of incarnation and its salvific power. I use Athanasius as a kind of personification of the logic of domination. One can dip into history at almost any point and find an equally appropriate candidate. As the author of orthodoxy who so ruthlessly defended the Nicene Creed, he seems like a good choice.

Divine transcendence cautions us against all of the idolatries we carry around in our heads and in our churches: ideas *about* God that displace the *desire for* the Good beyond even our best thoughts. After this initial purgation, we turn to the more cheerful topic of the mystery and goodness of Divinity. The argument is conducted in three parts: the theory and practice of divine transcendence as the root of incarnation (chapters 2–4), a theology of incarnation itself (chapters 5–8), and the theory and practice of gospel Christianity (chapters 9–10).

Chapter 2—"You Shall Have No Other Gods before Me": Incarnation and the Wisdom of One God. This chapter reflects on Scripture as a source for disidentifying our thoughts *about* God from the mysterious depth of divine goodness; in particular it engages in a *lectio divina* of the first table of the Ten Commandments.

Chapter 3—"God Is Love": Naming and Negation. Here we engage the theological tradition to remind ourselves of the unnamable depth of divinity. This chapter walks the negative way, by exploring the dialectic between naming and negation in the work of three theologians: Pseudo-Dionysius, Schleiermacher, and Mechthild of Magdeburg.

Chapter 4—"Arise, My Fair One": Contemplation and Incarnation. Theology invites us to a conceptual acceptance of the namelessness of Divinity. Contemplation augments this with a practice that moves awareness beyond conceptual apprehension.

The *via negativa* and contemplation prepare us to conceive of the incarnation as something that hinges backward toward Beyond Being, into the *Ungrund* that defies the limits of conceptual and even of doctrinal knowledge. But incarnation itself hinges forward toward the cosmos, history, and the scandalous particularity of personhood. For Christians, the incarnation is the intersection between time and eternity. Through it, the eternal fecundity of Eros becomes concrete and flows into creation: World Maker, Pain Bearer, Life Giver. But at the same time, through the incarnation we are able to move through the limits of thought and image to the unspeakable sweetness of the Good Beyond Being. This Good cannot be spoken, yet (to speak poetically) it yearns to express itself and so manifests itself as Wisdom. The next chapters meditate on Wisdom: the perfect image of the Good as it takes on form and concreteness.

Chapter 5—"Breath of the Power of God": The Emanation of Wisdom. Here we move to the first sense of incarnation, the initial manifestation of Good in concrete form, Wisdom, the "image of the invisible God" (Colossians 1:15). The author of Colossians calls Wisdom the firstborn of creation, which implies a secondary nature, almost an Arianism (!). But we might think instead of the eternal simultaneity between ungrounded Eros and Wisdom as these intertwine to manifest the fathomless depths of Divinity. Wisdom, as the first expression of the Divine Eros, expresses Divinity in cosmos. The incarnation is thus first Wisdom that enacts divine goodness in creation. This chapter concludes with reflections on the divinization of nature.

Chapter 6—"But Who Do You Say That I Am?" Union of Humanity and Divinity. This chapter considers what it might mean to say that Divinity is incarnate in the human being, Jesus of Nazareth. Behind the scenes is the question of "two-nature Christology," although this chapter does not take up the question in exactly that way. It begins with testimony and song to emphasize that christological claims are experiential more than doctrinal. It goes on to meditate on senses in which the Divine is embodied in Christ.

Chapter 7—"Every Spiritual Blessing": The Passion of Christ. This chapter begins a two-part reflection on Christ as savior. The first part considers salvation in relationship to suffering and the sense in which the passion narrative expresses healing power. It reflects the importance of the passion even if the doctrine of substitutionary atonement is rejected.

Chapter 8—"The Least of These": Salvation as *Theosis*. This chapter explores a second sense of salvation, perhaps more ancient, the restoration and healing of our divine nature. Seeing Christ in ourselves and one another is the deep healing expressed by the incarnation.

Chapter 9—"This Will Be a Sign": Gospel Christianity. The gospel knows Jesus not as cosmic savior but as a person with distinctive teachings. This chapter examines the teachings of Jesus, in particular exploring the distinctive representations of power and of community that it expresses.

Chapter 10—"They Disbelieved for Joy": Incarnating and Practicing the Gospel. The last chapter proposes ways to think about how we incarnate and practice faith. It does not propose particular things all Christians should do but imagines truth, compassion, and joy as signs of the gospel present in all of the ways contemporary Christians practice their faith.

I believe that the church can and does change over the years and centuries. I am grateful for the people whose energy and hope have opened up parts of the church for women, for lesbians and gay men, for transgendered people, for multicultural worship. But I do not expect any time soon to be spared a church that bludgeons people like me with Scripture to insist we are not fully human and the goods of society and church should not belong to us. I expect large swaths of the church to continue denuding itself of our gifts. I expect it to reinforce an atmosphere in which psychological and physical violence is tolerated. I believe that it will conspire with courts to steal children from lesbian and gay couples and to prevent these families from enjoying the securities that are afforded to other families: health insurance, social security benefits, medical prerogatives, adoptions, the sacrament of marriage, the right to inherit or to file joint taxes. I expect young people will continue to be harassed, humiliated, and bullied, driven to acts of desperation. Women will continue to be tormented as they choose between obedience to church prohibition against birth control and another impossible and dangerous birth. HIV/AIDS will continue to spread unnecessarily quickly as the church insists that human beings abstain from sex rather than practice it more safely. Women and men and children will go to church, savaged by family violence or sexual assault, hunger or fear, and hear about their sins and the horrific sacrifice God demanded to satisfy his justice. In other words, I do not expect the church to fulfill my own personal fantasies of what a community of justice and love might look like.

The revelation of the incarnation is not that a messiah came and magically changed the course of world history so the potency of might was no longer efficacious or that patterns of domination and hierarchy disappeared forever or truth suddenly became more powerful than deceit. Jesus came and left, and justice has yet to roll down like water. We are discouraged by this because we do not pay sufficient attention to the symbols with which Wisdom adorned herself when she became incarnate: in a stable, in a manger, in a conquered country, in the body of a wandering Galilean. The stories and symbols of the gospel and the fate of its first witnesses do not lead us to expect to encounter a power that will protect us from harm. But Jesus preached what was called "good news" to the impoverished and war-torn people of Galilee and its environs. They continued to call it "good news" even after generations of followers were harassed, and many tortured and killed. The good news inspires justice and compassion; it calls into existence a community organized not by social hierarchies but by the realization that we all bear the divine image; we are all Christ. This good news does not depend on the overthrow of the "powers and principalities" that control history and the church. With or without hope we act on the conviction "that when we act in this world with wisdom and compassion and concern for justice, it is the Spirit acting in and through us. What this will lead to, we don't know. The Spirit and therefore the Kingdom is present already. The not-yet will take care of itself. So the value of our actions is to be found in the actions themselves. . . . Whether they produce fruits or not—whether they bring about structural change in El Salvador or in the global marketplace or not—they are what we do when the Spirit touches us, when we wake up to our Buddha-nature or our being-in-Christ. We cannot not do them. We act not to gain the fruits of our actions but because this is how the Christ-Spirit or our Buddha-nature acts, though we rejoice when our actions do bear fruit."[12]

I sometimes feel that I cannot bear for Holy Scripture to be despoiled by those who would deceive us about the great beauty we offer the body of Christ. I refuse to allow "the tradition" to degenerate into a cultural conservatism forgetful of the great cloud of witnesses that sing of the tenderness of incarnate love. I admit that our current situation causes me pain and irritation. But I believe that the most countercultural practice of the kingdom is joy. This is a joy that embraces its own broken heart and the broken hearts of everyone else, not least those whose form of Christianity causes so much pain. The incarnation is the unspeakable joyousness that we dwell in at the intersection of Divinity and humanity. We do not have to wait for this. It is already here, abiding in us as we abide in love. The incarnation invites us into the joy of the brokenhearted "here below," now, within and among us.

The incarnation of Wisdom in Jesus of Nazareth is like a prism in a window: through it shafts of invisible light splinter into color so they can be seen. The divine empire is always present. It is the deep truth of creation. But we have trouble seeing it. Society incarcerates the logic of domination in its basic institutions. The deeper truths of creation are veiled. The incarnation is one of the places where a prism is placed in human history so the invisible truth can become visible. Like all great wisdom teachers, Jesus emphasizes love as the basic reality that connects Divinity to humanity and human beings to one another and to their world. In this kingdom there is only one command: love one another. Just as a prism makes light visible, the incarnation allows a world structured by love to be glimpsed. These glimpses are as brief and ephemeral as the rainbows splashed by a prism on the wall. But in witnessing a truth we cannot possess, we are privileged to bear the bitter-sweet pain of its absence.

---

12. Paul Knitter, *Without Buddha I Could Not Be a Christian*, 194.

Chapter 1

"He Feeds on Ashes"

Christology and the Logic of Domination

He feeds on ashes; a deluded mind has led him astray, and he cannot deliver himself or say, "Is there not a lie in my right hand?"

Isaiah 44:20 RSV

The Soul speaks to Reason: "I say, says the Soul, that on account of their rudeness I must be silent and hide my language, which I learned in the secrets at the secret court of the sweet country, in which country courtesy is law, and Love moderates, and Goodness is the nourishment. The sweetness draws me, the beauty pleases me, the goodness fills me. What therefore can I do, since I live in peace?"[1]

Snapshots:

In 2008 clashes between students and police in South Korea were becoming increasingly violent. Into this turmoil a priest entered carrying the Eucharist, followed by a white-robed retinue. Photographs show a long, sinuous line of white threading through the crowd, silent, utterly calm. This simple act of presence defused the violence and the impasse was broken. Dr. Min-Ah Cho, whose own research focuses on two women marginalized by the church, sent me photographs and wrote: "I believe that these pictures tell us why we still need institutional religions and how powerful religious symbols can be even in the twenty-first century."[2]

---

1. Marguerite Porete, *Mirror of Simple Souls*, chap. 68 (p. 143).
2. Thank you, Dr. Min-Ah Cho, for burning this image in my brain.

During a talk to a class of divinity students I referred to the church as an abusive parent. Many students were shocked and hurt by my characterization of an institution to which they were dedicating their lives. I was genuinely sorry that I had upset members of the class. At the same time, I could not help but think: How is it that they do not know this about the church? How could they be naïve about the legacy of violence in the church, its relentless misogyny, its harshness toward sexual minorities, its intolerance of theological diversity? Some churches refuse to permit the distribution of condoms in Africa because it is a "sin" to acknowledge that sex is not exclusively procreative. A woman works in a church, but her denomination does not ordain women and so leaves her uninsured because she is ineligible for clergy benefits. Frustration over these things, like sexual pleasure and pensions for women, is contrary to traditional Christian values.

A middle-aged Presbyterian pastor, chair of Tennesseans Against the Death Penalty, wife of a wealthy banker, mother of three children, drives three hours every month to visit a man on death row, an implacable witness to Christ's words about sheep and goats (Matthew 25).

On All Saints' Day the service opens with "For All the Saints." An image of my grandmother vividly pierces my mind's eye and I see a great chain of humanity linked across the abyss of death: "we feebly struggle, they in glory shine, but all are one in thee for all are thine." As the congregation sings, I weep.

During the early days when AIDS raged unchecked and mostly unmourned, members of the gay community in San Francisco condemned the pope's callousness through a performance of the Roman Catholic ritual of excommunication. A bell tolled as for one dead, and a candle was ritually snuffed out. My friend described how moving this event was for him, and yet even in the face of the church's betrayal and indifference to the ravages of suffering he could not but be horrified by a ritual that symbolically excised someone from the body of Christ.

This book addresses itself in particular to those who have felt the wounding power of the church: women, queers, the afflicted, and those who feel alienated by oppressive or empty qualities of the Christian narrative. One of its central claims is that "those driven away" are a vital part of the body of Christ who participate in a lineage of lovers that goes back to the origin of our faith. We are part of a tradition that cherishes the message of divine presence available in the Incarnate One, Mother and Lover Christ. In revisiting the idea of incarnation, I am relying on classical texts including canonical and noncanonical writings and theological literature from the first centuries and beyond. The *Didache*, Origen, John Scotus Eriugena, Mechthild of Magdeburg, Marguerite Porete, and their contemporary queer, womanist, and feminist counterparts allow us to encounter the incarnation again or perhaps for the first time. They do not all say the same thing but they open a window on new ways of understanding who we are, who God is, the significance of the incarnation, and the meaning of salvation.

Individually and collectively, these writings constitute part of the tradition that is underrepresented in theological education but that is crucial to our participation in a catholic Christian tradition that has spanned two millennia and found a home on every continent. This is a part of the tradition that has had to "be silent and hide [its] language." What is so terrible, so threatening about these strands of the tradition? It speaks of a sweet country in which courtesy is the law and Love the moderator and Goodness provides nourishment. The sweetness of this country provides a peace beyond understanding, but it has been constantly assaulted and rejected by the institutions of the church. Origen and Eriugena were considered heretics, mostly because they rejected the idea of a wrathful and violent deity. Mechthild's book was burned in a public square, and Porete was herself burned in a public square.

It is important to challenge particular teachings that justify the church in withholding ordination or communion, train us to despise our desires or ourselves, or disconnect our suffering from the balm of faith. It is also important to challenge the idea that there is a self-consistent tradition that has "always" believed and behaved in the same way. It is important to find a way of inhabiting tradition that recovers its diversity and richness while rejecting the conflation between particular church teachings and the eternal will of God. The incarnation is the sign for Christians of the joining of heaven and earth, of divinity and humanity. We are all embraced by that glorious "oneing" as Julian of Norwich puts it. Through the symbols, the sacred texts, the traditional writings, through liturgy and practice and community, Christians learn to participate in this beautiful and infinitely mysterious reality. It is not when the church rejects us or we reject the church that we fall away from this truth. There is nowhere to fall but into the love of the Beloved. If we find another language, another set of practices, that weave our divine eros into the great Divine Eros, we might move even deeper into this truth. But we suffer the pain of actual or interior exile from the land of our religious birth. We are defrauded of our first language of faith when it is used to abuse or exclude us.

Tradition is what bears faith through time. It is the accumulated wisdom of centuries. It is also the accumulated victories of power as these are sedimented in the church. The inescapable paradox of every religion is that it must be mediated by concrete institutions that remain permanently inadequate to the glory and mystery of the Good Beyond Being.[3] This is not in itself a terrible thing. We bear the divine image as finite, anxious, struggling beings. The church is everything that we are: kind, compassionate, confused, cruel, mundane, redemptive, murderous, wise, ignorant. But it claims an authority *as if* it could be free of the error and corruptions of human life. Through a theological sleight of hand, the bare-knuckled maneuverings through which one party gains a political victory over another become divine decree. It is our fate to seek the Beloved from within the human condition and not by magically circumscribing it. That the

---

3. For analyses of this paradox see, for example, Schleiermacher, *On Religion,* 238; Tillich, *Systematic Theology,* vol. 3, 98–106. This theme, however, is intrinsic to religion, and almost every theologian struggles with it in one way or another.

church shares our nature is not evil, any more than the human condition itself is evil. This is admittedly frustrating because we wish the church really were a magical place where sin and evil, oppression and ignorance were displaced by the unstained immediacy of the divine presence. We hurry to claim for it a perfection that it cannot possess. That we are beloved and precious does not make us perfect; that the church is beloved and precious does not make it incapable of error. The difficulty the church poses for us is that it too often compounds error with a view of its own inerrancy. In this way evil or only imperfection gain the potency of divine inspiration.

The synod and presbytery meeting, as much as the rack, torture the gospel into recanting its truth. I believe that it is an important spiritual practice, a faithful obligation, to challenge the narrative of sin and redemption that underlies so much Christian belief. It is a narrative that presupposes an irrational and inconsistent deity, split between his bloodthirsty rage and his infinite love. It steals our sense of mutual dignity and beauty by describing humanity as helplessly deformed and deserving of infinite punishment. It schools us to despise those who believe differently from ourselves. The doctrine of original sin and the sacrifice required to counteract it make participation in the church, or rather, whichever part of the church we believe teaches true doctrine, essential to salvation. This nest of beliefs and assumptions are not particularly resonant with the teachings of Jesus, but they are essential underpinnings to a view of authority that gives to the church, and to nothing else in creation, the power of salvation.

This chapter offers a purgative moment before engaging the more pleasant task of reflecting on meanings of incarnation. Many people have criticized the idea of passion and sacrifice, others have challenged the teaching on original sin. Still others have uncovered the seamy and violent history of the church; many books remind us of the times the church's allegiance to empires has trumped allegiance to gospel. I am indebted to all of these approaches. My own focus is on the struggle for orthodoxy, epitomized by the Nicene Creed. I use Athanasius as a kind of epitome of this strand of the Christian tradition. This is unfair, both because history is much more complex than one person and because Athanasius himself is probably more multivalent than his cynical strategies might suggest. But looking at the rhetorical and coercive strategies employed by Athanasius and his allies provides a "distant mirror" to contemporary struggles. The seamy and violent underpinnings of the struggle for "orthodoxy" cast a shadow on the church's appeal to a supposedly uniform and eternal set of theological and ethical practices. I focus on Athanasius as a way to surface the logic of domination that undergirds so much of our language for salvation. Christology's polarizing rhetoric and a forensic narrative are devices for domination, and I too add my voice to those seeking to demystify Christian theology so that a less oppressive vision of our faith might emerge.

For those of us wounded by the church, it seems important to reflect on how tradition works both to oppress and to heal. Most of this book is dedicated to reimagining the incarnation, but we pause here at the beginning to expose ways the story of our Beloved has been savaged by those who know how to play the game of power well.

THE COUNCIL OF NICAEA

It is, in a sense, natural that a reflection on the incarnation should begin with the Nicene Creed, which expressed the unity of divinity and humanity in the majestic poetry many still recite today: God from God, Light from Light, True God from True God, Begotten, not made, of one being with the Father. Light from Light—what a beautiful image, capturing the undiluted synthesis possible between humanity and ultimate reality: one taste, as the Buddhists put it. This is "high Christology" at its best, and I admit that the reflections on incarnation in this book rest in this sense of intoxicating oneing between humanity and divinity, rapturously, though not uniquely, accomplished in the person of Christ.

It is somewhat less edifying to examine the struggle through which the Creed became synonymous with orthodox Christianity, or more horribly, through which the idea that there could be such a thing as a uniform and orthodox faith gained ascendancy. The Creed is emblematic of the mixed nature of tradition: beautiful in its wisdom, powerful in its creation of a common and shared language, but violent in its methods and divisive in its effects. The Creed was eventually accepted as orthodox, but it reified divisions from which the church never really recovered. In describing it, Constantine papered over machinations of which Karl Rove would have been proud to celebrate a work of divine providence: "That which has commended itself to the judgment of three hundred bishops cannot be other than the doctrine of God, seeing that the Holy Spirit indwelling in the minds of so many dignified persons has enlightened them!"[4] The Holy Spirit was apparently hard-pressed and required an ingenious and ruthless strategist to assist her.

Examining the role of Athanasius in the triumph of orthodoxy is admittedly a vast simplification of patterns of thought that had been evolving probably since Paul's nasty attack on Peter for refusing to eat with Gentiles (Galatians 1 and 2). It is not that Athanasius single-handedly created a logic of domination and structured the church by it. But he exemplifies movements within the church, then and now, that create the illusion of unity by condemning and ostracizing opponents and abusing theology and Scripture until they support his case.

In the last decades of the third century, Christians experienced intensified violence and persecution. As the real stability of the empire deteriorated, symbolic shows of unity became all the more important.[5] Christians were increasingly

---

4. Constantine, "Letter to the Alexandrian Church," quoted in Michael Gaddis, *There Is No Crime for Those Who Have Christ*, 60.
5. First Decius, then Valerian and Diocletian launched efforts to "enforce religious unity and

threatened with execution, prison, and torture; with the razing of churches, the burning of Scriptures, and the appropriation of property. When Constantine came to power, he experimented with the opposite strategy for securing stability throughout the empire. In 313 he issued the famous Edict of Milan, which prescribed religious tolerance throughout the empire. Christians were no longer outlaws, but they now had to redefine themselves in light of a dramatically altered political situation. This transition from the era of periodic, if intense, persecutions to a time when Christianity became the dominant religion has preoccupied scholars for centuries. Eusebius saw in Constantine a new Cyrus, an instrument of the divine will who liberated an oppressed people. As H. A. Drake notes, Edward Gibbon saw in the ascendancy of Christianity the beginnings of "a violent suppression of variant beliefs that had continued unabated to his own day."[6] With all of its ambiguity, the transition to an "orthodox" Christianity furnished opportunities for those who understood how to align the fortunes of the church with the power and wealth of the empire.[7]

The Nicene Creed may be a beautiful tribute to the Trinity. But the struggle over the precise wording proper to Trinity, incarnation, and redemption proved to be an occasion for identifying Christianity with the idea there *could be* a best and only expression of divine being. Faith became contingent upon supporting the party that defended the correct verbal formulation. An ecclesial structure developed to police this support. The significant triumph of the orthodox party was that it emerged with the authority to condemn not only those with variant theological views, but also those who wished to remain in communion across theological boundaries. Drake points out that it is not difficult to imagine circumstances under which an inclusive and tolerant form of Christianity would have emerged in the fourth century. The centrality of the love ethic makes it "just as likely that the most committed Christians would be those who were the most irenic. To explain why, instead, militants succeeded in gaining control of the Christian message, a different principle must be invoked."[8] Willingness to use violence and deceit to secure its position does give a party a decisive edge.

The Council of Nicaea was called by Constantine in 325 to address conflicts over Trinitarian theology and other matters.[9] The issue of the Trinity had

---

stamp out Christian 'atheism.' . . . Diocletian and his colleagues envisioned a Roman people united in common loyalty to the traditional gods as a necessary concomitant to their hard-won restoration of security and political order" (Gaddis, *There Is No Crime*, 32–33). See also Rebecca Lyman, "Athanasius," in *Empire and the Christian Tradition*, 65.

6. Drake, *Constantine and the Bishops*, 21.

7. Two recent books that reflect on the integration between Christianity and imperial power are Joerg Rieger, *Christ and Empire;* and *Empire and the Christian Tradition: New Readings of Classical Theologians*, ed. Kwok Pui-lan, Don H. Compier, and Joerg Rieger.

8. Drake, *Constantine and the Bishops*, 421.

9. "The purpose of Nicaea, for Constantine, was to end the controversy by producing a consensus statement of faith to which all could subscribe. . . . It mattered little if some of them understood the creed in a different fashion from others: as long as all accepted the same language and maintained communion with one another, unity would prevail" (Gaddis, *There Is No Crime*, 60).

emerged in an increasingly bitter dispute between Arius, a presbyter and teacher in Alexandria, and Alexander, bishop of Alexandria. Most of this conflict was carried out by Athanasius, who replaced Alexander upon his death. Little can be directly gleaned about Arius's life or thought since his writings were burned and those who owned copies were threatened with the death penalty (a remarkably effective way of creating a uniform past). What remains comes almost exclusively from his opponents, especially his arch-rival, Athanasius.[10] Nonetheless, it appears that he had been admired as one who not only taught but embodied the "philosophical" life; that is, he was an esteemed ascetic, scholar, spiritual director, and preacher. At the time of the controversy he had been in Alexandria for some time, having remained there throughout the period of persecution that had emptied the city of so many of its leaders. Some seventy virgins were attached to his church and under his care. The reference to the seventy virgins is probably worth noting because it represents a different kind of authority from a bishop's.[11] Arius, spiritual leader who had remained in Alexandria during the last wave of persecution and was beloved by a community of women, represented a threat to the kind of church that Alexander and Athanasius envisioned entering the world stage.

Alexander became bishop of Alexandria, a large and important city in what is now northern Egypt, after the martyrdom of its previous bishop, Peter. The Alexandria he inherited was in tumult. Some clergy had fled or had gone into hiding, others were in prison or had been executed. By the time Alexander was ordained, many threads of conflict were roiling the Christian community. There was more than one line of ordination vying for control of the episcopal seat of this very large and affluent city.[12] The role and character of asceticism was also disputed. Sexual discipline was not perceived to be a matter of personal practice but central to the lines of authority in the church. Asceticism generated its own kind of authority, and ascetics tended to gather around adepts in philosophical schools, including that of Arius. These were small groups of women and men who joined together to study Scripture, contemplate, and experiment with ascetic discipline. These groups often understood ascetic practice as a way to move beyond sexual distinction. Asceticism later took on somewhat misogynistic connotations, but in the early church it was a way to empower and authorize women and slaves. Because it was available simply through personal discipline, it was an active manifestation of the relativity of social distinctions: in Christ "there

10. A particularly good summary of what can be known of Arius's life and thought is provided by Rowan Williams, *Arius: Heresy and Tradition*, 32.

11. "By ministering to the spiritual life of holy women in great cities, many cultivated clergymen were enabled to step to one side of the world of their bishops. . . . Men like Arius . . . gained no small part of their public reputation by giving spiritual guidance to devoted women, most of whom would have been virgins or widows, living in their family houses" (Brown, *Body and Society*, 266).

12. During the chaotic period prior to Alexander's ordination, Bishop Melitius of Lycopolis had entered Alexandria and ordained clergy, sending some to the mines and prisons to minister to those who had been incarcerated there. Many accounts of these controversies are available. See, for example, Brakke, *Athanasius and the Politics of Asceticism*, 5ff.; and Williams, *Arius*, 32–41.

is no longer slave or free, there is no longer male and female" (Galatians 3:28).[13] In the kind of Christian academy led by Arius, intellectual debate and embodied practices offered the primary modes of persuasion. Those dedicated to Christian asceticism, philosophy, and contemplation gained a measure of authority simply by their way of life, but this threatened the system in which authority was institutionally controlled and headed by a bishop.[14] That this form of Christian congregation tended to support a more substantive role for women in the church only made it more problematic from an episcopal perspective.[15]

In this time of flux, when the status of Christianity in the empire had been so dramatically and instantaneously transformed, those bishops committed to authority derived from clerical hierarchy perceived that with the backing of the empire, enormous power was available to them to determine the kind of Christianity that would triumph. Both Alexander and Athanasius were intent on establishing the dominance of episcopal authority over the spiritual teachers who had so deeply shaped the faith of Alexandria. They were among those who believed that a strong episcopal structure was crucial to the health of the church. As a way of establishing this authority and bringing more uniformity to the teachings of the faith, Alexander demanded that the presbyters of Alexandria provide him with a sample of their preaching. When Arius did so, Alexander rejected it as unorthodox, engendering an intense conflict. It is important to note that from Arius's point of view, the issue was partly a disagreement over theology but it was also resistance to an interfering bishop. Prior to this time, there was not a well-established mechanism that allowed a bishop to silence a presbyter. To the contrary, presbyters had been accustomed to act independently as colleagues. Alexander's insistence that he could control Arius's preaching was an attempt to assert authority where it did not self-evidently belong.[16] Arius's response to Alexander was a defense of traditional structures of power as much as

13. Susanna Elm points out that in some circles "the highest form of ascetic life is that of men and women together" (*Virgins of God*, 222). This point is a leitmotif of Brown's work; he describes, for example, the view (opposed by Tertullian) that sexual renunciation was a declaration that the power of sex (and its social implications) was "null and void. Possession of the Holy Spirit conferred by baptism was thought to lift men and women above the vast 'shame' of the human condition. To stand unveiled among the believers was to declare the fullness of the redemption brought by Christ. . . . Yet, in the church at least, an unveiled, continent woman was a stunning sight. Her open face and free hair summed up the hope of all believers: 'I am not veiled because the veil of corruption is taken from me; . . . I am not ashamed, because the deed of shame has been removed far from me" (*Body and Society*, 80–81).

14. Brakke, *Athanasius*, 65. In addition, Brakke describes Athanasius's strategies to subject the virgins of Alexandria to his control (ibid., chap. 1).

15. Elm points out that "though never mentioned explicitly, one subject of the reforms and of the doctrinal and legal struggles leading to their success was that of women. The decision between Eustathius and his Homoiousian model of ascetic life and that proposed by Basil directly affected the ways in which women could henceforth realize their ascetic ideals: they would act no longer in concert with their 'brothers in Christ,' and would be less and less involved in charitable works and direct doctrinal conflicts. . . . [though] it is doubtful that all forms of communal ascetic life, despite the impression generated by our 'orthodox' sources, disappeared entirely" (*Virgins of God*, 223).

16. Brakke, *Athanasius*, 58.

a defense of his theology. He was supported by bishops who considered Arius's thought within the broad scope of acceptable theology as well as by those who "were dismayed by Alexander's (and now Athanasius') authoritarian response to philosophical disagreement."[17]

Not long into the controversy Alexander died, and Athanasius took control of his bishopric in an ordination that was controversial at best.[18] Athanasius (c. 293–373) has been "described by some as a 'gangster' for his use of force to advance his theological beliefs and revered by others as a 'saint and martyr' for his unwavering opposition to heresy."[19] Certainly his political acumen helped propel both Nicene theology and the coercive tactics through which it succeeded to the forefront of Christian history. But the path was not smooth. By 335 he faced a number of serious charges: "not only that he had illegally seized the bishopric of one of the Empire's largest and most important cities but also that he maintained his position through violence and corruption. In his zeal to eliminate all dissident voices, as his opponents charged, he had beaten and imprisoned rival clergy and desecrated church property. In one incident that would haunt him for decades, opponents claimed Athanasius's goons had thrown over an altar and broken a holy chalice."[20] Athanasius spent many years in exile and in hiding. He was condemned by church councils for violations of church discipline, including accusations of embezzlement and extortion. The party supporting Arius and that supporting Athanasius swung back and forth for control. Yet by the end of his life, Athanasius was serving as Alexandria's bishop. The creed he fought so hard for was eventually accepted by most of the church. The authority of the episcopacy became firmly established, and the habit of declaring opponents to be heretics, excluded from the church and from salvation, became standard operating procedure. Ascetics were confined to monasteries, which were themselves brought under the authority of the bishop; virgins were separated from the public sphere, silent, and, ideally, submissive.[21]

In calling the original counsel, Constantine and many bishops thought they would calm the turmoil by agreeing to theological formulations designed to include a broad Christian community. Instead, Athanasius attempted to isolate and, if possible, destroy opponents.[22] Establishing the authority of clerical

17. Ibid., 8.

18. A detailed account of the reasons the ordination was disputed is provided by Barnes, *Athanasius and Constantius*, 18.

19. Lyman, "Athanasius," 63.

20. Drake, *Constantine and the Bishops*, 3. Barnes adds to these details an unsavory account of his manipulation of elections, his violence against opponents, arrest of opponents on false charges after which they were tortured, imprisoned, or sent to the mines; extortion; his consistent disruption of councils and agreements that attempted to heal schisms, *Athanasius and Constantius*, 17–27.

21. See Brakke, *Athanasius*, 11. His first chapter lays out in much detail the rhetorical and strategic methods Athanasius deployed to transform the role of Alexandrian virgins from a public, philosophical one to a private and silent one.

22. See Gaddis: "Such attitudes guaranteed that imperial attempts to reach unity through compromise would always encounter determined opposition from the extremes, even if the vast majority

hierarchy and defining Christian community as submission to this structure represented the heart of the conflict.[23] This conflation of doctrine with power politics has made me wonder how much the disagreements with Arius were inflamed *in order* to provide an occasion to redefine how authority would operate within Christianity. In thinking about this question, let us first turn to the benefits that accrued from this reconstitution of ecclesial authority.

THE REWARDS OF "UNITY"

The term "bishop" (Greek *episkopos*) came into Christian use very early and could be used for both men and women.[24] The role gradually expanded in authority but became limited first to men and eventually to celibate men. By the fourth century bishops were spokesmen for their local communities. When Constantine came to power, it was the bishops with whom he negotiated. They were in his eyes "players in the game of empire."[25]

Bishops exercised increasing control over what beliefs and practices would be tolerated in their communities, but their authority also had deeply practical and material significance. Bishops were elected for life and therefore were able to accumulate a great deal of personal power. "Large basilicas modeled on Roman assembly halls gave their liturgies and consultations a central place in the ancient cities. Bishops would become almost a parallel senate with significant influence on the emperor."[26]

Of particular significance was the struggle for control of the church's welfare system.[27] Bishops were responsible for collecting and distributing charity to their constituents. These resources could amount to very significant wealth.[28] Charitable giving was an important Christian practice; this charity was directed

---

of bishops went along. The clash between these two attitudes in turn reflected a larger battle between two conflicting ideas of religious community. Was the congregation of the faithful to be inclusive, universal, building upon consensus—or was it to be marked off by firm boundaries from known enemies, the exclusive preserve of the pure who saw compromise as the work of the devil?" (*There Is No Crime*, 61).

23. Williams, *Arius*, 46. See also Brakke (*Athanasius*, 4), who identifies the consolidation of episcopal hierarchy over both other claims to ecclesial authority and ascetical or spiritual forms of authority as the two-pronged agenda of Alexander and Athanasius.

24. Mary Jo Torjesen begins her excavation of women's church leadership—found and lost during the first centuries of Christianity—with a description of a mosaic dedicated to Bishop Theodora (*When Women Were Priests*, 9–10).

25. Drake, *Constantine and the Bishops*, 73. See also Brown's discussion of the bishop's parallel role to Roman civic leaders: "Poverty and Power," in *Power and Persuasion in Late Antiquity*, 90, *et passim*.

26. Lyman, "Athanasius," 66. Cf. Brown, *Power and Persuasion*, 90: "Rival churches competed by replicating the social services provided by their opponents. . . . From services to the poor to new basilicas, the Christian presence was heightened by men in a hurry. Each Christian group was anxious to leave a permanent mark on the city."

27. Brakke, *Athanasius*, 190.

28. Drake, *Constantine and the Bishops*, 396.

not only to the poor but also to virgins and others who were supported by the church. All of this was routed through the bishop.[29] Controlling this much wealth allowed bishops to channel resources to those parties and peoples of whom he approved. While their virtue added to his prestige, a bishop could make his support for virgins and widows, for example, contingent on their support of his agenda. This was significant in a time when virgins could still participate in theological controversies.

Not only Christians, but the emperor routed charitable giving through the bishops. In this way they became responsible for dispensing the large grain allotments granted by the emperor to a city. This gave them influence over grain shipments through which they could even "demand obedience from captains of ships."[30] Given the amount of wealth that flowed through a bishop's hands, it is not surprising that struggle for the bishopric of Alexandria, a very wealthy city, was intense. That many of the crimes of which Athanasius was accused concern the integrity with which he handled his charitable responsibilities is perhaps not surprising. He was accused of inhibiting shipments of grain and was exiled by Constantine for embezzlement. These accusations may not mean that he hoarded wealth for himself but that he was directing charity to his own party at the expense of other Christians.[31]

In addition to financial incentives, Constantine extended the judicial authority of bishops. Parties in a suit were allowed to appeal to a bishop, even if one party objected to the change of venue. Once the bishops ruled, there could be no further appeal.[32] In addition, the testimony of bishops obviated the need and even the possibility of other witnesses: once a bishop testified, no other witnesses could be heard. Bishops themselves became immune to secular courts of law, and only councils of bishops could address accusations against them. This concentration of financial and juridical power in the hands of the bishops made them powerful patrons in a society where patronage was the primary social lubricant. "In many ways, bishops could be equated with the traditional patrons and

29. "Laypeople were not to question how the bishop distributed their offerings, nor were they to give directly to the needy and so bypass the bishop" (Brakke, *Athanasius*, 117). Brown also quotes this fourth-century rule: "If any man should do something apart from the bishop, he does it in vain; for it will not be accounted a good work." But he notes that private giving remained a powerful form of patronage that was not always handed over to the bishop, though Constantine also preferred to route "charity" through the bishops (*Power and Persuasion*, 95, 98).

30. Lyman, "Athanasius," 67. She points out, "Bishops and deacons had become effective and unique urban mediators between the elite and the poor. Because bishops were elected for life, unlike Roman offices filled for set terms, and were protected from execution, they possessed an unusual longevity, influence, and cohesion with other leaders through councils. Large basilicas modeled on Roman assembly halls gave their liturgies and consultations a central place in the ancient cities. Bishops would become almost a parallel senate with significant influence on the emperor" (ibid., 66).

31. The issue of grain shipments is discussed in a number of places including Drake's *Constantine and the Bishops*, 396; Lyman, "Athanasius," 70–71; Brakke, *Athanasius*, 6.

32. Drake, *Constantine and the Bishops*, 325. Brown also discusses the judicial powers of the bishops in *Power and Persuasion*, 100.

elites of the ancient world, protecting their perquisites and their flocks as great magnates always had."[33]

Because the authority of the bishops concerned wealth, juridical power, deployment of violence, access to public funds, and confiscation of property, it is not surprising that theology became deeply intertwined with imperial politics. Some Christian bishops magnificently exploited access to imperial power. The kind of power and authority that bishops came to wield mirrored the kind of power the empire could support. Episcopal authority reasserted patriarchal authority over women, slaves, and the poor, reinforcing the alliance between bishops and empire. This alliance is also reflected in the identification of "catholic" bishops as the legitimate channel for power and money. Identifying fellow Christians as heretics or schismatics meant more than the pleasure of imagining them in hell. "Heretics" were obliged by Constantine to hand over their property to the catholic church.[34] The construction of heresy could be lucrative in a situation that allowed bishops to acquire significant benefits from a line between true and false belief.

THE RHETORIC OF BINARY OPPOSITION

Just as the emperors prior to Constantine had sought to imprint an artificial unity on the empire by eradicating Christian "atheism," those, like Athanasius, who were committed to a strong episcopal authority attempted to create an artificial unity of faith by eradicating "false" versions of Christian faith. In this way a fluid and diverse set of communities were split between truth and falsehood, catholicity and heresy. Through the long-protracted conflict over Trinitarian language, the habit of conceiving Christian community as a single, unified, orthodox tradition constantly defeating an utterly alien and demonically inspired band of heretics destined for hell became integral to Christian identity.[35] The transition that placed "the keys to the kingdom" in the hands of an ecclesial hierarchy required an ideological structure to support it. Out of the plural ways Christians had preached and lived, there would be one that would dominate all others. To accomplish this, Athanasius shunned consensus and sought to obtain unity through division and conflict, by identifying—even creating—and then excluding opponents. Through an appeal to "unity" he mounted a relentless assault on Arius, on those who tolerated diversity, on philosophical circles, on the autonomy of virgins, and on the independence of monastic communities. His "unity," by some estimates, made over half of Christianity "heretical."[36]

33. Drake, *Constantine and the Bishops*, 72.
34. Pagels, *Beyond Belief*, 174.
35. Elaine Pagels's *Origin of Satan* is a particularly careful and detailed account of how this opposition came to dominate Christian consciousness.
36. "A year before the bishops met at Nicaea, Constantine had tried to legislate an end to

For Constantine, the council was intended to create a unified understanding of Christianity to which all parties could subscribe.[37] Early on the council developed language broad enough to include both Arius's and Athanasius's ideas. Those seeking consensus proposed that technical language be removed to avoid offense: "we declare that the Son is like the Father in all things, as the holy scriptures indeed declare and teach."[38] But these efforts failed. For Athanasius, the point was not to find words upon which consensus could be built, but rather to clearly define opponents so they could be exiled from Christianity and, perhaps more importantly, from their bishoprics. Athanasius explained later "that while he certainly had no quarrel with more moderate formulations such as 'the Son is like the Father,' these were insufficient because they did not explicitly exclude 'Arian' interpretations. The mere fact that the other side might also find it acceptable was enough to make it unacceptable."[39] The intense focus on technical precision arose because the positions were so close that they required sword-like language to parse theology ever finer, lest a common ground was accidentally discovered.[40]

Conflict requires an opponent. Where one does not exist, it must be invented. The very idea of an Arian "party" reflects the success of Athanasius in transforming an intellectual debate with a respected fellow Christian teacher into a struggle against a heretical school. Through skillful polemics, those who opposed him at Nicaea became a single heretical party. "Arius and his original theology became irrelevant except as a heretical category to be attached to the opponents of Nicaea. Using conventional heresiological categories, a 'school' was created based on a demonically inspired teacher, and diverse opinions could be melded into a coherent sect relentlessly opposed to the apostolic truth of the orthodox. . . . Portrayed as philosophical not biblical, political not holy, and effeminate not masculine, Arians opposed the 'holy' Alexander and the council of Nicaea. This binary opposition . . . turned Arius from a historical opponent into a mythological heresiarch and the shifting theological alliances into a vast imperial and demonic conspiracy."[41]

Rowan Williams echoes this point, describing "Arianism" as a "fantasy based

---

'heretical sects,' which, by one estimate, may have included about half the Christians of the empire" (Pagels, *Beyond Belief*, 174). Brown points out that appeals to unity were often made by those who were themselves members of a minority faction (*Power and Persuasion*, 90).

37. Constantine's role at Nicaea is the subject of some debate. Gaddis characterizes his pursuit of consensus as a "'coercive harmony,' the violence of the center, [which] would underpin the religious politics of the Christian empire" (*There Is No Crime*, 65). Drake also sees Constantine's primary effort to forge a "big tent" type of Christianity that was constantly undermined by bishops such as Athanasius (*Constantine and the Bishops*, e.g., 421).

38. Barnes, *Athanasius and Constantius*, 139, 144.

39. Gaddis, *There Is No Crime*, 60–61. Lyman notes: "The term *homoousios* (of the same substance or being) seems to have been included only because it was rejected by Eusebius of Nicomedia and others" ("Athanasius," 70).

40. Lyman notes: "The battles became increasingly heated and technical not because of profound theological differences but rather because in fact so much was shared in common" ("Athanasius," 71).

41. Lyman, "Athanasius," 71.

on the polemic of Nicene writers, above all Athanasius."[42] But this "fantasy" was crucial for Athanasius. Arius was a preacher who expressed the relationship between the Son and the Father in a particular way. He was supported by women and men in his community. He was also supported by others who shared his theological views. Still others shared his view that truths of faith should be explored by philosophical debate rather than ecclesial fiat. Some agreed with the orthodox party but did not consider disagreements of this sort to be a reason to break Christian communion. All of these points of view were transformed into a heretical *sect* that opposed itself to "orthodox" *tradition*. Identification of a unified opponent became essential to the transformation of Christianity from a pluriform set of practices and beliefs into a unified Catholic Church determined by clear boundaries and regulated by an ordained, male clergy. Without this clear demarcation, episcopal authority has insufficient traction.

Constructing opposing points of view as "heresy" is a way of changing a debate into a struggle between merely human opinion and divinely inspired truth. Within a logic of domination, an opposing position is illegitimate simply because it is different from what a more powerful party has claimed to be true. When we go to church over the years and hear the same passages preached on, a virtually infinite set of meanings is opened. The trick of orthodoxy is not so much to deny this plurality of interpretation but to accuse those with whom one *disagrees* of projecting their own experiences while insisting that one's own interpretation stands in the tradition of the apostles. Faithful stewards of the divine Word "hand down only what they, in turn, received from the apostles, without adding or subtracting anything. By invoking the authority of the ancient consensus of the apostles they can claim, then, that what they teach is not only the *unchanging truth* but absolutely *certain*."[43] It is interesting to note how blithely Athanasius deploys his rhetoric of opposition. He concludes a long letter interpreting the Psalms with a defense of the practice of chanting rather than saying them. Not unlike Cynthia Bourgeault, he describes the meditative and somatic benefits of chant. But (unlike Bourgeault) he identifies anyone who speaks rather than chants the Psalms as a sinner: "Well, then, they who do not read the Scriptures in this way, that is to say, who do not chant the Divine Songs intelligently but simply please themselves, most surely are to blame, for praise is not befitting in a sinner's mouth."[44] A sinner appears to be anyone who disagrees with Athanasius on however minor a point.

Athanasius directs this reasoning against Arius's verbal formulation but also against the idea of Christianity as a path of wisdom. Arius represented a kind of

---

42. Williams, *Arius*, 82. This construction of an Arian "school" through Athanasius's rhetoric is a theme echoed by many historians; e.g., Barnes points out it is not a term people used to describe their own position but was a term of abuse hurled at opponents who disagreed with the "orthodox" party for a variety of reasons (*Athanasius and Constantius*, 15).

43. Pagels, *Beyond Belief*, 155.

44. Athanasius, "The Letter of St. Athanasius to Marcellinus on the Interpretation of the Psalms," in *On the Incarnation*, 115.

authority that a small community granted to the wisdom and spiritual practice of a particular teacher. It is somewhat resonant with the guru tradition of Eastern religions. It is not an institution that is the primary vehicle of religious transmission but the *shakti* of a spiritual adept. As a contemplative practitioner, I can only regard the impoverishment of this tradition as a tragic loss; but from the perspective of someone like Athanasius, corralling, controlling, and disempowering the tradition of spiritual teachers was crucial to the consolidation of episcopal power. Part of the strategy for this disempowerment was the construction of wisdom traditions as heretical. *Teachers* create new and unnecessary lines of thinking; *clergy* mediate truth handed down by Christ. Athanasius himself was an original theological thinker who did much to articulate a novel vision of Christian thought and practice. But this originality was occluded by his insistence that, in contrast to "teachers," he passively expressed an unchanging tradition.

The term *homoousia* (one substance), so important to his view of orthodoxy, is itself a rather dramatic break with biblical theology. But Athanasius insisted that he was merely a conduit for a tradition that had remained unchanged from the time Christ handed down correct doctrine (and presumably the admonition to chant psalms) to his male disciples.[45] No less creative and innovative than others, proponents of "orthodox" belief cloaked their own innovations in the appeal to a self-identical authoritative past while accusing their opponents of imposing private opinions on sacred texts. (This strategy has been powerfully deployed by advocates of "family values" in defense of a kind of family that did not exist before the modern period.) By characterizing controversy as conflict between apostolic truth and heresy, bishops who shared Athanasius's views of power and authority were able to create an impression that there was such a thing as an unalterable tradition and remaining true to that tradition was identical with fidelity to Christ himself—even though this unalterable tradition was being created in their own writings.

The potency of the construction of heresy is ratcheted up when those who hold variant views are not only one's own enemies but the enemy of God. "Opinion" is not only private, an arbitrary choice, merely subjective, but is demonically inspired.[46] Athanasius tapped into a tradition that deployed the rhetoric of demonology to frame the issues in a way that precluded a genuine exchange of ideas or a sympathetic encounter with various possible interpretations.[47] Even

---

45. Brakke, *Athanasius*, 68.

46. This demonization of opponents enables Athanasius to "redefine the very concept of Christian community, restricting it to only those who espoused Nicene Trinitarian doctrine and who remained in communion with himself. All others were pushed outside the boundaries and classified as 'persecutors' not fundamentally different from the pagans" (Gaddis, *There Is No Crime*, 72).

47. "Tapping into this tradition allowed Athanasius to undercut his opponent and deny them any right to a sympathetic or unbiased hearing—then as now, a far easier means of dealing with uncomfortable situations than the alternative of a reasoned give-and-take that more thoughtful forms of discourse require" (Drake, *Constantine and the Bishops*, 415–16). Compare Athanasius's rhetoric against Arius with that Irenaeus used against Valentinus, also a popular, erudite, and profound thinker, who became in Irenaeus's construction no longer a popular and erudite Christian philosopher but, with his followers, "sons of the devil" destined to eternal fire (Pagels, *Beyond Belief*, 156).

now it requires great mental discipline to conceive of Arius or the Valentinians or even Origen representing legitimate strands of Christian experience. The beauty of their lives, their compassionate interpretations of the gospel, and the devotion they inspired notwithstanding, they remain heretics, hostile to Christ and his church.

It was particularly ingenious to extend the rhetoric of demonization to those who did not think that theology should be grounds to break fellowship with fellow Christians. Monks, for example, considered hospitality, even to murderers (or those, like Athanasius himself, who were hiding from soldiers), a crucial element of their religious practice. But Athanasius insisted they demand theological credentials as a condition of hospitality. Offering hospitality to Arians or to those who associated with Arians was itself as bad as holding heretical views.[48] In a logical progression doctrine became a pathway to salvation; deviation from correct doctrine is demonically inspired and assures eternal damnation; an open communion tolerates those God rejects and is therefore another form of satanic perversion. Within this framework, it becomes not only logical but in a sense necessary to ease over from verbal to physical violence against one's opponents.

The excesses and horrors of Diocletian's persecution had led to a repudiation of state violence as a means of enforcing unity of belief. Against this trend, however, the "polarizing rhetoric of the heresy debates, with its emphasis on the evil nature of opponents, helped restore coercion as a legitimate means of protecting the interests of the state."[49] In the immediate aftermath of the Great Persecution that had so badly traumatized Christian communities, violence was turned on other Christians. For Christians and Jews, civil rights began to follow the fault line of orthodoxy.[50] Falling on the wrong side of the orthodox party could invite physical violence. Athanasius himself made use of a labor corps that functioned as "a virtual paramilitary force."[51] But he did not hesitate to make use of the state to carry out violence against his opponents, for example, arranging for bishops who opposed his ordination to be arrested and tortured by imperial soldiers.[52]

As the distinction between genuine and heretical ecclesial leaders took root, "orthodox" bishops could invoke state violence for their own ends.[53] At the behest of bishops, the emperor could and did order "'heretics and schismatics' to

48. Brakke, *Athanasius*, 134–35.

49. Drake, *Constantine and the Bishops*, 439.

50. The appalling history of anti-Semitism begins in early Christianity and the conflation of religion and civil rights. Pagels quotes Timothy Barnes: "Constantine translated Christian prejudice against Jews into legal disabilities" (*Beyond Belief*, 170).

51. Drake, *Constantine and the Bishops*, 397; Brown echoes this point: "By 418 the 'most reverend bishop' commanded, in effect, a hand-picked force of some five hundred men with strong arms and backs, the *parabalani*, who were nominally entrusted with the 'care of the bodies of the weak' as stretcher-bearers and hospital orderlies. The massed presence of the *parabalani* made itself felt in the theater, in the law courts, and in front of the town hall of Alexandria. The town council was forced to complain to the emperor of such intimidation. . . . 'Throughout the empire, the personnel associated with the bishop's care of the poor had become a virtual urban militia" (*Power and Persuasion*, 102–3).

52. Barnes, *Athanasius and Constantius*, 22.

53. Gaddis, *There Is No Crime*, 73; cf. Pagels, *Beyond Belief*, 180; Lyman, "Athanasius," 67.

stop meeting, even in private houses, and to surrender their churches and whatever property they owned to the catholic church."[54] It is noteworthy that it was not religious diversity itself that became the object of violence. Constantine did not penalize pagans for not being Christian.[55] The ability to enforce theological and liturgical uniformity through state violence channeled ecclesial power in the hands of the bishops and so diminished other sources of authority. As Rebecca Lyman points out, "Over the third century, episcopal power had concentrated over other church offices; traditional charismatic privileges such as the laity's right to preach, the teaching authority and mobility of widows, or the forgiveness of sins by confessors, were limited."[56] Over the decades, emperors shifted their allegiance from one strand of Christianity to another, and the violence moved in waves against various communities as the tides turned one way or another. But the pattern of making doctrine the primary site of Christian faith and using violence to maintain "unity" had gained ascendancy.

This violence is never actually done by the church or the clergy themselves: through the sleight of hand that makes human agents stand in for divine ones, it is always God who acted. According to his own rhetoric, Athanasius's writings, his withholding of grain shipments, his sacrilege against another cleric's altar, his use of thugs against enemies, his outright lies and prevarications, his hiding from the emperor or fellow bishops, his instructions to destroy texts that might support opponents' preaching are all God's activities. If the vote of a synod goes with him, it is because God willed it. If it goes against him, it is because Satan has infected the other bishops. God wished him to dispense charitable contributions in ways that reinforced his power. God, sharing Athanasius's anxieties about intelligent and articulate women and charismatic spiritual leaders, inspired strategies to shunt them to the margins of history. "We have here the very heart of human evil as it rationalizes itself. Once a finite, historical complex is given divine status, all means are justified in protecting that complex."[57]

CONSTRUCTING A NARRATIVE

The authority of tradition became identified with ordained clergy whose power was institutional rather than charismatic. Ostensibly, authority rested primarily

54. Pagels, *Beyond Belief,* 174. cf. Lyman, "Athanasius," 73: "Public orthodoxy created an official and public topography of authorized meeting spaces and holy places. Just as Athanasius wished to regulate private reading or ascetic households, other bishops banned private gathering or worship spaces."

55. In the fourth century, "Christians first used both a rhetoric conducive to coercion and the tools of coercion itself not against pagans but against other Christians. Heresy, not paganism, was the first object of Christian intolerance" (Drake, *Constantine and the Bishops,* 416). Pagels is among those who point out that the earliest demonization is against Jews; see, for example, *Origin of Satan.*

56. Lyman, "Athanasius," 67.

57. Edward Farley, *Ecclesial Reflection,* 168.

in revealed Scriptures, but it would be the bishops, the mouthpieces of God, who were to be the arbiters of scriptural interpretation.[58] It is they who would condense the true meaning of Scripture in creeds and doctrines.[59] These mechanisms of power were held together by a narrative that provided the theological underpinnings of episcopal authority. Unsurprisingly, Athanasius provided a primer of Christian theology.

On the Incarnation tells the story of salvation in a way that illustrated why the church and its clergy were the necessary gatekeepers of salvation. The story is probably familiar. Creation was brought into being from nothing as good and perfect by God. The first humans possessed the capacity to choose good and evil but were commanded to refrain from eating the fruit of the tree of the knowledge of good and evil. Adam and Eve, in an act of inexplicable perversity, "went astray and became vile, throwing away their birthright of beauty."[60] Eating the fruit caused them to lose their knowledge of God and become subject to corruption and death, falling ever more completely under the thrall of Satan and his violent and perverse works. This creates for God a "divine dilemma": "The thing that was happening was in truth both monstrous and unfitting. It would, of course, have been unthinkable that God should go back upon His word and that man, having transgressed, should not die; but it was equally monstrous that beings which once had shared the nature of the Word should perish and turn back again into non-existence through corruption."[61] Either of these scenarios would be unworthy of the goodness of God. But the punishment God was required to impose was deeper than anything repentance or good works could correct.[62] "He could not falsify Himself; what, then, was God to do? Was He to demand repentance from men for their transgression?" This would not do because "repentance would not guard the Divine consistency, for, if death did not hold dominion over men, God would still remain untrue."[63]

God ordained that the punishment for disobedience would be a transformation of human nature so severe that it could no longer help but sin. Since human beings no longer had the capacity to do anything but sin, they could neither repent of their disobedience nor prevent themselves from continually falling into new sin. Desire for God expressed in contemplation, study, prayer, and communities of prayer are themselves sinful because they are dedicated to transformation

58. See, for example, Brakke, *Athanasius*, 68. As Irenaeus puts it: "it is necessary to obey the priests who are in the church—those who have received the succession from the apostles, as we have shown, and who have also received . . . the certain gift of truth . . . but to hold in suspicion those who stand apart from the primary line of succession, and who gather in any place whatsoever, [and to regard them] either as heretics with evil intentions or as schismatics, puffed up with themselves, or as hypocrites" (*Against Heresies* 4.36.2–4, quoted in Pagels, *Beyond Belief*, 155).

59. Pagels develops a particular clear and concise account of the interlocking authority of creed, canon, and clergy in *Beyond Belief*, especially chaps. 4 and 5.

60. Athanasius, *On the Incarnation*, §3 (p. 29).

61. Ibid., §6 (p. 32).

62. Ibid., §7 (p. 33).

63. Ibid. (pp. 32–33).

rather than obtaining forgiveness. God is inspired by love to desire salvation but bound by his penal code to make it impossible. This "divine dilemma" is resolved by the sacrifice of the Son. In order to satisfy both his judgment and his desire for reconciliation, God sends the second person of the Trinity to become incarnate and take on death for humanity out of love. "Thus, taking a body like our own, because all our bodies were liable to the corruption of death, He surrendered His body to death in place of all, and offered it to the Father. This He did out of sheer love for us, so that in His death all might die, and the law of death thereby be abolished because, when He had fulfilled in His body that for which it was appointed, it was thereafter voided of its power for men."[64] Christians live pure lives and study the Scriptures in order to face Christ, who is no longer judged by humanity but "will Himself be Judge, judging each and all according to their deeds done in the body, whether good or ill. Then for the good is laid up the heavenly kingdom, but for those that practise evil outer darkness and the eternal fire."[65] The divine dilemma is resolved in one sense by satisfying the divine law. It is resolved in another sense by allowing God to express both his desire to destroy and his desire to save.

Notwithstanding his protestations to the contrary, this is an astonishingly creative retelling of the drama of salvation that enjoys little direct biblical support. There is in Genesis the story of disobedience, but there is no divine dilemma, no annihilation of human nature, no deformation of human agency so that it can do nothing but sin. Neither do the Gospels tell us anything about an atonement demanded by the Father in order to turn aside his destruction. It also represents a break with ways theologians had been translating biblical narrative into theology. Irenaeus described Adam and Eve as spiritual children who had to learn moral awareness, like all children, by making mistakes. He, like Origen and others, conceived of the passion as a ransom of humanity from the devil. Because God could not use violent means to redeem humanity, the Trinity conspired to trick the devil.

There are a number of odd things about this narrative. It seems strange that God, who is utterly unconstrained in his actions, devises a punishment that automatically destroys the thing he most desires. It is puzzling that the goodness of God is expressed so decisively in a law that initially requires the endless suffering of all of humanity and later requires the endless suffering of only most of it. Endless torment is apparently part of the original architecture of creation, desired for its own sake. Among human beings, only sociopaths desire in this way. It also seems strange that God can draw cosmos out of nothingness, wrestle Satan into submission, and re-create the cosmic harmony so tragically lost in Eden but cannot make use of anything in creation but an ordained clergy to actualize the salvation so dearly bought. It is true, technically, that Christ destroyed death and

64. Ibid., §8 (p. 34).
65. Ibid., §56.

reconciled humanity to God. But we do not have access to this unless we believe what the church teaches us. It is only through the church that the benefits of Christ's sacrifice can accrue. Without the bishops "Christ died for no purpose."

The insertion of the "divine dilemma" into the drama of redemption reconstructs salvation so that it becomes the sort of thing that can be delivered only institutionally. An institution cannot deliver love or compassion or wisdom or awakening. It can, like a court of law, condemn or remit punishment. Sin becomes identified with disobedience to law; its analogue is a crime through which one might end up in court. Divine punishment mirrors the penalty law courts mete out: torture and death that disfigure and maim human nature itself. The church, through its ordained clergy, functions like a court-appointed attorney who negotiates a reduced sentence if we agree to plead guilty.

The construction of the Christian narrative of redemption through the doctrine of original sin and substitutionary atonement narrowly aligns divine presence and ecclesial power. Everything outside the institutional church is stripped of significance. This is no less true after the Reformation, which continued to affirm that the primary benefit of Christian belief was that it enabled us to avoid eternal torment. Protestant churches continued to be committed to these doctrines and to the singular power of orthodox belief, mediated by churches, to save us from perdition. Nature, other religions, and even other forms of religious practice within the church are either irrelevant or demonized. The attack on Arius, like those on Valentinus, Origen, and Porete, reflect a perennial hostility to forms of faithfulness less dependent on clergy to mediate salvation.

In Athanasius's retelling the incarnation becomes less a story about the love of God for humanity than a greatly exaggerated threat of utter condemnation. It is a story of divine violence that blasphemes the eternal Goodness and obscures the human desire for this Goodness. *Extra ecclesiam nulla salus:* outside the church there is no salvation. Here we have the apotheosis of raw power projected onto God and embodied in the church's fantasy of control. The richness of the Christian tradition cannot be circumscribed by this narrative or by the binary logic and coercive strategies that accompany it. As we return to the incarnation and passion, it is important to remind ourselves that this orthodox way of telling the Christian story underwrites a logic of domination. Its captivity to this logic has tragically diluted the church's witness to the distinctive beauty and poignancy of divine love.

A SWEET COUNTRY

In Athanasius we see one example of an impulse within Christian tradition toward domination and exclusion. This impulse came to dominate the history of the church. Rhetoric that demonizes opponents and a theology that construes humanity to be utterly enthralled, subjectively and objectively, to evil conspire to make episcopal power the only means of salvation. From this perspective the erasure of native populations from the New World, the torture and death of thousands of women as witches and heretics, the entrance of Africans into Western history as chattel, millennia devoted to the persecution of Jews, the decimation of Irish culture, the suicides of gay Christians, and the sacrifice of untold others to sexual and domestic abuse all become collateral damage of the story of Christ's incarnation and passion. The costliness of this damage is evident, too, in the writings that have been destroyed, the voices silenced, the legions of lovers defrauded of the chance to grow spiritually and intellectually, and the impoverishment of a church that humiliates those whose charisms it desperately needs. Contemporary Christians will find much that is familiar in this distant mirror: the mendacious use of Scripture, the occasional but horrifying use of violence, the insistence that there is an eternal and self-identical version of Christian faith and ethics that is being created in the conflict itself, the use of theological terror whose god seems more like enraged homophobes than the Jesus of the Gospels.

Mark Jordan argues that "the history of Christian theology can be seen as a long flight from the full consequences of its central profession. The big business of theology has been to construct alternate bodies for Jesus the Christ—tidier bodies, bodies better conformed to institutional needs. I think of these artificial bodies as Jesus' corpses, and I consider large parts of official Christology as their mortuary."[66] In this chapter I have been at pains to draw attention to the logic behind this postresurrection burial of Christ in an effort to disenchant the narrative of original sin, atoning death, and salvation through obedience to church teachings. It is easy to remain in thrall to this story, whether we stay in or leave the church. The rest of this book experiments with other ways of understanding the power of incarnation to bring us good news of a sweet country where "Love moderates, and Goodness is nourishment."[67]

66. Mark Jordan, "God's Body," in *Queer Theology: Rethinking the Western Body*, ed. Gerard Laughlin, 283.
67. Porete, *Mirror of Simple Souls*, chap. 68 (p. 143).

Chapter 2

"You Shall Have No Other Gods before Me"

Incarnation and the Wisdom of One God

> *To whom then will you liken God or what likeness compare with the Beloved? The idol! A workman casts it. . . .*
>
> Isaiah 40:18–19 (my paraphrase)

> *If, however, divinity begins to show up in terms other than oneness—in terms of incarnation, on the street, at the crossroads of the peoples . . . then the uses to which divinity is put by humans for political purposes, for meaning in the midst of smoke and ash . . . may actually begin to open up to other possibilities, other endings—which are other beginnings—to the stories of the nations.*[1]

It is disheartening to consider the coercive strategies and the oppressive logic through which canon, creed, and theological narrative came to narrow our interpretations of the incarnation. But disenchanting the authority of a single stream of Christian thought liberates the other texts, narratives, and voices so they can contribute more openly to our meditations on incarnation. In this chapter, we begin that more fruitful task.

Within Christianity an ever-living stream of iconoclasm challenges excessive claims of religious authorities.[2] We see this in the prophets' savage assault on religious practices that cloak indifference to the poor. We find it in Jesus'

---

1. Laurel Schneider, *Beyond Monotheism: A Theology of Multiplicity*, 197.
2. Paul Tillich is one voice that reminds us of the dangers of religious idolatry. Many of the essays in *The Essential Tillich* describe the importance of retaining the Protestant principle: "It is obvious that the Protestant principle cannot admit any identifications of grace with a visible reality, not even with the church. . . . For Christianity is final only in so far as it has the power of criticizing

challenges to religious authorities. Reform periodically cleaves the church, and the one body is split into Eastern Orthodox and Catholic, splintered again in countless protesting denominations. Perhaps we can view this perennial impulse toward iconoclasm as a necessary antidote to the habits that are generated by authoritative institutions. Institutions by their nature preserve and concentrate their authority. The Protestant churches have been just as likely as Catholic ones to deploy religious authority to preserve patriarchal and heterosexist power and to justify cruelty and violence.

This vulnerability to religious authoritarianism is why the underside is crucial to faith's well-being. It may be despised and oppressed by institutional authority, but this underside remains a much needed companion and reminder of ways in which blind spots violate the body of Christ. Marcella Althaus-Reed claims the holiness of this underside: though authorities claim that God has "declared us, made us, irredeemably lost in the eyes of the church and Christian ethics, yet it is not we who are lost."[3] We are not only not lost, we are called to interpret the incarnation as a witness to the nonviolent and unlimited efficacy of divine love.[4] This love is the self-manifesting beauty of nondual Divine Eros: from the infinite and mysterious depths of Divinity, beauty emerges. Nonduality expresses something of this mystery; love expresses its healing efficacy. The incarnation reveals and heals because it expresses the nonduality of love in the world. Lovers of the Divine in the past and the present, many of whom are despised by the institutional church, bear witness to this nonviolent love. Their voices are crucial to remember as we try again to hear the love songs embedded in the Christian witness.

The story of the incarnation is central to the meaning of the Christian faith, and yet it is constantly drawn back into the violence that stalks the human imagination. It is easy to be discouraged by the apotheosis of violence in theologies of incarnation that see in it yet another excuse to condemn "others." God becomes the arch-abuser and his Son a justification of all the oppression and violence we humans visit upon one another. The consoling nearness of the Beloved suddenly becomes an abyss dividing the saved from the damned. John Calvin describes the human heart as a factory of idols.[5] Certainly nothing is easier than projecting onto God the desires and fears of our tyrannical ego. This is why it is important to engage in practices of love and nonduality as we inquire into the meaning of incarnation. These practices help us to better recognize the idols we have been worshiping. Love and compassion expose our tendencies to do violence to the face of Christ shining in those we allow the church to despise.

In our time, like all times, love is the test by which we discern spirits and call

---

and transforming each of its historical manifestations" (78, 79). In vol. 3 of his *Systematic Theology*, he sets out the ambiguities of history and the potential for demonic distortion more systematically.

    3. *Queer God*, 165.

    4. Carter Heyward describes this focus on relational love as "so foreign to most traditional Christian thought that . . . [it] necessitates . . . new symbols, or images, by which we might express the value of our shared power" (*Redemption of God*, 2, quoted in Cleaver, *Know My Name*, 83).

    5. Calvin, *Institutes* 1.11.8.

out the deceptions of false prophets. "Those who say, 'I love God,' and hate their brothers or sisters, are liars; for those who do not love a brother or sister whom they have seen, cannot love God whom they have not seen" (1 John 4:20). If we must be idolaters, let us be idolaters of love: love is the last name of the Divine before it slips beyond the help of language. Let us learn to worship Christ in the face of those we have not yet understood to be our friends.

The other aspect of the incarnation is its root in the nondual reality of Divine Eros. This is the element of Divinity that is always more, different, beyond our thoughts and even our traditions. Theologies and practices that remind us of this mysterious depth are crucial for untying attachments to whatever ideas we hold dear at any given moment. In order to avoid some of the more violent interpretations of the incarnation and passion, it is important to vivify awareness of the Erotic Abyss from which the incarnation emerges. As long as we hold pictures of God that make Divinity in some literal sense a monarch, we will inevitably load the story of incarnation with images of reward, punishment, violence, and domination. But any and all images are only pictures that help us orient our imaginations toward the Divine. In order to better understand the incarnation, it is necessary to enter into the formless nonduality of Divine Eros. Faith is always bound up with unworthy images and attachments. But Scripture provides a practice to help us relinquish these. That is, meditation with Scripture is itself a practice that allows us to inhabit its images more generously. This chapter will explore one way of using scripture to move into the apophatic depths of divinity.

Dwelling in nondual love is not easy. Relinquishing attachment to beliefs requires enormous courage. Rather than acknowledge these difficulties, too often we take on other, easier tasks—judgment, righteousness, true belief, guilt, shame. It would be wrong of us to berate ourselves for our inability to remain faithful to our Beloved. But we can explore reasons why fidelity to the incarnation of the Divine Eros seems no more possible than spinning straw into gold. If we notice that we grope toward the Beloved along a dusky, dimly light path, we might bear the challenges of faith with more compassion. That is, rather than condemn the human habit to worship idols, we might simply notice how deeply it is woven into the practices of faith—and how Scripture provides ways to weaken the hold of our favorite idols.

STRUCTURES OF FAITH AND IDOLATRY

From the Hebrew prophets to the ministry of Jesus, through desert ascetics, Calvin and Schleiermacher, Barth, Tillich, neo-orthodox, liberal, and liberation movements, theologians have been preoccupied by our tendency toward idolatry. Idolatry is not the false worship of the gods of other traditions. It is an intrinsic part of religious life; like the wheat and tares, it forms the tangled undergrowth of faith. In the previous chapter, I suggested some ways in which the desire for power accomplishes institutional victories that repress the plurality of ways Christians understand and practice their faith. Power dynamics seduce anxious egos that long for support against real or imagined enemies. Faith is the work of weaning ourselves from unwholesome nourishment as we gradually come to trust the Beloved. But this trust runs into an inherent tension; the path of faith is rocky and it is impossible to avoid stumbling.[6]

At the heart of faith is the paradox of loving something that is not present to us in any familiar way. This paradox generates various theological conundrums: the relationship between faith and reason, the significance of emotion or experience, the role of authority, and methods for designating the divine attributes. But more importantly, this paradox generates deep existential anguish. Because we name the Divine as the source of salvation, one of the most basic names of Divinity is Love. But this love is mediated to us in puzzling and indirect ways. We are spiritual beings incarnate in flesh, in nature, in culture. Our primary access to reality is through sense experience, language, emotions, and discursive reasoning as all of these are shaped by the societies in which we live. But our deepest longing is directed toward that which infinitely eludes our senses, our words, and our understanding. "Oned" with God in our creation, we are never separated from the object of our longing, and yet nothing we know, no word or image directly corresponds to God.

This paradox at the heart of faith is both cognitive and existential. It reflects the disjunction between the dimensions of reality most accessible to our experience and the dimension of reality we long for in our longing for the Divine. Most of our ordinary ways of knowing the world are based in the dualism between subject and objects, between ourselves and the things we know through sense and reason. Naturally, we use the language of reason and sense to give form to our desire for God. We inhabit metaphors and families of metaphors that are drawn from the world we know: king, judge, father, mother, lover, friend. We make arguments based on discursive reasoning and we participate in authoritative traditions that mirror the authority structures of family and government. But all of our ordinary ways of knowing are only imperfectly useful to faith. They fail to provide a conceptually reliable understanding of the Divine.

Existentially, most of our experience as persons is dominated by the primacy of ego-mind. Personhood is embodied, formed by emotions, physical experiences of pain and pleasure, hormonal and chemical fluctuations. It is embodied also in particular cultures and subcultures. Our experience of the world arises from this ego- and culture-centered awareness. Our pain and pleasure are very vivid to us. Our cultural constructions are very real to us. Naturally, we interpret

---

6. For a very fine feminist retrieval of faithfulness within the Reformed tradition, see Serene Jones, *Feminist Theory and Christian Theology: Cartographies of Grace*, 112. Joy McDougal's robust retrieval of a feminist interpretation of sin as an effort "to strengthen one's faith in the fellowship that is offered through the Spirit, and in this way to inspire believers with the passion and the creative vision to mend the broken fellowships in their midst," is another important contribution to this conversation (*Pilgrimage of Love*, 151).

the world in light of this ego-centered form of awareness and judge it according to how well it corresponds to our cultural expectations. Those things that are necessary or desirable to our ego-minds are attractive to us. Those things that frighten or harm our ego-minds we interpret negatively.

It is useful and appropriate to experience the world as centered in a duality between self and world. It is useful and appropriate to use our culturally conditioned sense of reality to navigate our corner of the world. But dualistic awareness does not work as well when it is directed toward something that is not an object in the world. Culturally constructed meanings are inadequate for a reality that inflames not only our tiny corner of the universe but all of space and time, all things seen and unseen: the movement of quarks and dark matter and realities that bend beyond our knowledge and our imagination. Ego-mind, structured by subject-object dualism, leery of the uncanny, and restricted to the tiny threads of life available to its unimaginably small scrap of time and space, is not prepared to understand divinely erotic, kenotic love. Karl Rahner points out that "*that* God really does not exist who operates and functions as an individual existent alongside of other existents, and who would thus as it were be a member of the larger household of all reality. . . . Both atheism and a more naive form of theism labor under the same false notion of God, only the former denies it while the latter believes that it can make sense out of it. Both are basically false."[7]

Catherine Keller reminds us that we usually flee from what she calls the *tehomic* depths, chasing instead order and safety. She quotes a Jewish tradition that envisions the Holy One sporting with Leviathan (Psalm 104:26). "To love the sea monsters and their chaos-matrix is consonant with affirming their 'goodness' within the context of the whole. It doesn't make them safe or cute. . . . But this tradition cannot be reconciled with the identification of chaos and its wild creatures as *evil*."[8] Though we dwell in the depths, we make sense of infinite complexity by constructing meanings through sense, culture, and symbol. Our minds create for us a nice, human-sized world. We invite our Beloved into this homey domicile. And, as Calvin says, God "condescends" to our capacity. We do not have to give up all of our thoughts, emotions, and traditions about God when we realize the disjunction between our way of knowing and the beyond-being superabundance of our wild lover. But we do have to learn how to inhabit our ideas about the Divine in ways the ego-mind initially finds uncomfortable. Dwelling ninety-thousand leagues over the deep, as Kierkegaard puts it, can be nauseating and vertiginous.

This discomfort affects not only individuals but religion itself. The subject matter of religion is primarily the transformation and healing of life as it participates in the great Goodness beyond and within all that is. But religion is itself part of creation and shares the dynamics of ego-consciousness as these are writ large in culture and history. We long for something that will meet the needs of

---

7. Karl Rahner, *Foundations of Christian Faith: An Introduction to the Idea of Christianity*, 63.
8. Catherine Keller, *Face of the Deep*, 28.

the ego and so we imagine the Divine through familiar images of power: king, judge, paterfamilias. Dynamics of worldly power and the oppressions they breed are internalized into religion itself. We use *God* as the term for what will bring the ego and its social environment security and defuse its pain.

Just as the world is encountered through the prism of our own ego-mind, our communities become the center through which all human communities are encountered, understood, and judged. As the center point of reality, our religious community is often thought to enjoy exclusive knowledge of God. Our tribe has a special relation to God. The good of our community or nation seems to be divinely ordained. Heaven itself is imagined as a place of endless pleasure for us, while hell assures the eternal suffering of our enemies. Our satisfactions and hatreds are projected onto eternity and God becomes the power that will realize the fantasies of the ego. As the infinite mystery of the Divine is drawn into the cognitive, existential, and political limitations of individual and communal egocentrism, desire for God resembles lust more than eros.

Revelation is often offered as a solution to this paradox: God reveals himself to us in Scripture so that we do not have to depend on our limited resources for knowledge of him. At this point I will only point out that since it is always "him" that does this for us, it is difficult to avoid the suspicion that these revelations reflect interests of patriarchal power. They do not circumvent human limitation and confusion. Tillich pointed out this problem in his otherwise sympathetic assessment of Barth's *Epistle to the Romans*. Both men were struggling with the dawning implications of National Socialism, and according to Jack Forstman Tillich assessed his colleague in this way: "Barth's brilliant criticism of all religion in *Romans* is flawed in that Barth should have acknowledged that his own understanding of faith is itself also religion."[9] We encounter even revelation only through our interpretations of it. It does not save us from limitation and error.

Instead of reifying any authority, we might explore faith as our capacity to dwell in the breach between our ignorance and our desire. Faith should not be confused with believing things that cannot be "proven" or assenting to authoritative teachings. Faith is one way of describing our capacity to desire beyond the ordinary habits of our ego-minds. Faith attempts to orient us to a reality nothing like the objects of the world. But since it is does so in company with the self-protective impulses of the ego, it performs its work as a task, a path, rather than an accomplishment. We might remind ourselves of Luther's emphasis on salvation by grace alone. We are already cherished and guarded; we do not need to do anything to make ourselves attractive to the Beloved. We do not need to rely on anything but this grace alone: not revelation, not Scripture, not true doctrine, not belief, not even faith—nothing at all. Neither faith nor revelation provides untainted access to the Divine. We are constantly tempted to draw back from this breach and live in more familiar territory. Our ego-minds are terrified

9. Forstman, *Christian Faith in Dark Times*, 108–9.

to relinquish religious intermediaries and dwell in this nothingness, this Divine Emptiness where we rest at peace with our divine lover. But faith reminds us that this intimacy was accomplished by the Beloved already before the dawn of creation. "I believe! Help Thou my unbelief."

Because of the intrinsic paradoxes of faith, the temptations of the ego-mind, and the dynamics of power, idolatry infiltrates faith. We transform our Beloved into an object of our lust and control—that is, an object cast by the workers in our own idol factories. Faith seeks the true God. But it is a puritanical fantasy to imagine that faith completely extricates itself from confusion and the consolations of power. The desire for pure or total truth seems laudable, but the cruelty of movements committed to this fantasy suggests that it is dangerous to imagine that we possess a correct belief. We do not so easily evade the human condition. We humans are limited, anxious beings tyrannized by the ego and constrained by the gods of our tribe. It is to us, the sick and wounded, that physician Christ has come, but this coming did not neutralize our condition; it did not eradicate vulnerability to error and violence.

Our tradition gives us clues how to dwell in the paradox of faith. It teaches us that love is the most fundamental reality and that this love is always more and better than our best thoughts about it. Faith affirms not only intellectually, but with our hearts and bodies, that the Divine is compassionately present throughout creation but can be *identified* with nothing in creation. The author of our salvation is not this or that thing in the world. Faith is the *practice* of trying to disarm the beguiling illusions by which the good things in our world become for us oppressive idols. This practice of faith liberates the heart for love. Love is the goal: we are drawn on toward ever deeper intoxication by the Beloved, especially through the divine cupbearers: all those who bear the image of our Beloved. Love is also the path. Walking with the infinite company of God-bearers, spangled across all space and time, we slowly recognize that we have been walking with the Beloved all along. Reflecting and meditating on Scripture does not save us from error, but it is a practice for walking the way of the incarnation.

LOVE AND BETRAYAL IN SCRIPTURAL NARRATIVE

Salvation history as it is told by Scripture is the repetition of a consistent pattern. Divine Love enters into relationship with humanity. Humanity, in its ignorance and confusion, botch the relationship. But the Divine Love continues to be faithful. This pattern begins with the myth of creation in Genesis. In this dream of origins, we are exiled from the childish simplicity of paradise, but God does not abandon us.[10] God prepares us for the hard journey into history, covering

---

10. Irenaeus is perhaps the first to use this image of childhood to interpret the story of Adam and Eve; see *Against Heresies*, IV.xxxix, IV.xxxvii.5, and III.xx.1.

us with warm cloaks and accompanying us into the wide world where life can be pried from death only through pain and hard work.

In the scriptural narratives, God enters into covenant to express the intimacy with which we are bound together. God provides rituals, texts, and institutions to orient us. But we humans seem always to distort the gifts of God, using them to obscure the divine call to compassion and to justify our ignorance. God sends prophets to remind us that it is not the rituals themselves that matter but the justice and compassion that they are meant to instill.

> What to me is the multitude of your sacrifices?
> . . . .
> Bring no more vain offerings:
> incense is an abomination to me.
> New moon and Sabbath and the calling of assemblies—
> I cannot endure iniquity and solemn assembly.
> Your new moon and your appointed feasts
> my soul hates;
> they have become a burden to me,
> I am weary of bearing them.
>   Isaiah 1:11, 13–14 RSV

This list of new moons, Sabbath observation, sacrifices, and assemblies is a list of the ways in which the children of Israel had been taught to worship the mysterious power of liberation beyond all images. Through the prophet, our Beloved describes these very liturgies as a burden. The Divine Eros hates them. They make God sick. If we were to transpose this to our context, the Beloved might have said:

> What is the multitude of your moralizing?
> Bring no more vain offerings:
> Pounding of Scripture is an abomination to me.
> I cannot endure iniquity and Sunday morning worship.
> Your hymn singing and gospel readings my soul hates.

The problem with new moon and Sabbath is not that God suddenly has a new idea about what kind of worship appealed to the divine aesthetic. The problem is that the children of Israel have been using revelation to deal corruptly. They are estranged from the Lord, not because they have betrayed authoritative cultic traditions but because correct worship has done little to constrain them from injustice. Through the voice of the prophets, the priority of justice over correct form is announced as the sign of fidelity. The forms were correct. But it is all in vain. Israel is whoring after other gods, not by forgetting revealed religion, but because "on your skirts is found the lifeblood of the innocent poor" (Jeremiah 2:34). This situation should not feel alien or ancient to us. We live in a period of time when religious rhetoric galvanizes hostility toward participation of same-sex lovers in civil and religious goods. "What we learn from situations such as Matthew Shepard's murder and Colorado's passage of Amendment 2 is that a loving God hates that fags might marry, adopt, or live happy lives in their sin; and, somehow, this strong religious rhetoric appeals to a national citizenry that is only partially religious."[11] Correct belief and worship accompany and even generate hatred and division now as they did not in the past.

The Bible is familiar with the use of religious rhetoric to justify social oppression and violence. It is accustomed to the eternal return of hostility through the very religious instruments designed to promote justice. God suggests a way to return to true worship:

> Wash yourselves; make yourselves clean;
> Remove the evil of your doings
> from before my eyes;
> cease to do evil,
> learn to do good;
> seek justice,
> rescue the oppressed,
> defend the orphan,
> plead for the widow.
>
> Isaiah 1:16–17

The children of Israel are castigated by the prophets, but condemnation opens onto the possibility of deeper understanding of covenant.[12] The prophets are breathtaking in their condemnations of Israel, but they do not break the pattern. "Come now, let us reason together" (Isaiah 1:18 RSV), begs God. Through Hosea, God remembers mothering Israel, teaching "Ephraim to walk, I took them up in my arms" (Hosea 11:3). God wails in pain at the intransigent betrayal of her people: "How can I give you up, O Ephraim? How can I hand you over, O Israel? . . . My compassion grows warm and tender. I will not execute my fierce anger, . . . for I am God and no mortal, the Holy One in your midst, and I will not come in wrath" (11:8–9).

The biblical narrative splits into two covenantal expressions, rabbinic Judaism and Christianity. Judaism preserved the worship of a just and merciful God through centuries of dispersion and appalling oppression. In the Christian part of the story, the Messiah comes, embodying a dramatic story of intimate and merciful love. But Christians immediately quarrel. Four canonical and countless other Gospels vie to tell the gospel story. The new community in which goods will be shared among everyone falls apart in the early pages of Acts. Peter and Paul fight over true Christianity. The Corinthian Christians are torn apart by discord. Paul's description of a community unbounded by the social divisions of Jew and Greek, male and female, slave and free is "corrected" by a later writer using Paul's name to reinstitute the household codes of Roman patriarchy.[13] Yet

---

11. Michael Cobb, *God Hates Fags: The Rhetorics of Religious Violence*, 6.
12. See Abraham Heschel's description of the divine pathos in *The Prophets*, vol. 2, chaps. 1–3.
13. See, for example, Gerd Lüdemann, *Heretics: The Other Side of Early Christianity*.

God remains in the story, and the scriptural part of the tale ends with a promise that tears will be washed away and death will be no more.

These narratives tell a story in which we continue to participate. We misunderstand, betray, and oppress and yet we are not ourselves betrayed by our beloved Mother. This is the great story of Scripture. As Augustine writes: "Scripture enjoins nothing but *caritas* [love], and censures nothing but *cupiditas*, and molds men's minds accordingly."[14] Faithfulness to this love is envisioned as a kind of spiritual monogamy: it relates us to the one, true, and living God. Compared to this one God, all others are impostors. The incarnation is the embodiment of this one God in history. The rest of this chapter explores the idea of one God not so much as a barrier against other faith traditions but as a barrier against the idols of our hearts. Fidelity to incarnation does not withdraw us to a narrow and singular religion that is alone true but rather witnesses to the grandeur of the Divine Eros everywhere in nature and history.

COMMANDMENTS TO FIDELITY: THE FACE OF THE DEEP

We are called to dwell in and as love, and the first three of the Ten Commandments give us some guidance about how to do this. I bring up the tablets of stone with some trepidation. We are perhaps most aware of the Ten Commandments through recent hostilities regarding their placement in courthouses. But why should this argument denude these words of richer theological luminosity? A more significant objection comes from colleagues in feminist theology who draw attention to the primordiality of multiplicity within the Divine. Catherine Keller, in her masterful and sustained meditation on the first lines of Genesis, reminds us that *Elohim* is "a flux of syllables, labial, multiple. Its ending marks it stubbornly as a *plural* form of *'eloh.'*"[15] She notes the "manful" protests through which this grammar is tamed, called back to simple unity. She unearths Rashi's (characteristically) beautiful notion that the plural grammatical forms suggest that God asked permission of the divine court before creating. She quotes Rashi: "In spite of the license given to heretics by this formulation, the text does not restrain itself from teaching the virtue of humility: the great one should consult with, request permission from, the small one." She continues: "this startling bit of hermeneutical democratization itself 'risks heresy' to counter the simple unity of the Aristotelian-Christian God, even as it challenges the dominological tendency of all monotheism."[16]

---

14. Augustine, "On Christian Teaching," 3.10.15 (quoted in Aaron Stalnaker, *Overcoming Our Evil*, 217).

15. Keller, *Face of the Deep*, 173. Cleaver expands this point, following Sally Gearhart's interpretation that the plurality of the name Elohim suggests an androgynous divinity (*Know My Name*, 66).

16. Keller, *Face of the Deep*, 174. She coined the term *dominology* earlier, pointing out the subjection to "the economics, the ecology, and the ecumenism of order. Theology has not outgrown the

In Keller's Trinity, *Tehom* becomes the unfathomable, quasi-chaotic depths where the divine trickster sports with Leviathan. *Elohim*, in their humility, engage the divine court, seeking approval before starting on the rash task of creation. *Ruach*, "spirit" or "breath," moves over waters: "thus this spirit will not transcend or obliterate differences; rather differences are intensified precisely by being brought into relation. So the third capacity thus signifies the relationality itself."[17] Her reading of the first sentences of Genesis interrupts our assumptions about monotheism. Instead of control, order, and unity, our imagination is nourished by the primacy of formlessness. Water, darkness, and relation become the primordial pluralities whose fecundity provides a beginningless origin. "In the beginning: a plurisingularity of universe, earth echoing chaos, dark deep vibrating with spirit, creates."[18]

Laurel Schneider echoes this challenge to the obviousness of monotheism. She tracks, with tender sympathy, the evolution of monotheism out of trauma. When war and impermanence eroded familiar theologies, a power untroubled by the rapacity of empire provided consolation. "Political life had become intolerably inconstant with consequent deep wobbles in the cultural traditions that gave meaning to the whole fabric of life. In both contexts [Jewish and Greek] the local gods were proving impotent against invasion and conquest. In both contexts, at roughly the same time, political trauma correlates with theological innovation toward ideas of cosmic divine unity."[19] Notwithstanding the consolations of monotheism, she relentlessly uncovers the logic of domination that this unity undergirds. "Eminently useful in the administration of imperial power, the logic of the One survived the fall of the Roman Empire, the splintering of the Greek and Roman Churches, and the convulsions of the Reformations," and comes to full flower in modern science's demand for "truths that do not change."[20]

Keller and Schneider remind us of the dependence of domination upon a logic of totality and unity. Their theological and historical genealogies are scathing in their denunciation of violence and delightful in their fecund explosions of pluriform imaginaries. Through multiplicity they bring us back to the disorienting depths of gospel wisdom that all creation is beloved. The *tehomic* depths celebrate our differences and provide the "rhythmic life of *all* creatures."[21] Schneider untangles the logic of love and washes us with its sweet immorality: "Love that is *presence* is promiscuous, willing to open the door to *whomever* the other is

---

subjection of the *oikos* to the *dominus*. The abiding western dominology can with religious sanction identify anything dark, profound, or fluid with a revolting chaos, an evil to be mastered, a nothing to be ignored. 'God had made us the master organizers of the world to establish system where chaos reigns. He [*sic*] has made us adept in government that we may administer government among savages and senile peoples'" (6, quoting Senator Beveridge in 1900 before the U.S. Senate).

17. Keller, *Face of the Deep*, 232.
18. Ibid., 238.
19. Schneider, *Beyond Monotheism*, 40.
20. Ibid., 72, 73.
21. Keller, *Face of the Deep*, 238.

now without demand for fidelity to promises made before, without regard for accompanying narratives or expectations. There is no contract. It is not that kind of love. . . . If we wish to say that God *is* Love, then we also say that God comes into being specifically, without abstraction. And this is multiplicity because it is presence in the world that is confoundingly multiple. . . . The multiplicity of divinity-in-love with the world speaks directly, in pentecostal fluency across the myriad unities of beings."[22] Both theologians underscore the limitlessness of love, spread out over all beings and nonbeings, and challenge our attachment to familiar peoples and local gods. They allow us to reconceive the commands in stone as condemnations of the idol factories in our heart so that we might open to the wideness of the Divine Eros, whose formlessness is infinitely fecund.

Returning to the magisterial commandment, "You shall have no other gods before me," after these shape-shifting theological poetics is not a relieved reassertion of unity after a drunken moment of divine lovemaking. It is rather another moment in the dance of nonduality in which neither one nor many has precedence. The tablets of stone do not defend a primordial One but teach us about ways we inadvertently abandon love and how we might open more deeply to the lapping of eros and agape.

DIVINE MYSTERY: THE FIRST TABLE OF STONE

Tradition delivers to us an understanding of God in which we "believe." "Tradition" is adept at identifying fragments of its past with unchanging and revealed divine truth. But tradition actually works out to be quite particular. It is not Christianity per se but our denomination or, rather, our congregation, or perhaps that faction of my congregation with which I most closely identify. Perhaps more accurately, traditional religious truth turns out to be identical to the ideas about religion that exist inside my head at any given moment in time. We imagine that our thoughts about God, as these are delivered by a local religious community, correspond exactly to God in God's own being. Avoiding the too obvious solipsism of belief, we pin our thought onto sentences or phrases from Scripture. We read that "the wrath of God is revealed from heaven against all ungodliness" (Romans 1:18), and that "God gave them up to dishonorable passions" (1:26 RSV). Such a text might engage our hostility toward women who raise children with other women or men who trouble our thoughts about male comportment. We slide over Paul's tirade against strife, malignity, gossip, slander, foolishness, faithlessness, heartlessness, ruthlessness (1:28–29) that might tangle us, too, in the divine wrath. We build whole religious and political movements around condemnation of homosexuality, unconcerned by his condemnation of malignant strife or his passionate assault on judgmentalism with which

---

22. Schneider, *Beyond Monotheism*, 206.

Paul concludes these reflections (2:1–5). Secure that our beliefs are identical to God's, we oppose this God inside our head with all of the lesser or false gods that exist in everyone else's heads: the heads of the Baptists or Catholics, the conservatives or the liberals, the Arabs or Yoruba. Faith often turns out to be an absolute confidence in the accidents of our own personal thought processes. This absolute confidence becomes the occasion for hostility toward everyone else: nonbelievers or the faction lobbying for hymns we do not like. This hostility to opponents seems not only justified by religion, but required by it.

The first three commandments expose ways anxiety mimics faith, confusing the god inside our head with the Divine Eros. The Ten Commandments describe how we are to be related to God. They are simple and straightforward, rules written on the kindergarten wall to provide basic guidance for living in community. They are also impossibly difficult, describing a state toward which we can aspire but which few attain, and they are endlessly reinterpreted. The first three commandments call us to allegiance to one God. They reflect in part the triumph of monotheism over polytheism. Read historically, this triumph is no more inspiring than the victory of one political and ethnic group over another.[23] YHWH is the one who used violence most efficiently against his enemies. From this perspective, the first commandment can be understood as an expression of an emperor demanding absolute loyalty. The subsequent political history of Western civilization indicates that this reading has found many devoted followers.

Laurel Schneider argues that monotheism functioned in a variety of ways in ancient Israel, but that exclusive monotheism emerges in conjunction with the "political anxiety" of the exile and Second Temple period (520 BCE—70 CE). The polemic against other peoples emerges as a weapon of survival in a perennially colonized people. "With the physical center of worship gone, the political and religious leaders in captivity far away, and the conquering powers ever present, such polemic makes sense as part of an attempt to keep the exiles, and perhaps particularly their children, from giving up and taking on the identity of their captors."[24] Monotheism prevents the dispersal of a fragile and threatened people. "A monotheism that transcends time and space but that binds a people as a people regardless of time and space took time to catch on but eventually made possible the retention of a distinctively Jewish identity in the face of relentless assault."[25] She continues:

> When a local deity cannot survive the conditions that war and cultural assault impose, that choice also is usually the same. What is remarkable is that most deities die because . . . they cannot change. In the case of Israel, the very human, expedient need was for the familiar and local warrior-king-

---

23. Jack Nelson-Pallmeyer, *Is Religion Killing Us? Violence in the Bible and the Quran.* See in particular chaps. 3, 4, and 5, which show the ethnic violence at the heart of Hebrew and Christian Scriptures.

24. Schneider, *Beyond Monotheism*, 33.

25. Ibid., 35.

patriarch protector and progenitor to merge into and with the more cosmic, abstract, and unfamiliar (and unnameable) source of all things, a single God now not only of the Israelites but of all the distant and unfamiliar peoples. It is this move (or recognition), grounded in cultural trauma and in the genius that necessity births, that reverberates through Christian monotheism and continues to help in shaping its concepts of the divine.[26]

Idolatry worships a tribal god but insists this god of our tribe is the most powerful, the "real" god.[27] It is a way of elevating my tribe—my religion, my congregation, my culture—over all the others. But read theologically, these first three commandments also reflect the perennial tension between anxiety and faith. Monotheism is more than the exploitation of religion in the triumph of local political and ethnic powers. It is also the intuition of faith that behind all of the local powers, all of the multiplicities of history, and all of our inexplicable sufferings something remains that is absolutely good. This is less a defense of dominating oneness than a foolish, faithful insistence that the tragedies of history and the hegemony of political power do not define us. In this sense monotheism is the intuition of infinite Goodness irreducible to the totalitarianism of power.

Walter Harrelson identifies three stages or types of biblical monotheism. The first is the prohibition of worship of deities other than YHWH, the God of Israel who brought liberation to them when they were slaves in Egypt. A second stage is an assault on rival religious claims. He cites Elijah's contest with the priests of Baal in 1 Kings 18. "For Elijah, apparently, the worshipers of Baal were to be humiliated and discredited, and their leaders destroyed. Religious conflicts around the globe today echo Elijah's understanding."[28] But a third stage points in the opposite direction. The prophets understood God to be a God not only of Israel but of all creation, "mysterious, merciful and compassionate, but also powerful, even irresistible."[29] Harrelson understands this version of monotheism and of the first commandment as not only tolerating but demanding religious pluralism. "If one worships God under any name, one worships the one God, for there is but one God. There are many ways of perceiving God, of experiencing God, of naming God, of worshiping God, but all that variety, by all its names and in all its nuances, is finally directed to the one God."[30]

Schneider makes this point from the opposite direction: "As the conceptual shape of divinity, multiplicity is therefore the embodiment of love. And love is

26. Ibid., 38. Schneider's excellent historical and theological reflections on monotheism are primarily taken up with an exposure of the ways the logic of "one" functions as an oppressive and destructive totality. Monotheism is conflated with monarchial imagery and God becomes not a transcendent Good imbuing all plurality with significance but an emperor at the head of an ecclesial hierarchy. Her analysis of the dangers of monotheism and her ethical alternative is fascinating and important.

27. See Richard H. Niebuhr, *Radical Monotheism*, especially ch. 2, "The Idea of Radical Monotheism," 25.

28. Walter Harrelson, *The Ten Commandments for Today*, 30.

29. Ibid.

30. Ibid., 31.

what divinity is because love cannot be One, as Augustine realized. Love, necessitating the existence of others, of difference, gravity, and encounter, is the divine reality of heterogeneity."[31] In this sense monotheism is more than the triumph of a tribal god or even a survival strategy of a traumatized people. It is a theological insight that my tribe or my ego is only one tiny drop in the infinite ocean of erotic exuberance and care. Divine Eros extends over all of creation, cherishing not only my tribe but everything that exists in any way. Nothing exists except through the gracious flow of this loving power. It is the power of healing and redemption, calling each being toward deeper intimacy.

It is appropriate to interpret the Ten Commandments and the triumph of monotheism in terms of the political struggles, the patriarchal powers, and the warfare of ancient Israel. This is not a particularly pretty history. But it is also possible to understand the Ten Commandments theologically, in terms of the Bible's countercultural and always alarming challenge to our idolatries, monotheistic or otherwise. To explore this more theological reflection, we should avoid thinking of this challenge as a royal command or divine loyalty oath. Instead, we might consider the first three commandments on the tablet of stone to be love letters, sent to us from our Beloved to guide our seeking when we become confused.

THE FIRST LOVE LETTER

"I am the Lord your God, who brought you out of the land of Egypt, out of the house of slavery; you shall have no other gods before me" (Exodus 20:2–3). This commandment no doubt arose from the particular context of ethnic and religious warfare and the complex conflict between matriarchal and patriarchal cultures, between tribes naming the Divine in various ways and worshiping in ways that reflected their values and fears. But if the Holy Spirit weaves herself through Scripture, then this history is not all there is to it.

"Our hearts are restless until they rest in thee," Augustine sings to God in the opening sentences of his *Confessions*. But it is difficult to rest in something we neither see nor taste nor hear. The dark emptiness that haunts our hearts is comforted with many images and many voices. This first commandment begins with a sign or rune that turns images into windows through which the breeze of the Spirit blows: I am the Beloved who brought you from the house of bondage. The sign of the Beloved is liberation. The exodus is not only one story among many; it is the iconographic story through which we learn to read the way the Beloved accompanies the Jewish and Christian people. Liberation is the signature of YHWH; it is the secret mark that identifies the Beloved amid all impostors.[32]

---

31. Schneider, *Beyond Monotheism*, 205.

32. See Peter Hodgson, who argues that the root meaning of God is as the one who "*gives* freedom or *sets free*. God's freedom is generative freedom. God sets the created world free from nonbeing, from its 'bondage to decay,' and God sets human beings free from their subjection to sin and oppressive

In fairy tales, when lovers or siblings are separated, they are given a sign, a ring, an amulet. Years later they recognize each other through this mark, this seemingly insignificant thing they have kept through all their tribulations. The rule of fidelity begins with this lover's knot. "By this mark you will always know me, whatever my disguise, however long we have been separated. I bring you from bondage. Know this and you will know me." This is put first, before the commandments proper begin, so we will have a key for interpreting everything that follows. Commandments are cast in the form of laws but they are framed as a path to freedom. What binds us, enslaves us, or tyrannizes us is not from the Beloved.

This engagement ring is important because we can be bound not only by Egyptians but by religion itself, by congregations that despise us, by church teachings that imprison us in dungeons of self-loathing. We may not be able to recognize our Beloved because her name is assumed by tyrants and oppressors. "You shall have no other gods before me" thunders the misogynist, the abuser, the moralist. It seems there is nowhere in the universe to go to escape this master of the universe who creates us only to despise us. Monotheism is deployed as a kind of "no exit"—there is nowhere to go if you are condemned by this god, the only god, beside whom there are no others. This song of faithfulness tells a different story. We are like the person in the riddle of two doors, one to life and one to death, each guarded by a soldier, one who tells only the truth and one only lies, but we do not know which door leads to life and which to death, and we do not know which soldier is the one who tells the truth and which one lies. There are masks of Divinity everywhere, and we have through our lover a clue how to tell which belong to the Beloved and which are death dealing. "I bring you out of bondage. That is how you can recognize me. That is the face of Divinity by which I will be known."

When we are confused, we project onto Divinity the fears and hopes that terrify or console us. We want a powerful divine king and bow to his tyranny even if it horrifies us. We hate ourselves because of the ugly portraits we see of ourselves in a racist, homophobic, class-conscious society and we enthrone our tormentor as a god. It is these idols against which the first commandment warns us.[33] From a theological point of view, it is not so much a commandment as a diagnosis. It describes for us our illness and prescribes medicine for us. We are confused and we worship at the altars of alien gods. But the issue is not the straightforward one of identifying which of the various gods we should worship: Baal, Astarte, Isis, Elohim. If Astarte brings a barren woman a child, we wor-

---

powers so that they might obtain to the 'glorious freedom' of God's children." Hodgson reminds us that Romans 8 is a scriptural example of this meaning. "Liberal" itself means "fitted for freedom" and so serves Hodgson as a particularly apt term "to designate the nature and content of theology" (*Liberal Theology: A Radical Vision*, 11).

33. John Shelby Spong reminds us that the numbering of the commandments is not universally agreed upon. There are actually nine injunctions. Sometimes the first one is split into two (you shall have no other gods, and you shall make no graven images). Sometimes these are united and the last commandment is split into two (*The Living Commandments*, 22).

ship her; if Elohim disperses Astarte's priests, we worship him. But the problem with idolatry is not about the different ways tribes name deity. God is the name of the power of liberation and healing, mighty in history (sometimes), mighty against our inner demons (sometimes). We use the name of God as cover for the idols of our hearts. This is the great danger of faith, to confuse our fears and desires with the Beloved.[34] It is against this universal temptation that the first commandment speaks.

The Divine Eros is not the name in which history's victors conquer. The Beloved Mother and Lover is the one who creates all things and liberates them for the fullness of their life. It was the genius of ancient Israel to have some intuition that Divinity is not only a tribal god but breathes over all creation, committed to the good of the whole cosmos and committed therefore to all of humanity. Monotheism wavers between awareness of Goodness beyond every name and befuddlement by the gods and goods of this world.

Emperor Constantine's conversion to a god in whose sign he won a great battle transformed Christianity from an outlaw cult to the national religion. His confidence in God translated into unsurpassed confidence in himself: "We have received from Divine Providence the supreme favor of being relieved from all error."[35] By a wonderful sleight of hand, this god gives victory in battle and vindicates the emperor, empire, and the policies he enforces. This is not a victory for monotheism; it is yet another, colossal, violation of the first commandment.

We are like the despairing slaves who escaped Egypt only to be left in the desert. We have Scripture, prophets, even an incarnation to teach us about the freedom that comes from compassion and justice. But our Liberator is hidden from us and we cannot bear this uncertainty and loneliness. "When the people saw that Moses delayed to come down from the mountain, the people gathered around Aaron, and said to him, 'Come, make gods for us, who shall go before us; as for this Moses, the man who brought us up out of the land of Egypt, we do not know what has become of him.' Aaron said to them, 'Take off the gold rings that are on the ears of your wives, your sons, and your daughters, and bring them to me" (Exodus 32:1–2). This story is not ancient at all. In our confusion we make our own gods from the rings of gold we admire and from the chariots we trust.[36] The first commandment warns us that though we do this to thwart our uncertainty and fear, it is in truth the way of despair. The way of faith is to yearn for the Beloved and to be satisfied with nothing less. "The mystery of God's inner being serves an enormously important purpose. It helps to protect the

---

34. George Eliot's character Bulstrode in *Middlemarch* is the great literary expression of the gymnastics the psyche performs to conceal genuine desires within a cloak of piety.

35. Quoted in Schneider, *Beyond Monotheism*, 67.

36. Joan Chittister argues that the significance of the first commandment is to reject our tendency to put our hope in worldly things (money, relationships, political supremacy, etc.) (*The Ten Commandments: Laws of the Heart*, chap. 1). Vincent J. Miller provides a much more sophisticated analysis of consumerism as it has infected our root experiences of desire, including religion itself, in *Consuming Religion: Christian Faith and Practice in a Consumer Culture*.

community from claiming too much about the meaning of God's revelation."[37] The Groundless Ground of liberation has many imitators but no rivals.

THE SECOND LOVE LETTER

This first song of divine fidelity diagnoses our condition as one of enormous confusion and attempts to give some guidance in our wanderings. In this we find comfort and consolation, hope that we are journeying toward and with the one true god. But the second commandment is like a splash of cold water, reminding us how infinitely difficult it is to follow the thread through the maze of religious possibilities. "You shall not make for yourself an idol, whether in the form of anything that is in heaven above, or that is on the earth beneath, or that is in the water under the earth" (Exodus 20:4). This seems terribly unfair. All the people of the earth, it seems, have images of the Divine to comfort and orient them. Even if they know that the images themselves are not literally gods and goddesses, they at least have something to inspire their imaginations as they worship and seek healing, protection, and guidance. The austerity demanded by this commandment is entirely alien to the human heart. But it is the tenderness and generosity of our Beloved to impose this hard commandment.

This prohibition is the key to everything else because it reminds us that there is nothing in the heaven above or the earth beneath or the water under the earth that is adequate to the creating and liberating power of the Divine. This power has no name, no image.[38] It is not like an angel in its fierce beauty or an animal in its superhuman power. It is not like a man or woman, even one removed from the confines of mortality or imbued with superpowers to bring rain, victory, babies, death, or mercy. This power is not *like* anything at all. When we tie this power down to our imaginations, we betray it, subjecting it to the small and limited things created by the Divine but which the Divine infinitely transcends.

The furor that is unleashed over whether male language alone should be used for the Divine suggests how deeply we cherish the images we form in our heads for God—and also how quickly these images translate into oppressive instruments of power. If there is nothing in heaven above or the earth beneath or the water under the earth that is adequate as an image for God, then certainly maleness is insufficient. It is a direct violation of this commandment to imagine God as male. But we cling to this image as if it were God itself. Elizabeth Johnson assesses this as "the equivalent of the graven image, a finite representation set up

---

37. Harrelson, *Ten Commandments for Today,* 33.

38. Harrelson suggests that another possible meaning of the second commandment is its connection with the language of image and likeness to the creation of humanity: "Might it be, then, that for Israel to have made images of God was forbidden because the only appropriate representation of deity in the creation was: frail and imperfect humankind!" (ibid., 35). This interpretation has interesting resonance with the parable of Matthew 25, which directs us to the poor, imprisoned, and sick as bearers of the image of Christ.

and worshiped as if it were the whole of divine reality. What is violated is both the creature's limitation and the unknowable mystery of the living God. . . . More solid than stone, more resistant to iconoclasm than bronze, seems to be the ruling male substratum of the idea of God cast in theological language and engraved in public and private prayer."[39] She points out that this theological idolatry "functions to justify social structures of dominance/subordination and an androcentric world view inimical to the genuine and equal human dignity of women, while it simultaneously restricts the mystery of God."[40]

Richard Cleaver makes a parallel point when he identifies the antigay agenda of the "focus on the family" as an expression of idolatry: "Idols are false gods that we worship because they are easier to manage than the real thing. We have made the bourgeois family into an idol because it, unlike the living God, gives us permission to confine our concern only to our own kin and kind. It tells us it is OK to worry above all about keeping our families safe from the rest of society. That is precisely the kind of family Jesus tells us to reject."[41] Whether it is men in general or a particular kind of family conducive to their hold on power, identification of these human constructions with the Beloved is exposed by this commandment as a kind of faithlessness.

This second love letter warns us of the dangers of identifying an image of something in creation with God. When we translate an image of God drawn from the earth directly into social and ecclesial structures, we end up defrauding women, queers, the afflicted, non-Christians, and most of the human race of their full humanity. Marcella Althaus-Reid shatters this kind of idol when she asks us to envision: "The God who has come out, tired perhaps of being pushed to the edge by hegemonic sexual systems in theology, has made God's sanctuary on the Other side. Our task and our joy is to find or simply recognize God sitting amongst us, at any time, in any gay bar or in the home of a camp friend who decorates her living room as a chapel and doesn't leave her rosary at home when going to a salsa bar."[42] When our idols are shattered we discover traces of the Beloved not only in a variety of images but in the face of the divine image sitting next to us.

THE THIRD LOVE LETTER

In the third prohibition, our Beloved arouses us to the consequences of our confusion when we translate our ignorance into action: "You shall not make wrongful use of the name of the Lord your God" (Exodus 20:7). Not able to recognize the Beloved, we nonetheless employ the name of God to justify and explain

39. Elizabeth Johnson, *She Who Is*, 40.
40. Ibid.
41. Cleaver, *Know My Name*, 78.
42. Althaus-Reid, *Queer God*, 4.

everything. Every cruel suffering that descends on us through natural disasters, plagues, droughts, illness, accident, and all of the tragedies to which a material world exposes us are explained by appeal to the name of God. Every injustice conceived and executed in the lust for power and domination is sanctioned by the name of God. "With god on our side" everything is permitted, everything is justified: every war, every slave, every child stolen from indigenous parents and incarcerated in "Christian" schools, every form of servitude and degradation become the will of God. Jim Crow laws in America's South, the pass-card laws in South Africa, the Nuremburg Laws in Germany, the humiliating exclusion of women or gay men from ministry, laws protecting the violence of men against their wives and children—all are given sanctuary through the name of God.[43]

This third warning exposes for our view the deep violation of the divine image we perpetrate in our confidence that we know how to wield the name of God. Walter Harrelson laments the potency of our confusion:

> We can see, therefore, that this third commandment has a burning import for our common life today, and in particular for organized religion. . . . God will not endure such a misuse of divine power designed to bring health and healing. When religion is turned perversely against the very means that it uses to bring blessing, then the springs are poisoned and little can be done. How massive is the damage that has been done by those who have lifted up God's name for mischief. Thousands and thousands struggle for health in mental institutions trying to undo, with professional help, the damage done by those who have driven them into psychosis by the warnings of eternal damnation. Unloved in this world by family and friends, as they believe, they have concluded that God too will not love them, cannot love them, until they do what the religious practitioner demands that they do. God, too, may then be identified as a deceiver and destroyer. These more subtle ways of abusing the power of God are far more destructive, I believe, than those prevalent in ancient societies.[44]

The violation of this third commandment is the most complete betrayal of our faith. It is not simply that we do not understand the Divine. This lack of understanding is fundamental to our condition and so is not itself a betrayal. But identifying our mistakes and baptizing our cruelties in God's name is the root violation of the intimacy between humanity and the Beloved. It betrays the divine love, it betrays our desire, it betrays our obligations to love one another. By naming one of our most characteristic confusions as a violation of the Decalogue, this third commandment exposes the root tragedy of the human condition: evil and destruction are justified in the name whose real power is creativity, healing, and liberation.

---

43. Dorothee Soelle describes this as theological sadomasochism in *Suffering*. Randy Newman's "God's Song" is a dark and ironic description of this masochistic piety from God's point of view.
44. Harrelson, *Ten Commandments and Human Rights*, 65.

TENDER MERCIES

Together these first warnings remind us of the threefold nature of our ignorance: 1) we cannot fathom the great mystery of liberation; 2) in our ignorance we fasten on symbols of power, desire, and fear as if these were themselves divine; 3) we magnify our mistakes and cruelties by perpetrating them in the divine name. In these ways we give infinite, even divine, sanctity to our errors and ignorance, our fears and our greed. This is a terrible violence we perpetrate on others, upon whom we inflict our certainty, and on ourselves, in the condemnations we inflict upon ourselves. Recognizing these habits might allow us to hesitate before we equate our community values with the divine will. We might imagine that those against whom we are fighting also have a story. We might entertain the possibility that the Liberator upon whose tenderness all reality rests may hold also our opponents and all those we know nothing about in the infinite abyss of mercy and love.

The diagnosis contained in these first commandments offers a great liberation. Not only does faith not depend on our certainty, faith is antithetical to certainty: utter confidence in the fabrications of our minds, of our tradition, and of our interpretations of the Bible is a massive violation of this first table of the Decalogue. Our thoughts about the Divine are no different from the "block of wood" that is mocked in Isaiah 44. Or perhaps they are worse. Ancient peoples probably knew that their block of wood was a representation and not Divinity itself. But we entangle ourselves in the confusion that our mental constructs are divine. In displacing the mysterious abyss of the Divine Eros with a "block of wood" we are blind to the utter goodness of the Beloved and blind to the preciousness of the divine image in one another.

There is a great mercy in this unmasking of our self-deceptions. In the unveiling of our idolatrous habits, faith becomes a task, a desire, and a perennial failure. We are seen by the Beloved in our sorriest and deepest deception and yet we remain cherished and adored. The intimacy of this mercy, moving so close against the raw wound of our fear, offers the opportunity to reroute the fruitless effort to deploy certainty against anxiety. When we undertake faith as a task, difficult and even impossible, the trustworthiness of the Beloved is illuminated in surprising ways. We do not have to have faith in what we do or believe or in our supposedly inerrant traditions. We have faith only in the Beloved, and this faith is completely warranted, no matter how imperfect it remains. But, like most things that come to us from the Beloved, this trust is deepened in paradoxical ways. There is a difference between the ways in which our ego-minds wish to trust in the Divine and the way in which this trust is actually satisfied.[45]

---

45. Porete is among those who give a particularly radical witness to this trust. Describing the soul who is completely absorbed into the divine Love she writes that they do not know "what is best for them, nor in what manner God wishes to find their salvation or the salvation of their neighbors, nor by what means God wishes to dispense justice or mercy, nor through what means God wishes to

Our ego-mind wants to be safe and well; we crave affirmation and certainty. These are perfectly reasonable expectations. In one sense, babies are fully justified in expecting and desiring to be cared for, fed, loved, cooed over, kept warm and safe. The impulse to provide for babies' welfare is deep in individuals and cultures. It seems to be a sign of particular depravity to be indifferent or cruel to a baby. We wish that the expectation of babies for good things could be fulfilled and as parents and as citizens make efforts to accomplish this. But babies do not have their needs perfectly met. Even if they are lucky enough to have parents who adore them, in this world they are still vulnerable to illness and injury, poverty and dislocation.

As we grow older and stumble toward adulthood we might navigate these frustrations and terrors with better grace and perhaps some understanding. But we do not stop wishing that our physical and emotional needs were met. We continue to experience frustration and misery when they are not. On the one hand, it is reasonable to expect and desire good things. The prophets' anguish over injustice suggests that from a biblical point of view socially generated suffering defaces the divine image. Jesus' ministry was dedicated to healing concrete miseries of illness, hunger, madness, and grief. There is little in Scripture to make us think that indifference to suffering reflects the divine goodness. Yet in this world we are not only vulnerable to all of these things, it is inevitable that many of them will befall each and every one of us. No one will escape unscathed the predations of suffering, any more than infants will have every physical and emotional desire instantly and unreservedly met. As Marilyn McCord Adams puts it, "God has created us radically vulnerable to horrors, by creating us as embodied persons, personal animals, enmattered spirits in a material world of real or apparent scarcity such as this. Sin is a symptom and a consequence, but neither the fundamental *explanans* nor the principle *explanandum*."[46]

This gap between legitimate desires and anxieties and what the world is capable of granting us generates many of the distortions that infiltrate our desire for the Divine. Just as it is natural to crave relief from suffering, it is natural to project onto the Divine the power to provide this relief. It is natural that the various levels of community we inhabit reflect this craving and organize themselves

---

give to the Soul the supreme gift of the goodness of His divine nobility. And for this the Unencumbered Soul possesses no longer any will to will or not-will, except only to will the will of God, and to accept in peace the divine ordinance" (*Mirror of Simple Souls*, 95–96). Her description of the peace with which such a soul encounters tribulation is all the more poignant since it was her fate to spend many months in a prison before she was burned alive in a public square.

46. Marilyn McCord Adams is unusually lucid in describing the inevitability of horror as a component of human experience. "Setting embodied persons in a material world such as this one—in which material creatures are allowed 'to do their own thing'—makes the embodied persons radically vulnerable to horrors, which *prima facie* deprives their lives of positive meaning. Letting matter such as this evolve into the most Godlike kind tends to get individuals whose lives are prima facie ruined." She raises the question why God permitted this species "so vulnerable to functional ruin" (*Christ and Horrors: The Coherence of Christology*, 39). Her book is an attempt to construct a theodicy that takes this functional ruin of human persons as an essential component of creation seriously.

both practically and symbolically to deflect suffering. This includes, of course, religion and its symbols. Much of religion's institutions and symbols reflect the desires of the ego for pleasure, happiness, and relief from suffering. God is envisioned as the power that can provide these things for ourselves and our group. We pray to God for rain, for victorious sports teams, for mercy in affliction. There is nothing wrong with this kind of prayer; indeed, it connects the Divine to our genuine experiences, weaving our desire for God into every detail of our ordinary life. But that the world does not continually support these normal desires of ego-consciousness alerts us that faith cannot simply reflect the desires of our ego.

Divine love does not intersect human faith as the ability to meet legitimate physical and emotional needs. If we think of God as the power that meets our needs, then when we experience the victory of suffering, it follows that God has abandoned us. If our child is not protected from violence or if liberation from slavery is postponed not for months but for generations, then it would seem that there is no God. This is the kind of reasoning that makes it easy to lose faith in light of the horrors of history or in the aftermath of personal disaster.[47] By exposing the dynamics of idolatry, these divine prohibitions point us in another direction.

Idolatry confuses human constructions with the Divine Emptiness we casually name God. This confusion is built into human consciousness as it struggles to accommodate to a universe that is often harsh. To the extent that religions are populated and run by human beings, this confusion is inevitably woven into all religion. We cannot expect that religion will magically enable us to escape the dynamics of idolatry or the misery that drives us to idolatry in the first place. But we can take up the task of faithfulness with an intuition that it provides something other than certainty or inerrancy. These things are alien to our human condition, and revelation does not change our condition.

Nothing changes our condition, but faith allows us to dwell in our condition with greater freedom. Instead of inerrancy we get desire. Desire is in accord with our nature; it is the bridge between ourselves and the Beloved. Faithful desire must accept that it is interlaced with errors, ignorance, and cravings. It must accept that all of the things faith uses to orient itself are themselves also interlaced with error. Faith is able to do this, even if only partially, occasionally, and imperfectly, because the Beloved has never abandoned us. We are not required to be error-free in order to be soldered in union with the Divine. This has already been accomplished in our creation as bearers of the divine image. This is what the incarnation reveals to us.

These first commandments suggest that we cannot trust our ego-consciousness and its craving for pleasure and relief from pain. This craving is part of us and should not be despised, but it is not the part of us that reflects the divine image. Neither can we trust religion. It can be a great gift and consolation; it can provide

---

47. See, for example, Richard L. Rubenstein, *After Auschwitz*; or William R. Jones, *Is God a White Racist? A Preamble to Black Theology*.

concrete ways through which we can seek the Beloved. But religion is not divine. These biblical love letters invite us to trust only the Divine Abyss, which is free of any image. Because of this paradox of yearning for what is in one sense wholly absent, faith is desire and trust. It is a desire for what is not present in anything we can touch or feel or believe concretely. It is a desire that is nonetheless already perfectly united with the object of its desire. It is trust that in spite of every failure of understanding and through every betrayal by religion, in the midst of every suffering that befalls us individually and in community, the sweet mercy of our Beloved is unwaveringly present to us.

We cannot expect to escape our condition and the distortions inherent in human life. We can only try to navigate them with greater humility and compassion. The good news is that the graciousness of the Beloved always precedes us and really has nothing to do with our efforts. The delight the Divine Eros takes in creation does not have to be generated by us. This delight is divine: infinite and eternal, unwavering, unchanging and unchangeable. This love and mercy do not even depend on our faith in them. Faith is not a work by which we surreptitiously bolster the (otherwise unreliable) divine mercy. Faith is nothing more than our awakening to what is already there. We do not create it. We only acknowledge it. By desiring it and participating in it more consciously, we do not draw it down to us, tacitly earning something that is freely given.

Desire and trust are ways to enjoy what is always there. It is the fabulous and unbelievable good news, the gospel, that we are precious regardless of what we do or believe. The *metanoia* ("turning," sometimes translated as "repentance") of faith is gradually allowing reality into our awareness. God is who God is whether we repent or not, whether we turn or not. This means that our lives are flooded with mercy and love at every second of life and over the boundary of death. *Metanoia* awakens us so that we can enjoy it, delight in it, and by burning with the joy of this intimacy we become ourselves lamps that radiate this love around us. This radiation is not a work or a responsibility. It is not by becoming good or kind or loving that we surreptitiously fulfill the obligations of faith. The compassion that burns off the faithful is simply the side effect of awakening to reality.

When young children are mad because they cannot have ice cream for dinner or are just generally tired and fussy, they may not be able to accept their mother's love. But such acceptance has nothing to do with the existence of the love. They may, eventually, recognize their mother's love, and that is a joy and consolation. But whether they do or not, their mother adores them and cares for them. Faith is only on the side of human beings; it is a joy and benefit to us. Julian of Norwich writes that she "saw no wrath except on man's side . . . for wrath is nothing else but a perversity and an opposition to peace and to love. And it comes from a lack of power or a lack of wisdom or a lack of goodness, and this lack is not in God, but it is on our side."[48] Our anxieties and frustrations are only on our side.

48. Julian of Norwich, *Showings*, chap. 48 (p. 262).

The Beloved is only love, mercy, and grace: "Mercy is a compassionate property, which belongs to motherhood in tender love; and grace is an honourable property, which belongs to royal dominion in the same love. . . . And when I saw all this, I was forced to agree that the mercy of God and his forgiveness abate and dispel our wrath."[49]

These prohibitions, these love letters, invite us to recognize the dynamics of idolatry so that we might be better able to desire and adore the Beloved. This divine presence seems not only deeply mysterious, but her gifts and pleasures are ridiculously alien to the goods anticipated by ego-consciousness. Both the security craved by the ego and the condemnations it inflicts are alien to the logic of love. Through faith, we practice disconnecting the needs of our egos or the failings of our communities with the divine will. These first three love letters are followed by a fourth: "Remember the Sabbath day and keep it holy . . . for in six days the Beloved made heaven and earth, the sea, and all that is in them, and rested the seventh day; therefore the Beloved blessed the sabbath day and hallowed it" (Exodus 20:8, 11, paraphrased). Augustine writes about this commandment: "This is holiness because here is the Spirit of God. This is what a true holiday means, quietness and rest. . . . We are offered a kind of Sabbath in the heart."[50] The tablet of stone enjoins on us peace and solace, a holiday from the cravings and fears to which we are so addicted.

The incarnation brings the Spirit of God near to us. As we become more skillful at recognizing the idols we hold dear, we become more skillful at recognizing the Spirit always so near us. The next two chapters experiment with the practice of resting in the Divine Eros, bathing in the Good Beyond Being who is holy in and beyond every name.

49. Ibid. (pp. 262–63).
50. Augustine, Sermon 8, "On the Third Commandment," quoted in B. Alan Wallace, *Mind in the Balance: Meditation in Science, Buddhism, and Christianity,* 56.

Chapter 3

"God Is Love"

Naming and Negation

But now, dear lady, I ask you, not as though I were writing you a new commandment, but one we have had from the beginning, let us love one another. And this is love, that we walk according to his commandments; this is the commandment just as you have heard it from the beginning—you must walk in it.

2 John 5–6

I certify to you, says Love to Reason, and I swear on myself, that everything which this Soul has heard about God, and all one can say about Him, is at best nothing (to speak properly) compared to what He is of Himself, which never was said, is not now said, nor will be.[1]

But this lesson is not placed in writing by human hand, but by the Holy Spirit, who writes this lesson in a marvelous way, and the Soul is the precious parchment. The divine school is held with the mouth closed, which the human mind cannot express in words.[2]

The incarnation is the embodiment of the Divine in a human form. The Goodness Beyond Being becomes meat (*carne*). Christians have been driven to make this audacious claim because of the experience of salvation that their encounter with Christ made possible. *Salvation* is derived from the word for healing: it

---

1. Porete, *Mirror of Simple Souls*, chap. 30 (p. 110).
2. Ibid., chap. 66 (p. 142).

refers not simply to feeling better about oneself or relieving old psychic wounds of their power or being declared innocent. Our deepest wounds of the soul and spirit disconnect us from our truest selves, from the divine ground, and from encounter with the divine image in humanity and in creation. The sufferings the world causes us blind us from our deep truth, and our blindness to reality immerses us in difficulties that further alienate us from this truth. Salvation heals all of these wounds. It heals us of the particular infection that suffering causes and it heals the deep wound of untruth. Salvation reweaves our spirit so that its unity with the Divine beyond being and in creation is restored. Only ultimate truth has the power to heal the deepest of our wounds; only the Divine saves.

The idea of incarnation is called forth by the encounter with healing power that was so luminous and potent in Christ. If healing, salvation, was and is available in Christ, it is necessary to say that in some sense Christ is divine. But Christians know that God is not a person who walks around, eats bread and fish, lives and dies. God is not like us. God is not even like a being. The impossible paradox of saying that God utterly transcends creation and thought but is also present in Jesus of Nazareth is captured in the symbol of incarnation. In order to begin our meditations on this, it is crucial to remind ourselves of what it is we say is being incarnate. If in Christ we have to do with the power of salvation, we will begin with reverence for the Good that transcends being, the Divine Emptiness from which flows all that is, the Infinite Eros whose fecundity is manifest in creation and whose mercy is manifest in healing. Those biblical and theological resources that help draw our mind toward the nonduality of Divinity will help us to dwell more deeply in the reality that we say is incarnate in Jesus Christ. This chapter considers the theological voices that have emphasized the nonconceptual reality of Divinity: the negative or apophatic way.

Lovers, besotted with their beloved, are not less but infinitely more acutely attuned to the way their beloved remains mysterious, evanescent, sun glittering on waves. Lovers taste the sweetness of life in their beloved, a dance, a light to be desired but never possessed. "Withered men" looked on the stars and the careless planets, only to "take their tablets and did sums"; but lovers remain "ignorant and wanton as the dawn."[3] Lovers of the Divine likewise fall more deeply into darkness and unknowing as they fall in love with the Beloved. Catherine Keller reminds us of a Renaissance lover whose "learned ignorance" allowed him to perceive something of the divine incomprehensibility: "The theology of negation is so necessary to the theology of affirmation that without it God would not be worshiped as the infinite God but as creature; and such worship is idolatry, for it gives to an image that which belongs only to truth itself."[4] Too many of us know the violence of so-called lovers who seek to possess rather than desire us. Too many of us know the violence of a religion that exchanges holy desire for pos-

---

3. Quoted from W. B. Yeats, "The Dawn," in *Poems of W. B. Yeats*, 146.
4. Keller is quoting Nicholas of Cusa (*Face of the Deep*, 205).

session of true belief. This chapter follows desire to places where ineffability and love flow into one another, distinct in thought, yet also "one taste" in essence. Meditation on this interdependence between ineffability and love is the essential foundation of reflection on incarnation. The relationship between naming and negation is at the core of Trinitarian and incarnational theology. As a practice, it deepens our freedom from the constraints of conceptual thinking, a kind of thinking that is necessary for theology and faith but also utterly inadequate to the Divine. The *via negativa* acts as a solvent that dissolves both what and how we think about the Divine Eros.

If we think about the incarnation primarily as a strange, paradoxical juxta-position of two alien and opposite substances, one divine (infinite, omniscient, simple, eternal, immutable) and one finite (bodily, finite, mortal, limited, pos-sessing at best partial knowledge), the idea of incarnation becomes all the more strange. We believe it as an act of will, but cannot really say to ourselves clearly how infinity clothed itself in a human body and wandered around an ancient town until the authorities arrested and killed him without changing. If Jesus was fully God and God is omniscient, did Jesus know everything? Could he do calculus? Did he know that Atlanta would be the capital of Georgia? Did he understand the relationship between the realization of emptiness and yogic samadhi? Did God the Father suffer on the cross? If he did, how can he be God since God does not have a body or a mind or any of the things you need to suffer; and if he did not, then in what sense was Jesus truly God?

These questions have exercised theologians for a long time, but I cannot say they exercise me very much. They seem to conceive of God as a sort of being with attributes, and these attributes are the opposite of the attributes a human being possesses (simplicity/plurality, changelessness/change, eternity/time, infinity/finitude, omnipresence/localized, and so on). The *via negativa* attempts to interrupt this way of thinking about Divinity. Rather than conceiv-ing of Divinity as a being with certain characteristics, this approach unpins our minds from the habit of conceiving of everything in terms of beings. Beings are the same as themselves and different from others. They have their own separate and distinct existence. They come into being and pass out of it. God is not a being, even a super-being; God is not a being at all. But even if we say this, together with all of the theologians and contemplatives who have come before us, it is difficult to apprehend what it means. The entire structure of our mind is shaped by language and by the senses, both of which allow us to divide the world into objects that can be experienced in various ways. It is natural and automatic that we would conceive of God in the same way, even if we tried to modify this way of thinking by making God a superior being. Conceiving of God as a being limits us spiritually. We remain spiritual children, not wrong or sinful but not growing into the deeper recesses of our souls where the Beloved awaits us. We content ourselves with milk and never grow into a diet of meat. God as being also limits the way we think about the incarnation. We may be more likely to think of Jesus as God in such a simplistic way that God can be nowhere else, and so non-Christians are all condemned to eternal alienation from their divine source.

The idea of God as a person, a being, with omnipotent powers is essential to the logic of domination by which some are saved and others damned, some orthodox and others heretics, and by which women and sexual minorities, the afflicted and the rebellious, remain perennial outsiders. In her own attempt to break up this dominating logic of a single, divine being, Catherine Keller expressed her frustration with the word *God*: "God. *Gott*. Its consonants grind like teeth. G-d. Who, saying this name, does not take it in vain? I have hardly been able to write it, to subject it to sentences that start 'God is,' 'God does.' As though 'God' identifies something, some One, rather than, as Meister Eckhart insists, 'a non-God, a nonspirit, a nonperson, a nonimage.'"[5] Paul Knitter also struggles with the difficulties of a God who is simply another being in the universe, an upholder of the dualistic order of things. He learns from Buddhists the language of emptiness, groundlessness, energy, inter-being. He quotes his teacher, Karl Rahner, who believed that "in the future Christians would be mystics or they would be nothing."[6] He finds his prayer more oriented to something that "bears a much greater resemblance to *Sunyata* and InterBeing than to the prevalent Christian image of God as the transcendent Other."[7] The great Emptiness or Groundlessness that connects all that is in deep and compassionate relationship seems to him more consistent with John's representation of God as love. The First Letter of John says not that God is a divine Father who loves but that God *is* love. "To love is to move out of self, to empty self, and connect with others. Love is this emptying, connecting energy that in its power originates new connections and new life. The God who, as Dante tells us, is 'the love that moves the moon and the other stars' is the InterBeing of the stars and the universe."[8] These contemporary writers are not seeking language for Divinity outside the conceptuality of being and person because they are postmodern, death-of-God, new-age, sensitive folk. They are doing so because this is the path that lovers of the Divine have been taking for many thousands of years. If we have forgotten this path it is not because it does not exist—it has merely been overgrown by institutions that are not served by it and practices that are less likely to discover it.

The more urgent reason for prefacing meditations on the incarnation with the *via negativa* is that it allows us to see Christ not as the juxtaposition of two opposite substances but as the human form in its fully realized and natural expression. The Divine Eros names a dimension of reality that is nondual, nonconceptual, and yet, to speak poetically, yearns to realize itself in creation itself and in the sublime intimacy of incarnation. This Divinity is the groundless ground of all that is and is also the deepest truth of the human soul. It is this erotic ground-

---

5. Keller, *Face of the Deep*, 172.
6. Knitter, *Without Buddha*, 15.
7. Ibid., 17.
8. Ibid., 18.

lessness that constitutes our own divine image. Both to protect ourselves from unworthy concepts of God and also to move more gracefully into our own imageless depths, we turn to the way of negation, the intertwining practice of naming and negation.

THE WAY OF NEGATION AND THE PRACTICE OF COMPASSION

The distinction between Divinity and our human constructs is protected by the first three commandments. But the insistence that the Divine Eros is irreducible to our thoughts and images does not leave us with an empty black box. Within Christianity a dialectical practice has arisen that integrates awareness of divine mystery with transformation by and for love. This interdependence means that mystery is not mere agnosticism but is rooted in a positive experience of the Divine as the rock of salvation, as the fountainhead of healing. Gregory Palamas is among those who explicitly link the utter transcendence of the Divine with the practice of love: "it is because of their love of men that the saints speak, so far as this is possible, about things ineffable, rejecting the error of those who in their ignorance imagine that, after the abstraction from beings, there remains only an absolute inaction."[9] But what is the love, the action, for which the way of negation prepares us? St. Isaac, bishop of Nineveh, an ascetic from the seventh century, opens a window on the compassion he perceives to be the essence of Christianity (I have modified the exclusive language):

> And what is a merciful heart? It is the heart's burning for all of creation, for human beings, for birds, for animals and even for demons. At the remembrance and at the sight of them, the merciful person's eyes fill with tears which arise from the great compassion that urges their heart. It grows tender and cannot endure hearing or seeing any injury or slight sorrow to anything in creation. Because of this, such a person continually offers tearful prayer even for irrational animals and for the enemies of truth and for all who harm it, that they may be guarded and forgiven.[10]

Because salvation is healing for this ever more intense and universal love of creation, it is natural that we retain love as one of the most potent names of redemptive power. But redemption itself points toward a source that is irreducible to our understanding. When we fall in love with the source of our salvation, we do not fall in love with a discrete object, a thing, an entity that is known or knowable like objects or persons in the world. The dialectic between naming and negation is inherent to the dynamics of faith. Dwight Hopkins draws

---

9. Gregory Palamas, *Triads* 1.3.19 (p. 36).
10. This is quoted from *Mar Isaacus Ninivta, De Perfectione Religiosa*, ed. P. Bedjan (Paris, 1909), 507, by Mary Hansbury, translator of St. Isaac of Nineveh, *On Ascetical Life*, 12.

connections between apophatic theology and the liberation of humanity. He identifies the "old, gray-haired, white god [as] one of the deepest causes for black self-hatred." God is black for African Americans because the "divine compassion for those on the bottom of society's scale [chooses to manifest] in the 'little ones' of the earth. . . . Human speech gives various verbal symbols for this divine spirit of liberation and freedom . . . [but] the Spirit cannot be contained within one human symbol."[11] In order to undo some of the violence done in the name of religion we move from oppressive names to an unnamed God. In eroding ideas unworthy of Divinity, we also challenge ideas unworthy of ourselves. We "unsay" the woman, bisexual, transgendered person who is demeaned by patriarchy and heterosexism. We "unsay" the violence that has stained our psyche. The blinding luminosity of the divine image shines through us in the specificity of our unique beauty—female, queer, afflicted.[12] Negation is not merely theoretical or conceptual. It is ultimately a practice of love that enables us to dismantle obstacles that block us from remembering our true name and the name of our Beloved. The method or technique of the negative way focuses on the structures of mind to break the domination of dualistic thinking.

Each sapiential theologian has a distinctive way of walking the path of negation, the way of "unknowing." This metaphor of unknowing, which is found in many apophatic theologians, paradoxically expresses a nonconceptual mode of awareness. In the words of Augustine: "If you have understood, then it is not God. If you were able to understand, then you understood something else instead of God. If you were able to understand partially, then you have deceived yourself with your own thoughts."[13] Pseudo-Dionysius, Schleiermacher, and Mechthild of Magdeburg are among those lovers whose writings dwell in the liminal space where we know only that we do not know. Dionysius names Divinity through the logic of causality and negates these names by dissolving conceptual thought. Schleiermacher questions the logic of causality itself, which had provided Dionysius the leverage for the practice of negation. He engages a proto-phenomenology, examining the deep structure of consciousness to expose a dimension of mind that is itself nondualistic. This opens an area in which not only causality but the difference between self and other dissolves. Where there is no self and no other, no soul and no (personal) God, there is no cause and no effect. Both Dionysius and Schleiermacher deploy philosophy to implement the limitations of language. Mechthild of Magdeburg bends language in the

11. Dwight Hopkins, *Heart and Head*, 99, 100.

12. But since faith is entangled in distortions, even the path of negation can recapitulate oppressive theologies, so we must remain "vigilant about the ways in which the categories that name and define the spiritual life—redemption, salvation, soul, self, God, virtue—as well as the process or stages of mystical ascent—purgation, dark night, union—repeat subtle forms of gender, racial, or social violence" (Lanzetta, *Radical Wisdom*, 22).

13. Augustine, Sermon 52, "The Trinity," §16, quoted in Mayra Rivera, *Touch of Transcendence*, 17. Johnson also quotes this passage of Augustine as she develops her own argument for the crucial role of divine incomprehensibility for classical and feminist theology (*She Who Is*, 105).

opposite direction, saturating her theology with concrete images drawn from bed chambers and imperial courts. Her theopoetics nonetheless demand yet another negation. In addition to the renunciation of concept, language, causality, self, and other, she invites us to renounce sovereignty as an image for divine power.

The disorienting effects of these negative paths let us inhabit religious language differently: we compose "images that reveal the traces of the passing wind . . . in faithful response to the unsettling caress of an indescribable God."[14] But the way we understand the object of negation governs how we undertake the act of negation. A residue of conceptuality survives our efforts to move beyond the constraints of language. When the practice of negation, even spread out over three such different thinkers as Dionysius, Schleiermacher, and Mechthild, remains within the conceptual framework of theism it is difficult to leave behind pictures of God as a man in white robes, as a terrifying or tender father, as a judge who condemns or sets free. Another way to practice negation is to expose the framework itself to the solvent of a nontheistic tradition. Meditating on emptiness or studying the eight limbs of yoga, for example, presses us to sacrifice still more of our ideas, in obedience to an ever more unrestrained devotion. But this extreme sports version of negation will await another opportunity. For the moment, we will remain inside the symbolic and conceptual universe of Christianity.

In the last chapter, we observed how false certainty shadows and mimics faith. The first commandments guard against the violence spun from idolatries that form in our minds and in our communities. The *via negativa* takes another step by proposing a practice that dismantles ideas about the Beloved, allowing the living love of Divinity to flow more unrestrainedly. Contemplation of the Divine Emptiness prepares us for the radical and universal love to which the gospel calls us. Protecting the divine mystery is in this sense not only a prophylactic against idolatry but intrinsic to the practice of love. As Gregory Palamas emphasizes, the practice of negation is what makes possible "the highest state of all, the love of God," through which one "will put in practice and acquire a pure and perfect love for his neighbor."[15]

NAMING AND NEGATION: TWO TRUTHS

There is a version of the *via negativa* in every theological writing. Karl Barth's *Epistle to the Romans* thunders against the identification of religion with God. Paul Tillich tracks the proximity between religion and the demonic that haunts

---

14. Rivera, *Touch of Transcendence*, 17.

15. Gregory Palamas, *Triads* 2.2.19 (p. 55). There is an echo of this complete interdependence of loving God and neighbor, abandoning oneself to the Divine Abyss as the only path to radical love, in the Buddhist representation of wisdom and compassion as the mutually interdependent paths and fruits of awakening. See, for example, Knitter's discussion of this in *Without Buddha*, especially 33 but throughout much of the text.

Christianity.[16] Negation is rooted in awareness that divinity is always more than our ideas about it. Some intuition that the Beloved is not a local deity that fits inside our heads is built into virtually any genuine religious sentiment.[17] When the gospel song croons "Jesus is on the mainline, tell him what you need," few people grab the telephone and expect to hear the voice of Jesus of Nazareth speaking Aramaic on the other end. Names and images for the Divine bring solace and comfort to the human heart, rendering the proximity of the divine love to our imagination. But as Schleiermacher puts it, religious people "know that it is only in speech that they cannot avoid the anthropomorphic: in their immediate consciousness they keep the object separate from its mode of representation."[18] We humans need concrete images and yet we know these images do not literally correspond to the Divine.[19]

The distinctive stability and consolation of faith are unlike anything else in the world. Built into the familiarity of images is the intuition that the power behind the name cannot be tamed either by homey metaphors or esoteric attributes. Our mode of speech and thinking derive from the primary ways we experience the world: we exist in the world of nature where subjects and objects are distinct from one another and names are convenient ways of designating ourselves and everything we encounter. As Nicholas of Cusa points out, we name things in order to distinguish things from one another, in particular by way of contrasts.[20] Objects are discrete, particular, the same as themselves and different from other things. They are "out there," "not me." Experiencing the world through language that distinguishes subjects and objects makes it possible to move around in creation in human form, interacting with other beings. But the divine cause of this cosmos does not share its mode of existence. It is not a being among beings, part of the furniture of the cosmos. The divine attributes as they are specified in Thomas Aquinas or other classical theologians do not attach to God in the same sense that ordinary objects have attributes: Graham has red hair, God is immutable. They function best as backhanded negations, specifying some of the senses in which the features of creation distinguish it from its creator. Every thinkable object is composed of parts; God is simple, that is, God is not made up

16. See, e.g., Tillich's *Systematic Theology*, vol. 3. William Franke's two-volume work, *On What Cannot Be Said*, provides short excerpts from numerous religious and poetical works, giving a good sense of something of the range of the apophatic strand of religious writings.

17. In response to the question why apprehension of redemption requires qualification or negation, Edward Farley argues that all speaking about God includes this dialectic of qualification: "Both worshipers and theologians sense the inadequacy, the non-immediacy, the mythological character of their language of praise and concept" (*Divine Empathy: A Theology of God*, 101).

18. Schleiermacher, *Christian Faith*, §5 Postscript (p. 26).

19. St. Isaac, bishop of Nineveh, points out that meditation on Scripture is an important part of what he calls ascetic practice: "Until one receives the Paraclete, he needs written indications to fix profitable memories in his heart by means of images, to renew the incentive for virtue by constant meditation on them, and to see in his own soul vigilance against the subtle ways of sin" (*On Ascetical Life*, 110).

20. Nicholas of Cusa, "On Learned Ignorance" 76 (*Selected Spiritual Writings*, 21).

of parts. Every being changes as it passes through time, coming into and passing out of existence; God is eternal and unchanging. But trying to think simplicity or immutability not only as a negation (not having parts, not changing) but as something positive is difficult. Trying to think a reality that in no way changes, we end up imagining only boring stasis. Thinking changelessness itself directs the mind away from everything it knows about existence. Changelessness is literally inconceivable: we cannot form a concept of it.

The exercise of trying directly to think these attributes indicates not only that they are literally unthinkable but also that they are not attributes in any ordinary sense. Meditation on the divine attributes begins the task of dissolving the normal way conceptual mind holds on to ideas about God. Through this practice, one is gradually driven toward dimensions of one's own mind that are not governed by discursive reason. Premodern theologians drew a contrast between reason and intellect. Reason equips us to operate in the world of nature and culture, but intellect allows us to apprehend dimensions of reality unbound by space and time. Nicholas of Cusa characterizes reason as "much inferior to the intellect."[21] John Scotus Eriugena goes further, meditating on the prologue to the Gospel of John: "At the furthest distance from all reason and intellect, the blessed Evangelist reveals the divine mysteries."[22] All of these writers use language to run up against its limits.

The dawning awareness of the inadequacy of language exposes every attempt to draw the Divine into the structure of thought as a failure.[23] Faith dwells in the gap between the living reality of Divinity and the god that is constructed by language, belief, doctrine, and ideas. The dialectic between *kataphasis* (naming) and *apophasis* (negation) arose within Christianity to express a double truth of religious life. We require names because our minds and our language, our thinking and therefore our religious life all depend on images. But the Divine completely escapes language and ideas that enable us to relate to created things. We must speak God's name, but there is no name adequate to the Holy Trinity. So we name God as the cause of the beauty of creation and of the transformation that arises through our redemption. We name God as Creator, Redeemer, Sustainer; the Good Beyond Being; the Father, Mother, Lover; the Rock of Salvation;

---

21. Ibid.

22. John Scotus Eriugena, *Voice of the Eagle*, 84.

23. As Edward Farley argues, the reality of redemption is the basis of our knowledge and worship of God, but redemption itself includes awareness of God as nonidentical with anything in the world. God is the referent of existential meaning and desire in a way that nothing in the world can satisfy. But what we humans can name are always the things in the world: "The failure, the *non capax*, to mean God is not overcome by redemption. The paradox is that God does come forth as a designated content (redeemer, founder) but never as a being, a discrete entity, or specific content. Thus, the belief-ful conviction of God's reality is from the very beginning both a symbolization . . . and a negative theology. The facticity of redemption, not God and the puzzle of the world, is then the original and deepest root of negative theology. From the very beginning the God who comes forth as God is the one who breaks and surpasses specific meaning designations." Otherwise, God would be part of the world and not the savior of the world (*Divine Empathy*, 73).

Almighty, invisible, God only wise. But Divinity is not a person who creates or a mother or father or almighty or invisible in any of the senses that we are able to directly think. Names are qualified by the practice of negation. Negation enables us to spiral through the unconscious ways in which we subject Divinity to our own thoughts and to the structures of creation. The Divine Eros is not a sense object, not an emotion, not a person, not a thought, not being, not nonbeing, not darkness, not light. "The fact is that the more we take flight upward, the more our words are confined to the ideas we are capable of forming; so that now as we plunge into that darkness which is beyond intellect, we shall find ourselves not simply running short of words but actually speechless and unknowing."[24]

But the dialectic of naming and negation does not simply take back what one says about the Divine: Jesus is on the main line; no, Jesus is not on the main line. God is Father; no, God is not a father. God is eternal; God is not eternal. This kind of negation does not really withhold the structures of thought from the Divine. It is almost a theological ping-pong that bounces from a yes to a no, but does not fundamentally challenge our dualistic and conceptual forms of thinking. Passing through layers of thought, we bring to awareness ways we continue to confuse our thoughts about God with the Divine itself. The issue is not that certain attributes do not apply to God: God is not a rock, does not exist in time. These negations imply their opposite: God is spiritual and timeless. This backhanded naming is still a kind of knowing. Negation shows us that the mental act of attribution is an imperfect way of orienting the heart toward the Divine. Names can be sweet. But the negative way describes a deeper fidelity. The lover breaks free of images and concepts, "renouncing all that the mind may conceive, wrapped entirely in the intangible and the invisible, he belongs completely to him who is beyond everything. Here, being neither oneself nor someone else, one is supremely united to the completely unknown by an inactivity of knowledge, and knows beyond the mind by knowing nothing."[25]

The *via negativa* requires us to use language as a solvent that dissolves the very structures of conceptual awareness. It is inadequate to say that God, in a positive sense, is or is not in time. Rather, the idea of time itself is withheld. This does not mean God *is* timeless, but that the idea or category of time is inappropriate to Divinity. Yet grammar itself betrays Divinity. The unassuming little verb *is* reduces God to a personal pronoun and negation to an attribute. This makes the practice of negation quite difficult because we are denying not only a particular attribute but concept and language. It is easier to think timelessness and then apply it to God than it is to hold in one's mind a mode of reality for which time *and* timelessness are equally irrelevant. The difficulty of this meditation indicates how hard it is to think past the limitations of the ordinary structures of experience. But we cannot bring Divinity directly into concept and say what it is or is

24. Pseudo-Dionysius, "Mystical Theology" 3.1033B-C (*Complete Works*, 139).
25. "Mystical Theology" 1.3, 1001A (*Complete Works*, 137).

not. "We make assertions and denials of what is next to it, but never of it, for it is both beyond every assertion . . . it is also beyond every denial."[26]

Negation is a way of moving more deeply into unsaying so that we experientially disconnect from our thoughts *about* the Divine.[27] The thinker most associated with the development of apophatic theology is Pseudo-Dionysius, the Areopagite. He is the "pseudo" Dionysius because his writings were originally attributed to Paul's acquaintance mentioned in Acts 17:34. In part because of this association his writings enjoyed near canonical status for a millennium or more and deeply shaped the evolution of Christian thought. But through the humanistic methods of scholarship that evolved during the Renaissance, it became apparent that these writings could not have been produced before the sixth century, probably by a monk in Syria. Somehow it seems appropriate that this foundational expression of the *via negativa* is produced under a pseudonym. Dionysius was deeply formed by the study of Neoplatonism, and so we will allow Plotinus to help us understand his thought.

PSEUDO-DIONYSIUS

Dionysius's texts, "The Divine Names" and "Mystical Theology," not only describe negation but engage the reader in the practice of negation. They are theology in the more ancient sense of sapiential wisdom, that is, theology that invites the reader into the way of unknowing. "Indeed the inscrutable One is out of reach of every rational process. Nor can any words come up to the inexpressible Good, this One, this Source of all unity, this supra-existent Being. Mind beyond mind, word beyond speech, it is gathered up by no discourse, by no intuition, by no name."[28] One can see here that Dionysius is not reminding us of the gap between language and the Divine. He is stretching and contorting language so that language itself breaks up. Conceptually, speaking the divine unspeakability is a failure of language. But sapientially, this failure contributes to the dissolution of conceptuality that opens toward . . . what? Toward what is known only in unknowing, in learned ignorance, in annihilation.

But the Divine is not mere absence: "the Good is not absolutely incommunicable to everything. By itself it generously reveals a firm, transcendent beam, granting enlightenments proportionate to each being, and thereby draws sacred

---

26. Pseudo-Dionysius, "Mystical Theology" 5.1048B (*Complete Works*, p. 141).

27. Beverly Lanzetta points out the "dialectic of naming and un-naming, illumination and darkness, revealed and hidden [without which] our spiritual life would cease to grow toward integration and wholeness. Yet he [Pseudo-Dionysius] also cautions us to 'not conclude that the negations are simply the opposite of affirmations, but rather that the cause of all is considerably prior to this, beyond privations, beyond every denial, beyond every assertion'" (*Radical Wisdom*, 15, quoting Elizabeth Johnson, *Truly Our Sister*, 23). Lanzetta is a particularly interesting interpreter of the *via negativa* because she does so in light of the distinctive path of contemplation for women.

28. "Divine Names" 1.1.588B (*Complete Works*, 49–50).

minds upward to its permitted contemplation, to participation and to the state
of becoming like it. . . . Nor do they go tumbling downward where their own
natural inclinations would take them. No. Instead they are raised firmly and
unswervingly upward. . . . With a love matching the illuminations granted them,
they take flight, reverently, wisely, in all holiness."[29]

For Dionysius, the first step of this ascent is Scripture. For him, Scripture is
not a collection of correct sentences but a bridge between naming and negation.
Because it is imbued with the power of the Holy Spirit, it enables us to move
beyond the limitations of discursive reasoning. Dionysius invites us to "look
as far upward as the light of sacred scripture will allow, and, in our reverent
awe of what is divine, let us be drawn together toward the divine splendor."[30]
Contemplation with Scripture allows us to move beyond awareness of sense and
cognition toward the ineffable Divine. Scripture is words and language, but
ones that bear the power of the Divine, and therefore they move into the region
beyond being. Through the power of names they move us toward and beyond
the negation of names.

We ascend by naming God according to the logic of causality. God is not
anything in the world, but God is the cause of the world. We call God beautiful
because God is the cause of beauty; we call God being because God is the cause
of being. We call God living because God is the cause of life. "It is the Life of the
living, the being of beings, it is the Source and the Cause of all life and of all being,
for out of its goodness it commands all things to be and it keeps them going."[31]

But spiraling down the logic of causality that connects us to the Divine, we
discover that all of our thoughts and images are structured by creation. All we
seem to have is the trace of the cause as it is imprinted on creation. If we remain
at the level of our discursive reasoning, at the level of language and image, we
cannot move beyond this trace. The great paradox for Dionysius is that we are
created to desire the Divine. But the modes of knowledge and experience most
characteristic of us—sense, reasoning, feeling—are inadequate to God. "Just as
the senses can neither grasp nor perceive the things of the mind . . . by the same
standard of truth beings are surpassed by the infinity beyond being."[32] That is,
just as we do not grasp geometric proofs with our ears, we cannot grasp Divinity by the faculties appropriate to knowledge of created beings. Scripture guides
us and grounds our desire for God; through it we are better able to bear our
desire as created beings for that which is infinitely beyond being. For Dionysius
and other advocates of the *via negativa*, names of God can be used as prayer, as
gratitude, as a kind of caressing of our Beloved. But through names we are carried beyond names. Names carry us into the infinite sweetness and desirability
of God. Infinite desirability makes the names of God sweet in our mouth. Just

29. Ibid., 1.1.588C–589A (p. 50).
30. Ibid., 1.1.588A (p. 49).
31. Ibid., 1.3.589C (p. 51).
32. Ibid., 1.1.588B (p. 49).

as human lovers caress one another with love letters and tender names, lovers of the Divine use words to express and attenuate their longing. "And so it is that all things must desire, must yearn for, must love, the Beautiful and the Good. . . . And we may be so bold as to claim also that the Cause of all things loves all things in the superabundance of his goodness, that because of this goodness he makes all things, brings all things to perfection, holds all things together, returns all things. The divine longing is Good seeking good for the sake of the Good."[33] For Dionysius this mutual longing is the fundamental energy of existence: the divine longing calls the cosmos into existence and into deeper intimacy, human longing yearns to return to its spiritual source.

This yearning for deeper intimacy moves from concrete or sensual images (father, rock in a weary land, mother, rose of Sharon) to more abstract or cognitive images. We move from homey images to more strictly conceptual images: for example, we say that God is one. "The name 'One' means that God is uniquely all things through the transcendence of one unity and that he is the cause of all without ever departing from that oneness."[34] This is a relatively straightforward beginning. God is the creator of all things; the great plurality of all things is created by one reality, one power. This is the basic meaning of monotheism. Amid all other powers of any sort, there is a single power upon which all else depends. But if we continue to explore this notion of divine unity, we realize that a concept of absolute unity is not really available to us. That is, we can think of one thing: one apple, one person, one world. But one is always implicitly in the company of more than one: one apple left on the tree, one apple to divide among three children. This one is also many: composed of stems, core, seeds, flesh, skin. To think unity itself, a unity that is neither one thing nor a temporary unity that slides between larger and smaller pluralities, is much more difficult. "But the transcendent unity defines the one itself and every number. For it is the source, and the cause, the number and the order of the one, of number, and of all being."[35] The One that creates the infinite plurality of beings is not "one" in the sense of one object. It is the *power* to make actual, concrete beings, particular and separate from other beings. As Plotinus points out, "It is in virtue of unity that beings are beings."[36] That is, we can say that something is an army because we draw together the parts of it to conceive of it as a particular thing. When an army disperses, going back to civilian life, it is no longer an army. Its unity has ceased and so it no longer exists. I can exist as a psychological being because in some sense I am one person, albeit composed of many parts and related to an infinite cosmos. But I am Wendy by being this one person, this one body. Unity is in a sense illusory because it obscures the interior and exterior relations and

---

33. Ibid., 4.9.708A–B.
34. Ibid., 13.2.977C (p. 128).
35. Ibid., 13.2.980D (p. 129).
36. Plotinus, *Ennead* VI, 9.1.

parts. But to conceive of any being in the world, we must do so through this abstraction or illusion of unity.

We name the power of the Divine to create entities that are themselves one, and we name the Divine as the one power behind the multiplicities of creation. But to say God is one in the same sense that the beings are one would mean that God is a being among beings. Through the work of the intellect we can form an idea of unity, but this idea points toward a mode of reality that cannot be either one or many. Thinking with intellect and abandoning intellect we perceive Unity that generates everything but that is "neither thing nor quantity nor quality nor intellect nor soul; not in motion; not at rest, not in place, not in time: it is the self-defined, unique in form or, better, formless, existing before Form was, or Movement or Rest, all of which are attachments of Being and make Being the manifold that it is."[37] Dionysius makes a similar point. The idea of unity discloses its own impossibility and unfolds the namelessness of . . . the One we cannot name. "There is the transcendent unity of God and the fruitfulness of God, and as we prepare to sing this truth we use the names Trinity and Unity for that which is in fact beyond every name, calling it transcendent being above every being. But no unity or trinity, no number or oneness, no fruitfulness, indeed, nothing that is or is known can proclaim that hiddenness beyond every mind and reason of the transcendent Godhead which transcends every being. There is no name for it nor expression. We cannot follow it into its inaccessible dwelling place so far above us."[38]

Nicholas of Cusa echoes this point. He reminds us of the divine simplicity that is necessary to undergird the multiplicity of creation. If God were not "one," God would be simply one more thing in the universe. "Indeed, 'Unity' seems an even closer and more appropriate name than 'All in One.'" But he goes on to say, "'Unity,' however, is not the name of God as we assign the name or understand unity, because just as God transcends all understanding, so God is, a fortiori, above every name." We think objects by contrasting them with other things, thus "according to the movement of reason, plurality or multitude is opposed to unity. Hence, it is not a unity of this sort that properly applies to God, but the unity to which neither otherness nor plurality nor multiplicity is opposed. This unity is the maximum name enfolding all things in its simplicity of unity, and this is the name that is ineffable and above all understanding."[39] We know what "one" means by contrasting it to "two" or "many." But this act of distinguishing one thing from another is not appropriate to the cause of all things, which is not one more thing in the universe. Whatever meaning "unity" or "simplicity" has when applied to Divinity is quite different from what these terms mean when they are applied to things in the world. There is a sense in which it is meaningful

---

37. Ibid., 9.3.
38. "Divine Names" 13.3.981A (*Complete Works*, 129–30).
39. Nicholas of Cusa, "On Learned Ignorance" 76 (*Selected Spiritual Writings*, 121–22).

to say that God is simple or unitary, but as we stay with the name, we are led by its inadequacy to the ineffability of the Divine.

Plotinus is sympathetic with the painfulness of this effort to think beyond concept: "The soul or mind reaching toward the formless finds itself incompetent to grasp where nothing bounds it or to take impression where the impinging reality is diffuse; in sheer dread of holding to nothingness, it slips away. The state is painful; often it seeks relief by retreating from all this vagueness to the region of sense, there to rest as on solid ground."[40] But entrusting our heart to the reality we seek, we can continue. It is important to notice that even for an adept such as Plotinus, this practice requires courage as much or more than intellectual prowess. The obstacles we come to in the negative way are not so much that it is difficult to understand these writings (though that is certainly the case!) but that we become somewhat nauseous as our mental structures—mind and language and understanding—begin to soften and give way. Plotinus emphasizes that his writings cannot speak of it, they can only inspire the desire to travel a road toward one's own seeing. For him, the driving motivation is love. Speaking of those who do not practice this way he says: "The soul has not come to know the splendor There; it has not felt and clutched to itself that love-passion of vision known to the lover come to rest where he loves."[41]

If we follow the pathway of one of God's names, we realize that the name was a caress or a signpost but was not literally attached to God. The way of naming leads inexorably to the way of negation. Through the *via negativa*, fidelity to divine ineffability is led not to sterile arguments about transcendence but to an ever more intimate awareness of our Mother and Lover's goodness and love. Negation is not simply a list of the ways in which the Beloved is not creation. Negation is the negation of our own inner idols so that the living goodness of the Divine Eros can more deeply vivify our faith. Religious speech "never definitively possesses or masters its subject but leads the speakers ever more profoundly into attitudes of awe and adoration."[42] The anxieties of the ego-mind are assuaged by the reliability of a world in which subjects and objects know their place, where desire is satisfied by possession, and knowledge is satisfied by facts. Fidelity to mystery opens us to the space where these reliabilities temporarily evaporate. The structure of the world is displaced by the structure of ecstasy, ecstasy in its literal sense of standing outside our ego-mind. Dionysius describes standing outside oneself: "This divine yearning brings ecstasy so that the lover belongs not to self but to the beloved."[43] The structure of eros is not the structure of the ego-mind. It desires but it does not possess; its knowledge is immediate connection rather than comprehending external facts. It is the dissipation of the ego-mind so that the deeper self, which is not structured by the duality of self and other, gains

40. Plotinus, *Ennead* VI, 9.3.
41. Ibid., 9.4.
42. Johnson, *She Who Is*, 105.
43. "Divine Names" 4.13.712A (*Complete Works*, 82).

temporary priority. The metaphor of sexual union captures the double meaning of ecstasy as blissful and as dissolution.

Apophatic theology moves beyond meditation on the names of God, opening onto the Divine Abyss, revealing the darkness of ineffability lying beyond, a blissful "unknowing" that sweetens and qualifies every thought. A lover lingering on the specific wonders of the beloved is all the more drawn into the realization that it is not something about the beloved that is loved: it is not the silky hair, the soft skin, the good humor, the tender smile, the strength of mind, the small acts of kindness. Each of these may be cherished but they are not the cause of the love. It is the mysterious depth of personhood that love permits us to enter with deeper and deeper intimacy that is loved. Love takes us beyond what we see and know with our bodies and minds to some secret garden that betrays every attempt to speak it.

> Yet I would not have all yet,
> Hee that hath all can have no more,
> And since my love doth every day admit
> New growth, thou shouldst have new rewards in store.[44]

Surely what John Donne celebrates in human love is all the more true of divine love.

The riddle of eros is its infinite giving of what was never a thing to be possessed. The *via negativa* walks the lover's way of naming as well as the devotee's way of negation and finds these to be one path.

SCHLEIERMACHER

Dionysius challenges us to surrender our attachment to names and enter into the darkness of unknowing. His emphasis on the beauty and interdependence of beings has important implications for ecological sensibilities. If we jump several centuries ahead, we find Friedrich Schleiermacher transposing the pattern of naming and negation for a new epoch. This "prince of the church" preached to huge crowds every Sunday at the Trinity Church in Berlin. He befriended religion's despisers, seeking to make Christianity intelligible to them by disconnecting it from the ossifications of authoritarianism and dogmatism. Like Thomas Aquinas before him, he reenvisioned Christian thought in light of advances of scholarship. In all of these ways, he attempted to translate the deep wisdom of Christianity for the modern world. Yet as much as or more than any modern theologian he remains fundamentally shaped by the ancient ideal of divinization. The namelessness of Divinity enters into us and we are part of it. The incarnation is the center of reality for him because it is the divine nature to communicate

---

44. John Donne, "Lovers infinitenesse," in *Complete English Poems of John Donne,* 61.

itself and it is human nature to become divine. The incarnation is the point where this occurs most fully. The divine love is the self-impartation of the Divine: it is not the motivation for but the content of redemption. God-consciousness is not awareness of God but awareness through God. It is consciousness transformed by constant awareness of the infinite: "Every finite thing . . . is a sign of the Infinite. . . . Every event, even the most natural and usual, becomes a miracle, as soon as the religious view of it can be the dominant."[45] That the human mind is capable of this intensity of focus in which divine consciousness totally absorbs personal consciousness while still allowing it to function is accomplished in Christ. We become Christ not by imitating him but by allowing God-consciousness to infiltrate our own mind. The Divine Eros "builds up, from all that has otherwise been developed in man, that part of the soul in which He specially dwells, manifests His immediate operation, and mirrors Himself, and thus makes His sanctuary quite peculiar and distinct, and if you only noticed how He glorifies Himself in it by the exhaustless variety and opulence of forms."[46] Ernestine, a mother in Schleiermacher's dialogue on the incarnation, describes this universal Divinity as something mothers in particular are able to recognize: "'In a way I feel she did not say too much when she thought that I might well be the mother of the blessed child. For I can in all humility honor the pure revelation of the divine in my daughter, as Mary did in her son, without in the least disturbing the proper relation of mother to child.' 'We are all of one mind on that,' added Agnes.'"[47] For Schleiermacher, all women are Mary and all children are Christ. Divinization as the essential expression of the Divine and of the human shapes a different sense of the *via negativa*. It is mind itself that is capable of immediate consciousness of the nonconceptual reality of the Divine, and so Schleiermacher pursues the negative way through an analysis of the structures of mind.

More, or perhaps differently, than Dionysius, Schleiermacher challenges the logic of causality itself. In clarifying the sense in which creation is "utterly dependent" on God, Schleiermacher writes: "I do not think that God can be placed in such a relation as a cause."[48] This is not so much a denial of dependence as an extension of the practice of negation. Since causality is itself a category appropriate to relations among beings, it too must be withheld from Divinity. As the practice of negation is pursued, the method used for one moment of negation must itself be negated. Schleiermacher's path of negation leads toward the dissolution of the duality of subject and object that constitutes the basic structures of self-conscious or personal awareness. His manner of exposition relies on a transcendental analysis of mind. He is, unfortunately, often understood to be analyzing conscious awareness and thus reducing religion to subjective experience. This is not the case. He analyzes the nondualistic structure of consciousness

45. Schleiermacher, *On Religion*, 88.
46. Ibid., 229.
47. Schleiermacher, *Christmas Eve*, 36.
48. Schleiermacher, *On Religion*, 103.

that is embedded in the architecture of the human mind. This is one way of saying that the human mind is capable of awareness of ultimate reality. This is not an isolated moment of experience (mystical or otherwise) but a dimension of the human mind.

For Schleiermacher, the dialectic between naming and negation is held together by the structure of consciousness itself. There is an aspect of consciousness that is appropriate to the practice of naming. Sensible self-consciousness is our normal way of encountering the world. It is structured by subject-object duality, my consciousness encountering a world that is not-I. This is the way we experience ourselves, our world, and our religion. Scripture, preaching, sacraments, community, and prayer all relate to our self-other mode of awareness.[49] When we think about any emotional or cognitive experience, a memory or an intention, that is, any conscious awareness, we are in the realm of sensible self-consciousness. But in examining our ordinary experiences of self-awareness, Schleiermacher became aware of another layer of consciousness not characterized by this subject-object duality.

Consciousness has a smoothness and unity to it. It is not isolated bits of data or free-floating memories or anxieties. Personal consciousness is experienced as an integrated whole in a more or less coherent world in which we are ourselves particular persons. This is not to say that consciousness is not complex, but normal consciousness is characterized by a quality of being "mine." Amid great flux and contradiction, I am still (for better or worse) Wendy. Sense data, memory, and the flow of consciousness are bound together into a meaningful world coordinated by a personal "I." But this binding together is not itself a moment of experience. Schleiermacher calls the principle by which the unity of consciousness is accomplished "immediate self-consciousness." Because it provides the underlying condition for sensible self-consciousness but is not itself a particular object of consciousness, it remains simple and self-identical, independent of outwardly given objects. It is the region of mind in which "the antithesis [of subject and object] again disappears and the subject unites and identifies itself with everything which, in the middle grade [sensible self-consciousness] was set over against it."[50] Underlying and supporting the possibility of ordinary consciousness is a layer of consciousness that is not itself reducible to the flux of experience. One might think of the top of the ocean, on which ducks paddle, turtles swim, fish dart, algae blooms, waves lap, and so on. But beneath all of this action, the depths of the ocean remain calm. The deep makes possible the life on its surface but is not itself troubled by it. Immediate self-consciousness is the unity of con-

---

49. It is characteristic of Schleiermacher's method to try first to describe the distinctive character of religious consciousness and then describe the communities and practices that shape consciousness. Thus the famous Second Speech, which provides a kind of eidetic analysis of religious consciousness, is followed by the Third, Fourth, and Fifth Speeches, which describe the various religious communities that nurture and specify piety. For him, there is no religion without the variety of religious communities.

50. Schleiermacher, *Christian Faith*, §5.1 (p. 20).

sciousness that connects sense data, memories, emotions, thoughts, and decisions together and gives us the experience of existing as a particular person. But this unifying structure is not itself a particular thought or desire or emotion.

Because sensible consciousness requires a form of consciousness that is not divided into the subject-object distinction, there is built into the very possibility of consciousness a capacity for nondual awareness. Just as Divinity is the cause of creation but is not itself an object within creation, nondual consciousness upholds everyday consciousness but is not itself a direct object of thought. It is this capacity for nonduality that provides the potential for God-consciousness. We have available to us in the very structure of our minds a way of transcending the duality that subjects Divinity to conceptual thought. Because mind is built this way, God-consciousness is part of our primordial psychic makeup. God-consciousness is this nonduality that underlies ordinary awareness. The formal structure of immediate self-consciousness is the arena in which God-consciousness develops and can be integrated into sensible self-consciousness.

At the level of sensible self-consciousness, the best name of God is "love" because everything we know about God concerns the impartation of the power of redemption that allows us to participate in the love of God and neighbor. But this dualistic, conceptual naming of the Beloved is complemented by nondual awareness through which we can enjoy a "sense and taste for the infinite."[51] Religious speech has these two qualities: it names, but it also negates. Because religious people recognize its inadequacy, language is able to carry them more deeply into relationship with the unnamable author of our salvation. In his writings to the despisers of religion, Schleiermacher seeks metaphors that are not strictly theistic to evoke this nonduality: dew breathing on a blossom, a maiden's kiss, a bridal embrace. "It fills no time and fashions nothing palatable. It is the holy wedlock of the universe."[52] The paradox of describing this or even experiencing it is that it flees discursive awareness. "The incoming of existence to us, by this immediate union, at once stops as soon as it reaches consciousness."[53] Schleiermacher is not here describing mystical or ecstatic moments of experience but the modification of consciousness through the integration of nonduality with ordinary awareness. This integration allows the normal flux of pain and pleasure to become stabilized by a quality of awareness that Schleiermacher calls "blessedness." God-consciousness is not consciousness of a particular thing, an idea, a momentary experience or emotion. It is a more or less stable integration of nondualistic awareness into everyday awareness. Religion consists not in beliefs or words but in this integration of nonduality with everyday life: "while man does nothing from religion, he should do everything with religion. Uninterruptedly, like a sacred music, the religious feelings should accompany his active life."[54]

51. Schleiermacher, *On Religion*, 39.
52. Ibid., 43.
53. Ibid., 44.
54. Ibid., 59.

This "blessedness" is the characteristic sign of life that has discovered its roots in the Divine.[55] To the extent that immediate self-consciousness enters into relationship with sensible self-consciousness "*with ease*," life will bear "the stamp of joy."[56] The modification of consciousness does not remove life's difficulty but eases its tyranny. Immediate self-consciousness is not a particular emotion or thought but accompanies all emotions, thoughts, and actions, giving them a more beneficent quality. In particular, equanimity and inclusive love are marks of the more stable integration of immediate and sensible self-consciousness. In his "Dialogue on the Incarnation," Schleiermacher personifies "blessedness" in the character of Joseph. Coming in on a cold Christmas Eve, Joseph embodies the equanimity that arises as the soul finds its home in Divinity: "The long, deep, irrepressible pain in my life is soothed as never before. I feel at home, as if born anew into the better world, in which pain and grieving have no meaning and no room any more. I look upon all things with a gladsome eye, even what has most deeply wounded me. As Christ had no bride but the church, no children but his friends, no household but the temple and the world, and yet his heart was full of heavenly love and joy, so I too seem to be born to endeavor after such a life."[57] Putting an end to the contentious theological disputations through which the other men have nearly spoiled the Christmas party, Joseph calls for music. The dialogue ends with the women and men, adults and children united in song.

God-consciousness expresses itself as love and compassion, in which tyrannical self-love is submerged in sympathy for others. When nondualistic awareness becomes more integrated, nothing is "more natural than the most heartfelt compassion with all the bitter suffering that must arise from this unequal strife, and with all the stripes which awful Nemesis deals out on every side."[58] This love is by its nature not only interpersonal but social. He dismissed the idea of eternal damnation on the grounds that it is inconsistent with the work of redemption. Like Isaac of Nineveh he envisioned the heart of Christianity as the intensification and universalization of compassion: "If the perfecting of our nature is not to move backwards, sympathy must be such as to embrace the whole human race, and when extended to the damned must of necessity be a disturbing element in bliss."[59] If even those only imperfectly capable of love find hopeless suffering of humanity intolerable, it is impossible to imagine that Love itself could sanction it.

---

55. Schleiermacher makes this point poetically in the Second Speech to religion's despisers: "The legions of angels with which the Father provided His Son, exercised no power over Him. They had no call to help Him in any doing or forbearing, but they poured serenity and calm into a soul exhausted with doing and thinking" (*On Religion*, 60). "Angels" here serves as an image of what occurs in immediate self-consciousness, accompanying action, thought, and emotion without significant power to dictate their content but rather to integrate them into the serenity of God-consciousness.

56. Schleiermacher, *Christian Faith*, §5.4 (p. 24).

57. Schleiermacher, *Christmas Eve*, 86.

58. Schleiermacher, *On Religion*, 78.

59. Schleiermacher, *Christian Faith*, §163, appendix, "On Eternal Damnation" (p. 721).

For Schleiermacher, the self-impartation of Divinity transforms us for love, recalibrating consciousness itself. This occurs in the immediacy of consciousness. Nonduality integrates with the subject-object awareness of ordinary life. Since this transformation is the truest and best thing we know about God, we can affirm love as our primary name for God. But if we reflect on the structures of consciousness, we discover a nonduality upon which speech and concepts founder. Tracking the name of love through the way of negation, we do not find a concrete entity that has attributes of love and wisdom. The logic of divine love drives us toward mystery. It dissolves our attachment to concepts so we can move more directly to relationship with the way of "unknowing." Here again naming and negation interpenetrate as nondual immediacy and as love, each one driving toward the other.

MECHTHILD OF MAGDEBURG

The *via negativa* is a way of expressing the deepest possible intimacy between Divinity and creation. The Good Beyond Being is oned with the deepest recesses of the human soul and the remote ecstasies of black holes and dark matter. The Divine Emptiness is proximate to everything because it is itself nothing—nothing, no thinkable thing. Because the traces it leaves are the beauty of creation and the fecundity of healing, we caress it with names like Good, Love, God. Divine lovers celebrate creation shot through with the "grandeur of God" (Gerard Manley Hopkins). But they are also especially sensitive to the distortions that arise when the Creator is displaced by idolatrous attachments to creation. Among the names of the Beloved are those that seek to understand the strange dance of nearness and difference, of intimacy and mystery. Schleiermacher was accused by his opponents of being a pantheist. But this accusation is itself embedded in a simple reversal of the logic of duality. Instead of thinking of God as "totally other" than creation, God is conceived of as "the same" as creation.[60] For apophatic theologians the distinction of same and other, so crucial for beings, is irrelevant to Divinity. Applying either side of it, sameness or otherness, to God can have a kind of truth to it, but both are equally problematic. The ways we name the relationship between God and the world have particular potency for consolation as well as vulnerability to distortion. We call God "King" because a divine king calls the injustice of human kings to account. Or we call God "King" because we want to imbue human kings with divine right. We have seen the *via negativa* practiced as a way to move beyond conceptuality. We have seen it

---

60. Paul Knitter also rejects the accusation of pantheism. He uses creation as "a pouring forth of God, an extension of God, in which the Divine carries on the divine activity of interrelating *in* and *with* and *through* creation. I can hear the objections: this smacks of—or simply is—pantheism. Everything becomes God. But it's not pantheism. It's what we called, for lack of a better word, nonduality: God and creation are not two, but neither are they one!" (*Without Buddha*, 22).

practiced as a movement toward nonduality. In this section, we turn the practice of negation toward symbols of divine power.

Much of Christian theology is governed by the metaphor of sovereignty, the cosmic emperor who, unlike merely human ones, effects a total symmetry between his will and the outcome of events.[61] This metaphor does not feature strongly in the way of negation. This is partly because the logic of sovereignty often reflects an uncritical conflation of one of the more decadent forms of human power with divine being. It is a flagrant violation of the second commandment. But more deeply, the image of a divine monarch fails to convey the deep intimacy that compels lovers of the Good to cry: "I move not without thy knowledge" (Epictetus). Lovers "accept the experiences befalling you as good things, knowing that, apart from God, nothing happens."[62] But they imagine the divine efficacy quite differently from that available to kings. As we have negated language, concept, causality, it is necessary also to negate this imperial image of power. The association between sovereignty and divinity is particularly durable, making it difficult to conceive of divine power as entirely different from the power of patriarchs and rulers. But walking the way of negation, we might say that God becomes divine through the renunciation of sovereignty. Mechthild of Magdeburg was a beguine, a lay contemplative, living in the late thirteenth century in what is now Germany. Her negation of the logic of sovereignty helps us extend the way of negation in another direction.

We are introduced to the paradoxes of power in the opening lines of her text. The Lord God says that he is himself the author of her book: "I made [*gemacht*] it in my powerlessness [*unmacht*], for I cannot restrain myself as to my gifts."[63] God is powerless to hold back the powerful flow of love toward humanity. God longs for occasions to let this power flow. When Mechthild begs for the souls of condemned sinners, her Lover responds: "Indeed, when two wrestle with each other, the weaker must lose. I shall willingly be the weaker, though I am almighty."[64] In this poetic rendering, God is able to accomplish the desire to save humanity by renouncing the kind of power that impedes love. It is God's powerlessness and God's weakness that express divinity.

Mechthild's divine Lover is happy to play at becoming weak and powerless in the intimacy of their bed chamber. But this pillow talk becomes more serious when it is transposed into the heavenly court where the Trinity is alone with itself. Here the Father is "adorned in his Person with the robust character

61. See Sally McFague's *Metaphorical Theology* for a trenchant discussion of the monarchial metaphor. Admittedly, theologians from Athanasius and Augustine to Calvin and Barth have worried that without a strong view of sovereignty we cannot properly appreciate our dependence on divine grace. But it is difficult to ignore ways in which this point of view affirms patriarchal and imperial power structures. Barth argued strenuously that women's subordination to men was the eternal will of God, a convenient credo for one who kept his mistress in the household with his wife.

62. *Didache* 3.10 (Milavec's translation).

63. Mechthild of Magdeburg, *Flowing Light of the Godhead* 1, preface (p. 39).

64. Ibid., 6.10 (p. 236).

of omnipotence."[65] But the magisterial Father is unable to bear fruit. Creation itself depends on renunciation of sovereignty. Enclosed in Trinitarian bliss, the omnipotent Father is plucked by the Holy Spirit and drawn out of barren bliss. Succumbing to the importunities of the Spirit, he acknowledges: "a powerful desire stirs in my divine breast as well, and I swell in love alone. . . . I shall make a bride for myself who shall greet me with her mouth and wound me with her beauty. Only then does love really begin."[66] Still unused to the ways of love, the Father is tempted to reject the soul he has created when she falls into sin. But he is drawn back to his true self by the Spirit and the Son. The "Father then bowed to the wills of them both with great love" and agreed to help.[67] The Father is reformed by the intercessions of the Spirit and the Son and gladly joins the project of salvation. In his reformed state, the suffering of the lost is too heavy a burden for the Heart of Compassion to bear: "My soul cannot endure that I banish the sinner from me. And so I pursue many of them on and on till I have them in my grasp."[68] The Father renounces omnipotence in order to be wounded by love. He then renounces justice when the bride proves incapable of the luminous lovemaking he desires. These renunciations provoke "God's justice" to complain that God's "mercy" took "from me what was rightfully mine . . . The true Son of God . . . robbed me of my strictest justice with his mercy."[69]

Mechthild understands the renunciation of power to be the work of Lady Love: "Then [the] true love of God revealed itself to me. It was like a noble empress. The outline of her body was refined, white, and rosy in the blossom of youth. . . . When I gazed upon her properly, my dark house was all lit up. . . . Then I said: 'Ah, dearest of ladies, you are more than a thousandfold above me, and yet you serve me with such great honors, as though I were more than an empress.'"[70] Here is yet another renunciation. In order to create, omnipotence is renounced; in order to redeem, justice is renounced. In this image of God as a beautiful empress who waits upon her servant, the honor-clad feudal hierarchy is renounced. The marks and motivations of power are abandoned in order for the true love of God to become visible.

Mechthild plays with an image of an almighty deity who is impotent until Love flows through him. It is Lady Love (*Minne*) who is the true principle of divinity. In her absence the Father is paralyzed. A god who sits in sublime and perfect sovereignty does not create, because he cannot tolerate any limit to power. Even the smallest worm that moves violates his supremacy. Such a god does not redeem because his craving for honor occludes his compassion. In Mechthild's

65. Ibid., 3.9 (p. 114).
66. Ibid. (pp. 114–15).
67. Ibid. (p. 116).
68. Ibid., 6.16 (p. 246).
69. Ibid., 7.62 (p. 331).
70. Ibid., 7.48 (pp. 316–17). This inversion of feudal hierarchy is found again on the opening page of Mechthild's book: Lady Love, the principle of Divinity, addresses Mechthild as "Mistress and Queen."

gender-bending theology, it is Lady Love, the true Empress, the marrow of divinity that recalls the Father to his true self. Redeemed by Love, the Lord becomes powerless to restrain his gifts.

> He surrenders himself to her,
> And she surrenders herself to him
> . . . .
>
> Dear friend of God, I have written for you this path of love. May God infuse it into your heart![71]

According to the logic of Mechthild's theopoetics, true power arises when sovereignty is abandoned. Those things that tempt God to set aside his yearning for his beloved humanity—omnipotence, honor, justice, punishment, control—appear as nothing in the light of Lady Love. Here poetry rather than paradox acts as a solvent on our normal patterns of thinking: the way of unknowing reduces to nothing those powers that exercise most control over human lives. In the emptiness that is opened, another name, another image for omnipotence emerges.

Instructed by Love, the Almighty Lover draws creation ever nearer in the way that all true lovers do—without doing violence to the integrity of the beloved's unique existence. Love allows us to enter into intimacy with others, but only as they can tolerate it. The Great Healer, our Savior, not only loves according to our kind, but also loves us into healing and wholeness; love creates the capacities for deeper love. But this is a delicate work, moving in the depths of our soul so that we are better able to tolerate the flow of love into and out of ourselves.[72] Origen understands God to undertake this delicate work for as long as it takes and by any means necessary. Like Mechthild, Origen portrays the powerlessness of God to turn aside from the yearning for salvation: "It is on this account, moreover, that the last enemy, who is called death, is said to be destroyed; in order, namely, that there may be no longer any sadness. . . . Not that its substance which was made by God shall perish, but that the hostile purpose and will which proceeded not from God but from itself will come to an end. It will be destroyed, therefore, not in the sense of ceasing to exist, but of being no longer an enemy and no longer death. *For to the Almighty nothing is impossible, nor is anything beyond the reach of cure by its Maker*" (emphasis added).[73] The negation of omnipotent control feeds the trust that the divine activity cannot be thwarted. Origen, whose own life began and ended in persecutions, wrote in total confidence of the time when "all things are restored and become one and then 'God shall be all in all.'"[74] He could not

---

71. Ibid., 1.44 (p. 62).

72. Mayra Rivera touches on this interplay between intimacy and transcendence on which love thrives: "the Other . . . incites feelings of wonder, that preserves the difference necessary for the unfolding of desire. . . . Interhuman transcendence takes place in the singularity of each encounter. This interhuman transcendence . . . is grounded in God's intracosmic transcendence" (*Touch of Transcendence*, 97).

73. Origen, *On First Principles* 3.6.5 (pp. 250–51).

74. Ibid., 3.6.6 (p. 251).

envision a cosmos in which this process fails to come to fruition. Anything less than this would be unworthy of Almighty Love. But the power to redeem arises when the power to coerce is abandoned.

Lovers of the Divine Emptiness cannot conceive of Divinity stained by violence or deterred by sin. The logic of sovereignty is from this perspective a failure of nerve that has lost faith with the efficacy of divine love. The logic of sovereignty does not give to God *too much* power but too little. Nothing has the power to permanently interrupt the love that flows through the cosmos and caresses even the most destitute human soul. Terrible and destructive suffering does not have the power to unmake the divine love for us. Periods of utter destitution, suffered individually or collectively, the bitter reality of affliction and cruelty, do not have the power to tempt God away from erotic, abysmal divinity. The Beloved, the Great Mother, is always the divine one, the Holy One of Israel who comes to save. The lover of the Good Beyond Being can join with others to sing "victory is mine" or "there is power in the blood" not because an exacting sovereign justifies even the worst of our misery but because nothing, not even the most depraved moments of human history, separates us from the love of God. The author of the *Gospel of Truth* celebrated this nonviolent Divinity, insisting that those who approach the face of this Divine Emptiness "by means of kisses" do not "lack the glory of the Father nor did they think of him as small nor that he is harsh nor that he is wrathful, but [that] he is a being without evil, imperturbable, sweet."[75] Followers of the negative way can testify with this anonymous author that divine lovers have no anxiety but "are set at rest, refreshed in the Spirit."[76]

FIDELITY TO THE UNNAMED GOD

We use names we know from human love and from ordinary experience as metaphors for a love and healing that have no real analogue. Reflection on the names of God carries us toward a darkness beyond being where language loses its power. Opening to mystery and transcendence, we are brought into the presence of the "ray of the divine shadow which is above everything that is."[77] The way of negation is not the logical opposite of naming; naming and negation are twinned ways of perceiving ineffable love. These are united in the *via negativa*: as we walk the "way of unknowing," we become detached from the thoughts and beliefs that structure our minds, and this makes it possible to be embraced by deeper strata of love. As we fall more deeply into the divine love, its inexpressibility and mystery open ever more fully.

75. *Gospel of Truth* 41.34–42.5, trans. Harold W. Attridge and George W. MacRae, in *The Nag Hammadi Library in English*, ed. James M. Robinson, 50.

76. *Gospel of Truth* 42.30 (ibid., 51).

77. Pseudo-Dionysius, "Mystical Theology" 1.1.1000A (*Complete Works*, 135).

The *via negativa* teaches us how to practice fidelity to the Beloved. It exposes us to ways we have become attached to ideas inferior to the Divine. It disciplines our way of naming God so that the deep mystery of redemption can transform ordinary names into pathways to the Divine. Fidelity requires that we remain vigilant in our effort to distinguish the working of our minds from the Divine Eros, allowing the erotic depth of divine mystery to transform our ideas and names.

Trust in the way of unknowing works against the temptation to turn the imaginations of our heart into golden idols. But there is an opposite danger against which fidelity must also struggle. When we run up against the failure of our ideas about the Divine, or despair of the religious communities in which we have been raised, it can seem as if God no longer exists. If we must give up a particular way of believing in God, it seems that there is nothing left but atheism or cynicism. The way of negation transforms the darkness in which our beliefs fail us into the darkness of unknowing, a darkness in which God covers us under healing wings. Doubt is the way toward deeper and more stable fidelity. Faithfulness is not belief in a particular idea about God, or Christianity, or Scripture, or the church. Faith is radical trust in the mysterious wisdom and compassion of the Good Beyond Being, which "out of love . . . has come down to be at our level."[78] As ideas *about* God get burned like chaff, faith lives over the abyss of the divine darkness without a net, and yet ever more confident that one can fall nowhere but into the gracious love and mercy of Eros. The negative path can be terrifying. We feel stability through strenuously insisting on the truths of our beliefs. But the inside of our mind is not God. The *via negativa*, in the dialectic of naming and negation, sanctifies our names of God even as it releases us from the anxiety that these names must do all the work. Our best names disappear into the mysterious Divine Emptiness, the Abyss of Love into which we are all always falling.

The practice of the negative way provides us with criteria for reflecting on how to live a Christian life in our own time. It reminds us of the provisional character of everything we believe about God, ourselves, our tradition, and our faith. But at the same time, it fills us with trust that nothing we do or believe or doubt can "separate us from the love of God" (Romans 8:39). Just as Jacob wrestled with the angel until he blessed him, we wrestle with our ideas of God until we are blessed and they let us go. For a contemplative Christian, this wrestling and love-making is the heart of faith. This is a kind of theology. It is also a contemplative practice. These two together prepare us to reflect on the Divine Eros incarnate in Wisdom and in Christ.

---

78. Pseudo-Dionysius, "Divine Names" 2.10.648D (*Complete Works*, 66).

Chapter 4

"Arise, My Fair One"

Contemplation and Incarnation

> *My beloved speaks and says to me:*
> *"Arise, my love, my fair one,*
> *and come away;*
> *for now the winter is past,*
> *the rain is over and gone.*
> . . . .
> *let me see your face,*
> *let me hear your voice;*
> *for your voice is sweet,*
> *and your face is lovely.*

Song of Songs 2:10–11, 14

> *I am what I am, says this Soul, by the grace of God. Therefore I am only that which God is in me, and not some other thing. And God is the same thing that He is in me, for nothing is nothing. Thus He is Who is. Therefore I am not, if I am, except what God is, and nothing is beyond God. I do not find anything but God, in whatever part I find myself, for He is nothing except Himself.[1]*

The incarnation is a pathway back to our divine root. The last two chapters have lingered over the ungroundedness of the Divine Eros rather than moving directly to a reflection on Word or Christ or Jesus. In order to remember the divine source of the incarnation, it is useful to undermine dualistic habits of mind. A

---

1. Porete, *Mirror of Simple Souls*, chap. 70 (p. 145).

dualistic theology of incarnation might conceive of God as an entity or being and then try to imagine that entity as somehow juxtaposed with humanity in the body of Jesus. This mental habit that conceives everything through the dualities of subject and object, of same and other, is shaped by our life in the natural world but it does not directly apply to Divinity. The *via negativa* shows that Divinity is not an object in any ordinary sense but is a kind of anti-object: neither nothing at all nor an entity in the cosmos.

The incarnation dwells in this nondual reality even as it manifests according to the dualistic structure of the space-time continuum. As Karl Rahner puts it, this establishing of divine creativity in something that is (in a sense) nondivine is the "grammar of God's possible self-expression."[2] That is, the perfection of the Divine Eros lies in its self-communication; the perfection of humanity lies in openness to the Divine Eros. The incarnation is the grammar of this coincidence of opposites, this indwelling of nonduality in the medium of duality. We human beings can think in this direction because we ourselves share this nondual root. "Like knows like," as Plotinus puts it. The incarnation is possible because humanity, created in the divine image, shares nonduality with its divine source. But conceptual thought does not provide adequate access to this nonduality. It is desirable to nurture another kind of awareness in order to develop a better sense of the place of connection between divinity and humanity.

Contemplation shows us that neither divinity nor human beings are merely things in the world, egos wrapped in a body. Because it attends to nondiscursive dimensions of reality, contemplation lies open to the apophatic quality of the incarnation. Preoccupation with images of things "in heaven above, or that is on the earth beneath, or that is in the water under the earth" (Exodus 20:4) draws our minds away from the erotic Divine Abyss. We become attached to ideas unworthy of ourselves and unworthy of the Divine. It is therefore useful to practice forms of prayer that weaken, if only temporarily, the structuring of mind by images. The *via negativa* is a cognitive way to do this; contemplation experiments with other ways to discipline and open awareness.

The intellectual practice of naming and negation gives way to the contemplation of the Divine Emptiness in which the transformation of mind opens upon "vision beyond negation."[3] As Evagrius Ponticus puts it, "The spirit that possesses health is the one which has no images of the things of this world at

---

2. Rahner, *Foundations of Christian Faith*, 223. Rahner's analysis of the "supernatural existential" is behind much of my own understanding of incarnation. It is the perfection of God to communicate God-self; it is the perfection of humanity to receive as fully as possible the Divine. "If immediacy to God is not to be an absolute contradiction right from the start, it cannot depend on the fact that what is not God absolutely disappears when God draws near. As he does not have to find a place by having something else which is not him make room. For at least the presence of God as the transcendental ground and horizon of everything that exists and everything which knows (and this is a presence of God, an immediacy to him) takes place precisely in and through the presence of the finite existent" (ibid., 83).

3. Gregory Palamas, *Triads* 1.3.4 (p. 33).

the time of prayer."[4] This objectless contemplation allows the soul to drop into the Divine Abyss, no longer tyrannized by images and attachment to images. Through contemplation, ineffability is not an infinite qualitative difference but a flame that connects Beloved and lover. Desire is a medium through which nonduality and duality dwell together.

Because discursive reasoning—thoughts, beliefs, ideas—are only one part of the human mind, theological reflections address only a relatively small part of our awareness. That is, even if we cognitively accept ideas about divine love and mystery, much of our actual experience, layered through the density of conscious and unconscious mind, remains unaffected by our belief. Contemplation is one way to move belief more deeply into the recesses of heart and mind. Or, to make this point from the opposite direction: contemplation modifies belief by tapping into the visceral reality of apophatic divinity. Contemplation is a practice that enacts the apophatic dimension of self. It may result in various benefits, but its significance lies in the practice itself. To practice contemplation for any length of time—even ten seconds—enacts a deep truth of our nature. Even ten seconds spent desiring to begin a contemplative practice enacts this truth: desire is the royal road to the Divine.

Contemplation is a journey of self-knowledge in which we come to know ourselves and all other beings as God-bearers, luminous through connection to all creation. Indra Devi (the first Western woman to train with a yoga master) points out that contemplative practices are available to anyone who wishes to practice them. "It is only through proper and unselfish meditation that the student can finally enter the temple of the undistracted and abstract mind, and in silence and solitude come to the realization of the One Ultimate Reality and reach the peace beyond all understanding."[5] Her tireless teaching of introductory yogic practices reflects her belief that this vocation is not restricted to dedicated adepts but is appropriate for all human beings. This chapter considers the significance of contemplation for ordinary lay Christians. The expectation is not that everyone should become a contemplative. But normalizing these practices might make them accessible to a broader community and more integrated into our sense of what ordinary Christian practice can entail.

THE SONG OF SONGS

Not everyone is drawn to contemplative practice; with Origen, it is important to acknowledge many types of faith and practice. But for those called to this discipline it is a method to deepen awareness of the formless source of

---

4. Evagrius Ponticus, *Praktikos* §65.

5. Indra Devi, *Yoga for You*, 215. Indra Devi was born in Russia in 1899. She was the first woman to be accepted as a yoga student by Krishnamacharya. She traveled the world teaching yoga until her death in 2002.

incarnation. In recent decades, Christian contemplative practices have undergone a significant resurgence. They have moved from their monastic home to lay communities. They have shed the penitential emphasis that has dogged much Christian imagination. Opportunities to integrate centering prayer, retreat, *lectio divina*, and walking a labyrinth are increasingly available even in the Reformed traditions.

Origen provides an ancient foreshadowing of these recent developments: like others in Alexandria, he considered contemplation to be a practice available to any Christian. He was among those early Christians who thought of Christianity as a path of divinization. For him, this path was worth prison, torture, and death, but it was itself fundamentally joyous. He is one of the first Christians to undertake a sustained meditation on bridal imagery, underscoring the eroticism of contemplation.

In his long meditation on the Song of Songs, Origen imagines the contemplative soul as a bride longing for her lover. Just as children have not awoken to the passion of love and are satisfied with milk, many of Christ's followers find satisfaction in the initial practices of religion: the study of Scripture, the rejection of hedonism and violence in popular culture, acceptance of the church's teachings. But Origen likens these practices, as important as they are, to the friends of a bridegroom. After a while, the bride ceases to be satisfied with these friendships and longs for the deeper intimacy of the bridegroom. Preliminary practices are like children's songs: they are precursors to adult faith, but as a girl matures into womanhood, it is not children's songs that she desires: "the Bride no longer wants the Bridegroom's friends to sing to her, but longs to hear her Spouse who now is with her, speak with His own lips; wherefore she says: *Let Him kiss me with the kisses of His mouth.* Rightly, then, is this song preferred before all songs. The other songs that the Law and the prophets sang, were sung to the Bride while she was still a little child and had not yet attained maturity. But this song is sung to her, now that she is grown up, and very strong."[6] Teachings and ethical discipline are important, but they do not replace the intimate and ineffable qualities of contemplative prayer.

Beguiled by the beauty of the Divine, we yearn ever more painfully for the Beloved. When we fall into the abyss of love, names and images fail to provide adequate nourishment. We want meat, not milk. Origen contrasts the stirring of love by the mere name of the Beloved with the intensification of desire by the Beloved himself:

> if His Name only, that became as ointment emptied out, had such effect and stirred the maidens so . . . what do you think His very Self will do? What strength, what vigour will these maidens get from it, if ever they are able by some means to attain to His actual, incomprehensible, unutterable Self? . . . They would no longer walk or run, but, bound as it were by the bands of

---

6. Origen, *The Song of Songs: Commentary and Homilies,* 46–47.

His love, they would cleave to Him, and would have no further power ever to move again. For they would be one spirit with Him.[7]

For Origen, the Song of Songs was an expression of the desire for the Beloved that lies at the heart of faith. Its descriptions of erotic longing and tenderness provide images for prayer that open the deepest levels of spirit to the healing and joyous touch of the Divine Eros.

Mechthild of Magdeburg also depicts contemplation through bridal imagery. She complains that her senses offer her only secondhand teachings about the Divine: "That is child's love. . . . I am a full-grown bride. I want to go to my Lover."[8] Desire inflames desire; when a spark of longing for the divine awakens, desire becomes the vehicle that ferries the soul ever more deeply into the divine heart. But this desire is of a different nature than the desire for objects. The Divine Emptiness cannot be possessed or grasped. Divine desire moves toward and within this healing Emptiness, learning the art of nonpossessive intimacy. Desire for the Divine is slaked and inflamed at the same time. As Gregory of Nyssa argues, because God is infinite goodness, and it is our desire to completely share in this, desire itself is without limit, moving ever onward, "from glory to glory."[9]

The more one enters into the Divine Abyss, empty of names and concepts, the more one longs for the Beloved. "The deeper I sink, the sweeter I drink,"[10] as Mechthild of Magdeburg puts it. Desire confirms what Scripture reveals: there is no name adequate to Divinity (Exodus 3:13–14). The admonition of Exodus 20 ceases to be a commandment, a song of the Bridegroom's friends; it is transformed by contemplative prayer into a way of life, a longing that is unafraid of the disorientation of the Abyss.

CONTEMPLATION AS ORDINARY LIFE

Contemplative practice is not something esoteric or special. It is not to get something else. It simply expresses who we are. It does not generate divine love but is a response to the love that is already being showered on us. As Father Basil Pennington puts it: "And this is our Beloved's delight. Perhaps one of the things that most undermine the development of our intimate relationship with God is our inability to realize and accept the fact that God does really want an intimate relationship with us, that we are really important to him. He made us for no other reason than to enjoy us and to have us enjoy him. . . . Such absolute gratuity is difficult for us to comprehend. Our whole training and the attitudes that

7. Ibid., 77.
8. Mechthild of Magdeburg, *Flowing Light of the Godhead* 1.44 (p. 61).
9. This point is made in several places in Gregory's writings. See, for example, *Life of Moses*, prologue 5–10; Jean Daniélou, *From Glory to Glory: Excerpts from Gregory of Nyssa's Mystical Writings*, 82, 84.
10. *Flowing Light of the Godhead* 4.12.

prevail in today's world reinforce the conviction that one has to merit love, that everything we get has to be paid for. Not so with God."[11] Contemplation effects nothing but simply acknowledges what is already the case. It embodies Luther's insight that we are saved only by grace.

Beverly Lanzetta uses feminine imagery for divine graciousness but makes a similar point. Ideas of exchange or domination are "a distortion of Her compassion and mercy. The ego structures that undergird a religion's quest for dominance and superiority violate Her cooperative relationality, which brings all to Love. She loves us even when we do not deserve love; She desires us even when we are undesirable; and She longs for us even when we deny our own longing."[12] Contemplative practice is a way of integrating this dimension of reality into ordinary life. In this way the identities delivered to us by the church and society are tempered by awareness of the infinite lushness of love that constantly surrounds us. The gracious intimacy between lover and beloved is not generated by contemplation, but contemplation can help us recognize this part of our identity, to live into it, and to live out of this love. The primary purpose of contemplative practice is not to achieve anything. But through it, we nourish the truest part of us.

Contemplation connects us to a part of ourselves that is ordinarily largely ignored: our capacity to dwell in love. John Newman points out that psychoanalysis can unmask "the illusions of our false loves," but it is contemplative practice that trains us for rightly ordered love.[13] Because love is our natural, healthy state, at one level contemplative practice is like brushing teeth. Contemplative practice is an ordinary practice that turns our attention to the nearness of the Divine, a nearness that is always present but to which our attention is less often turned. This regular practice of attention is simply hygiene: care for ourselves as spiritual as well as physical beings. It signals to us that we are spiritual beings, that we are cherished by incarnate Wisdom in ways of which we are hardly aware. We do not need to strive for anything, or judge the "success" of our practice. In this sense, contemplative practice is not teleological, we do not do it for any end other than itself.

When we linger with our lover, even for a moment or two to reconnect after a busy day, after dinner, before the dishes, we are not really trying to achieve anything. We are simply living out our life together, living into the connection because the connection is itself precious to us. It is not an ecstatic weekend away. It is not the drama of falling in love. It is simply the utterly ordinary connection with someone we love. We are also probably aware of what happens when these ordinary connections somehow get lost in the busyness of life. The relationship itself can feel more fragile, and we deprive ourselves of the ongoing nurture of daily love and care. We forget that this love is one of the deepest and most

11. Pennington, *Centering Prayer*, 68.
12. Lanzetta, *Radical Wisdom*, 199.
13. Newman, *Disciplines of Attention*, 191.

precious truths of our lives and allow it to get pushed out by work, schedules, responsibilities, traffic: all of the things that entangle us as we get through the days and years of life. Without the ongoing nurture of our relationships, we forget something about who we are. We become formed by the minutiae of our lives and the claims of responsibilities that, though pressing, are not deeply life-giving.

We are formed not so much by what we believe about ourselves, though naturally this is important. We are formed by what we do. This is true even at the level of cognitive processes.[14] What we do creates the specific structure of our brain, creating pathways that are wide and deep or trivial. Spiritual, psychological, and emotional habits are created by doing particular things. When what we mostly do is look at a computer screen, fight traffic, metabolize stress, these things dominate our identity. Practices that interrupt the domination of daily tasks rehabituate our experience of who we are. This happens when we spend a moment with our lover in between the endless string of obligations we undertake. It happens chatting with children as we put them to bed. Contemplative practice connects us to another dimension of our love life.

Keeping this part alive nourishes us in a way that is disproportionate to the time we spend on it. Even dedicating extremely modest amounts of time to contemplative prayer provides a kind of cushion against the assaults of stress, frustration, and confusion that constitute so much of our ordinary days. It is a respite that changes the quality of the entire day. When we experience any kind of good human love—a lover or spouse, a child, a friend—we experience some qualification of the claims of the world on us. If we come home and play the piano for a few minutes or volunteer on the weekends, we have some way of limiting the things that tyrannize us and dominate our awareness. We can put aside the frustrations of work because we know they may be real, but they are not ultimate. There is something else in the world that is important. Stresses and demands that might otherwise take on much more importance are put in their place.

Contemplative practice is like this. It creates more space in our awareness so that the things we desire and the things we fear are located in a larger context and their power over us is diminished. Slaves in the American South would sometimes steal away to the "invisible institution" for spiritual practices.[15] This did not change the conditions of their servitude or the brutality of their lives. But it provided a space that was not only a temporary escape but a way of claiming a different identity. Slavery did not wholly define who they were. Contemporary Americans, enthralled to a consumer society, are far from the conditions of chattel slavery. But the resilience of slave spirituality is a dramatic reminder of

14. The constitution of subjectivity through love (and its absence) is a theme of the little gem by Thomas Lewis, Fari Amini, and Richard Lannon, *A General Theory of Love*; see especially chaps. 3, 4, 6, and 7.

15. See, for example, Dwight Hopkins, *Down, Up, and Over: Slave Religion and Black Theology*, 135–45.

the human ability to interrupt the power of even the most notorious regimes of power to define who we are. Reinventing contemplative practice for contemporary situations is one way of interrupting social, religious, and psychological tyrannies that would defraud us of our identity as bearers of the divine image.

CONTEMPLATION AS THERAPY

At one level, contemplation is a pedestrian practice that helps keep our indwelling in love healthy by qualifying the ordinary demands of life. Commitment to contemplative practice can also effect psychic change. In comparing Carmelite spirituality with Buddhist insight meditation, Mary Jo Meadow, Kevin Culligan, and Daniel Chowning point out the psychological dimension of the process of purification: "besides preparing us for transformation in God, purifying our spirit in faith, hope, and love also heals our personalities."[16] Contemplative practice can help free us from the distorted images of God as a "punitive parent that keeps us imprisoned in neurotic fear and guilt. Hope can release us from painful memories that bind us emotionally to negative experiences of the past . . . love can heal dysfunctional human relationships."[17]

Father Thomas Keating also emphasizes the psychological dimension of contemplation, pointing out ways in which centering prayer connects to the unconscious.[18] The emotional detritus, junk, and wounds that shape fundamental experiences are allowed to rise up through centering prayer and be released. The "traumatic emotional experiences from earliest childhood are stored in our bodies and nervous systems in the form of tension, anxiety, and various defense mechanisms. Ordinary rest and sleep do not get rid of them. But in interior silence and the profound rest that this brings to the whole organism, these emotional blocks begin to soften up and the natural capacity of the human organism to throw off things that are harmful starts to evacuate them."[19] Like good hygiene, contemplation promotes the cleansing of those obstacles that trouble our faith.

This gradual cleansing of psychological obscurations can make us more awake to our connection to the Divine. As Cynthia Bourgeault describes it: "What

---

16. Meadow et al., *Christian Insight Meditation: Following in the Footsteps of John of the Cross*, 108.

17. Ibid., 109.

18. Keating's innovative articulation of contemplative practice through a psychological model can be found in his series of books, including *Open Mind, Open Heart* (1986) and *Invitation to Love* (1992). A 24-volume video series was also produced that films him teaching the theory and practice of contemplation. Some of the psychological apparatus might seem somewhat anachronistic now, and indeed he has more recently modified his description. But the basic description of the connections between contemplation and the unconscious remains intriguing and helpful. However one evaluates the particularities of his psychological framework, watching his good-humored and charming presentation is itself an inspiring introduction to the efficacy of contemplation.

19. Keating, *Open Mind, Open Heart*, 93.

really happens when one enters the cloud of unknowing, resting in God beyond thoughts, words, and feelings, is a profound healing of the emotional wounds of a lifetime. As these wounds are gradually surfaced and released in prayer (one simply lets them go non-possessively, rather than retaining them for inspection as in psychoanalysis), more and more the false self weakens and the true self gradually emerges."[20] From this perspective, descending into the ungrounded abyss of love requires also a descent into our own personal wounds. Because "meditational prayer loosens repressed material in the unconscious, the initial fruits of spiritual practice may not be the expected peace and enlightenment, but destabilization and the emergence into consciousness of considerable pain."[21] One must acknowledge that contemplation is not for the faint of heart.

Classical accounts of psychological purgation cast these transformations into the language of sin. Meadow, Culligan, and Chowning provide a contemporary example of this rhetoric: through the process of purgation, "the fears, delusions, compulsions, projections, and jealousies that subtly motivate our behavior are finally revealed to us. We recognize that for years we have been unconsciously working to establish our own illusory self rather than the kingdom of God. We are deeply embarrassed and ashamed to see all of our inner workings; yet, we also trust that this painful awareness is healing us to that in everything we can live and act for God's honor and glory alone."[22] In putting it this way, the authors are indebted to the familiar duality between the ego and God that interprets natural egocentrism as sin. But it might be more accurate to say that shame and guilt are themselves part of an illusory self that requires transformation. Shame and guilt are among the detritus of wounded psyches that need to be burned away by the Beloved.

The need to question the symbolism of sin, shame, and guilt is especially acute among women, sexual minorities, and the afflicted. The journey to self-awareness and the painfulness of that journey will take distinctive forms among those for whom suffering or denigration are underpinnings of the psyche. Contemplative literatures have been written largely by and for male monastics and, to a lesser extent, celibate women. The path that is traversed through the inner pathways of consciousness will not be identical across different strands of social experience. Father Keating and Cynthia Bourgeault have helpfully emphasized that contemplative practice effects a sometimes painful therapy upon the soul. This process takes on distinctive forms and intensities when practiced by those the church has taught to despise themselves.

Beverly Lanzetta points out: if "women have been systematically denied the ability to see themselves imaged as divine, then a woman's quest for her true self

---

20. Cynthia Bourgeault, *Centering Prayer and Inner Awakening*, 96. Bourgeault provides an excellent description and updating of Keating's position in part III of this book, "The Psychology of Centering Prayer."

21. Ibid., 97.

22. Meadow et al., *Christian Insight Meditation*, 132.

cannot be resolved without understanding the impact of gender on the mystical roots of her being. . . . While the classical accounts of the soul's journey provide important resources for seekers along the way, there comes a point in a woman's spiritual life where she is in uncharted territory. She must forge her own path, because even her religious traditions fail her."[23] Lanzetta's point should be emphasized also for sexual minorities and for anyone who suffers violence and affliction.

The limitations of classical accounts of contemplative life make it necessary to continually reinvigorate contemplative theology and practice. Otherwise a monastic template will distort or erase the experience of those with different backgrounds. Grace Jantzen makes this point more strenuously in her objection to "those who want to be able to tell one true story, whether about rationality, sex, or even God, and make their story compulsory for all."[24] She objects to the masculine sexuality, queer and otherwise, that has spread "false generalizations over the tradition of Christian spirituality and with it something so central to Christian thought as what it might mean to experience the love of God."[25] Same-sex desire in general and lesbian desire in particular is misrepresented by what is said and what is left out in our interpretations of contemplative practice. I do not know of many people writing at the intersection of contemplation and queer theology. Our understanding of human spiritual wisdom can only be enhanced as we speak more openly at this crossroad of interhuman and divine desire.

The absence of sexual minorities from our guidance in the practice of contemplative prayer becomes even more wounding by the presence of unforgiving teachings on sexuality characteristic of many Christian churches. Same-sex desires call forth contorted readings of Scripture and doctrine. It alone of human activities places people outside the great democracy of sin and grace.[26] But because of the importance of erotic desire to spiritual life, the inability to tell "truths about our loves" distorts our ability "to tell loving truths about Jesus."[27] Contemplative practices, in unearthing repressed strata of consciousness, can disclose some of the ways interior consciousness has metabolized false or demeaning accounts of gender and sexuality. It can surface wounds caused by contorted homophobic church teachings. In this context the language of shame and guilt seem to have little place.

If this process is painful and disorienting, it is also a way of recovering a healthier relationship to the particularity of our individual life stories. After all, "the erotic powers with which we were created were given not only for this world, hence not only for reproduction. They were given as instruments and enactments

---

23. Lanzetta, *Radical Wisdom*, 34.
24. Grace Jantzen, "Promising Ashes," in *Queer Theology*, ed. Laughlin, 245.
25. Ibid., 247.
26. James Alison, "The Gay Thing: Following the Still Small Voice," in *Queer Theology*, ed. Laughlin, 56.
27. Mark Jordan, "God's Body," in *Queer Theology*, ed. Laughlin, 290.

of intimate union. That union culminates in union with God."[28] Finding ways that unite our different strands of erotic desire dedicate us to healthier spiritual, religious, and interpersonal relationships.

The purgation of internalized oppressions, of debilitating shame, of submission to prevaricating church authorities is an essential therapy of the spirit. But because disjunctions between experience and doctrine make the journey into psychological depths all the more complex, it is important to engage contemplative practice in relationship with a trustworthy spiritual director, a community of practice, and sometimes a therapist.

CONTEMPLATION AS THEOLOGY

The interpretation of contemplative practice in conversation with psychological paradigms is quite helpful. It speaks in the lingua franca of contemporary American society. Instead of a preoccupation with sin, the dynamics of healing predominate. Especially for those for whom the penitential and debasing language of the church has been personally wounding, a psychological paradigm is an essential component of the transformation of mind.

This therapeutic language does not displace a theological account of what happens in contemplative practice. Nan Merrill employs poetic language to awaken readers to the transformation that is available to them:

> Why grope in darkness when the Beloved abides within your heart?
> Chaos transformed becomes beauty, a dancing joy.
> Awaken! . . .
> You are created for love! More precious
>   Than all the world's treasures
>   Is the heart alight with love!
> Once you experience the Beloved of your heart,
>   Ever present at each moment,
> You will never again feel alone.[29]

Basil Pennington insists that the primary purpose of contemplative prayer is not limited to physical or psychological well-being. For Pennington, contemplation is a way to connect to our identity as bearers of the divine image. We are one with Christ, and when we rest in our center, we are our truest self and dwell where Christ is. We participate in the truth of Christ's own consciousness that "I and the Father are one," not just "in heaven" but "within the Trinity, within the movement of Love, the torrential cascade of Love that is the Spirit, flowing from Father to Son and from Son to Father and wholly embracing them and engulfing them and us in the one Love."[30] Even though much of our lives might

---

28. Ibid.
29. Nan Merrill, *Lumen Christi—Holy Wisdom: Journey to Awakening*, 75.
30. Pennington, *Centering Prayer* 72.

be seen as headlong flight from this truth, it remains the reality of who we are. "We look outside ourselves, or seek to construct a false self, a very fragile shell, whose all-too-obvious fragility leaves us in a constant state of fear and defensiveness. We need to reverse our direction to see and accept our true selves. With the discovery that our contingency rests on a God of infinite love, intimately present, what security, what affirmation we experience! . . . And what could be more affirming than the fact that at every moment the infinite God is present to us, bringing us forth in his creative love? If we are so loved by God, how lovable we must be!"[31] Meadow, Culligan, and Chowning acknowledge that meditation can improve physical, emotional, and mental health: lower blood pressure, improve concentration, reduce worry. But for Buddhists and Christians alike the purpose of meditation is reconnection to "unmanifest Ultimate Reality, Nibbana, the only unconditioned, unborn, undying, unmoving, unchanging reality. Insight practice directly prepares us for this."[32]

Here too modifications of even the most generous traditional language will be required as contemplation is transposed by a spiritual underside. Reconnecting to unmanifest ultimate reality is refracted differently in the context of suffering or exclusion.

Womanist thinkers draw attention to ways traditional doctrines have been distorted to exclude or debase large portions of humanity. The great declaration that we are created in the divine image has done little to help us recognize the full humanity of all persons. Without this most rudimentary acknowledgment the root symbols and practices of Christianity suffer horrendous distortion. When the revelation in Genesis that "all of humanity reflects God in God's great diversity" must traverse a wilderness of humiliation, new language for spiritual practice emerges. Diana Hayes reminds us of "women such as Hagar, abused and misused by both her master and her mistress, yet taught by God how to survive in the wilderness as African-American women had to do for centuries in this land."[33] Both the difficulties and wisdom of womanist spirituality will contribute unique perspectives on contemplative practice.

Another humiliation is the religious teaching that maleness alone resides at the intersection between humanity and Divinity: "The incarnation of the Word took place according to the male sex: this is indeed a question of fact and . . . cannot be dissociated from the economy of salvation. . . . That is why we can never ignore the fact that Christ is a man."[34] From this perspective Christ is a norm that makes women unrecognizable as bodies capable of bearing the divine image. "Women cannot materialize in the economy of salvation as other than

---

31. Ibid., 73.
32. Meadow et al., *Christian Insight Meditation*, 21.
33. Diana L. Hayes, "Standing in the Shoes My Mother Made," in *Deeper Shades of Purple: Womanism in Religion and Society*, ed. Stacey M. Floyd-Thomas, 67.
34. Sacred Congregation for the Doctrine of Faith, quoted by Karen Trimble Alliaume, "Disturbingly Catholic: Thinking the Inordinate Body," in *Bodily Citations: Religion and Judith Butler*, 93.

recipients, while men may be recipients and/or conduits of that salvation. . . . If Jesus is the standard or norm cited by Church leadership, to which women do not conform, then they fail to 'matter' in relation to this standard."[35]

Karen Trimble Alliaume is indebted to Judith Butler's philosophy, which makes it possible to see more clearly that "bodies and identities that do not successfully approximate communal norms are not recognized."[36] They fail to matter. The maleness of Jesus and even of God creates an essential obstacle; women cannot become sufficiently "purified" to see God, except perhaps by becoming "female men of God"—by renouncing our gender and sexuality. For women to identify themselves as Christian requires us to accept the humiliation of a partial, incomplete, passive, and dependent identity. Alliaume goes on to argue that the church's inability to see women is not a failure of women to matter but a failure of the church to matter. Divinization becomes thinkable, like the ordination that Alliaume is discussing, "because Christ is the 'other' upon whose address they [women] are fundamentally dependent for their identity as children of God, and Christ does not materialize only in the confines of the institutional Church."[37] Both Hayes and Alliaume limit human power to constrain divine graciousness, but struggling against regimes of power that define us out of existence, spiritually as well as socially, affects the way in which contemplation is practiced and experienced. Patriarchal and racist imagery for the Divine is endemic in Christian theology. The tradition that provides a contemplative path mines it with idols. We are constantly blown up by idolatrous images and self-defeating teachings.

Abjection also creates novel opportunities. Robert Goss describes homodevotion to Jesus: Jesus' initiation of a young man into homoerotic love as part of initiation into the higher secrets of God in the *Secret Gospel of Mark*, Paul's "thorn in the flesh," and the transference of homoerotic love into contemplative practice in the Middle Ages and beyond. He quotes Michael Warner: "Jesus was my first boyfriend. He loved me, personally, and told me I was his own." Goss himself describes the transformation of sexual feelings "through contemplative prayer from erotic fantasies to imaginative moments of grace and divine love."[38] He sees in gay sexuality a potential gift to erotophobic religious traditions because many "gay men view sexuality as a necessary and authentic part of their spirituality."[39]

Christopher Hinkle sees in St. John of the Cross's poetry a potential resource for queer contemplation. "Theology must address the multifaceted relationship of sexual desire to desire for God in order to speak to those who, having felt the full force of the challenge queerness presents to traditional Christian doctrine, still sense . . . that sexual practice can lead us towards God. . . . Although there

35. Ibid., 106.
36. Ibid., 105.
37. Ibid., 109.
38. Goss, *Queering Christ*, 138, 139.
39. Ibid., 78.

is a risk here of confusing sexual desire with desire for God, St. John directs us towards practices of discipline and discernment which, in correctly aligning the two, prepare us for the fulfillment in intimacy with God."[40] Hinkle is sensitive to the way in which St. John's project, though open to the gift of sexuality, depends on a conviction that there is a form of desire that is neither socially constructed nor satisfied by human sexuality. For St. John, sensual attachments give way to unmediated desire for God and nondiscursive contemplation. But because St. John is able to recognize sexual and divine desire as "means towards an intimacy with God," he is able to continue "to act as a spiritual guide for contemporary queer Christians whose own divine desires lead towards a queer theology . . . but is directed towards God."[41]

Contemplation as theology reminds us that the deep truth of our nature is the "mind of Christ." But it also reminds us that connecting to this in a healthy way will traverse the spiritual and theological wilderness in which the heterosexual white male is imagined as the normative form for spiritual life. The contribution of other bodies to the accumulated wisdom of contemplation may make the radiant opulence with which Christ bodies forth in humanity more evident.

CONTEMPLATION AS LOVE

The recovery of one's identity as a bearer of the divine image is, by itself, "too light a thing" to express the lure of contemplative practice. Dwelling in love requires the healing of our own distorted self-love. Especially for those whom the church has marginalized, this distortion can take the form of self-loathing and internalized oppression. But the healing of such distortion is not an end in itself; it is the precursor to joyous compassion for an ever-widening circle of beings. The Jesuit priest Father Yves Raguin acknowledges that contemplative practice can stall out and limit itself to a self-enclosed spirituality. But love is by its nature relational; and contemplation, by easing the constraints of egocentrism, expresses itself in compassionate relations. Father Raguin reassures us that by continuing through stages of darkness as well as light, the heart of the contemplative beats with one love for God and for humanity.[42] Neither the therapeutic nor the theological model understands the human being to be a self-enclosed ego satisfied with self-affirmation, but they might focus on personal transformation in a way that minimizes the relational quality of contemplation.

Love is our deepest identity, and healing the wounds of the ego free us for

40. Christopher Hinkle, "Love's Urgent Longings," in *Queer Theology*, ed. Laughlin, 196.
41. Ibid., 197–98.
42. Raguin's own language is evocative but so gendered I found I could not bring myself to quote it in the text: contemplation allows one to enter into a "new dimension of himself which unites him by a fraternal bond with everything that exists and most especially with all men, in the brotherhood of the sons of God. The heart of man, which is thus at the center of the universe, beats with one and the same love for God and for his brothers" (Yves Raguin, *Paths to Contemplation*, 128–29).

love, even as love tends to the wounds of the ego. Contemplation is one way to move more deeply into this circulation of justice and compassion. Cynthia Bourgeault argues that contemplation is an important, perhaps even essential method for nourishing the radical love described in the Gospels: "Only when the mind is 'in the heart,' grounded and tethered in that deeper wellspring of spiritual awareness, is it possible to live the teachings of Jesus without hypocrisy or burnout. The gospel requires a radical openness and compassion that are beyond the capacity of the anxious, fear-ridden ego."[43]

One of the disturbing things about reading the hagiographies of saints is the radical, self-sacrificing, even self-mortifying love attributed to them: St. Catherine of Siena licking the wounds of a mangy dog, St. Kevin holding a bird's nest in his hand until the eggs hatch. But the love that emerges from contemplative practice is neither an obligation nor self-sacrifice. These and other "near enemies" of love such as self-righteousness or moralism can be neutralized through a sustained practice of contemplation. Of course, contemplation, like everything else, can also become an occasion for self-righteousness, exhaustion, feelings of obligation or accomplishment. But when it is able to ease the intensity of our own fears and restless desires, the proximity of other beings is more evident to our experience. The easing of the tyranny of the ego creates more room for sympathy and compassion.

Love for others is not a goal to be achieved through contemplation but its natural expression. Beverly Lanzetta describes the ethic of a "feminist mystical theology" as arising "out of a mystical connection to the whole family of creation. This means that the depth of our being is in solidarity with the depth of all beings. The divine spark in the center of our soul is sustained by and has a stake in the flourishing of all other souls and life forms."[44] Out of contemplative experiences "flow kindness, patience, long-suffering, benignity. When we sense our oneness with others, when we are filled with compassion, how can we not be kind, patient, benign?"[45] Contemplation can stabilize and deepen capacities for joyous compassion. But contemplation is not itself a work nor is it justified because it culminates in ethical actions. Resting in the Divine is an end in itself; joy and compassion are the perfume of this rest.[46]

---

43. Bourgeault, *Centering Prayer and Inner Awakening*, 117.
44. Lanzetta, *Radical Wisdom*, 196.
45. Pennington, *Centering Prayer*, 103.
46. Meister Eckhart and Marguerite Porete are good teachers here. Both emphasize that they do not work, and indeed work is another effect of the ego that interferes with the divine presence. See, for example, Eckhart's Sermon 52, or "Why God Often Lets Good People, People Who Are Really Good, Be Prevented from Doing Their Good Works" (in *Talks of Instruction* or *Table Talk*, collected among other places in *Meister Eckhart, from Whom God Hid Nothing: Sermons, Writings, and Sayings*, ed. David O'Neal. Eckhart is in this influenced by the writings of Porete, for example, *Mirror of Simple Souls*, chaps. 56, 69, 77, 81–82, 84.

CONTEMPLATIVE PRACTICE

There is a woman I pay to clean my house every other week so I can do things like write this book. She cleans. I write. She meditates as she cleans. She identified this as common ground between us, though I have no idea how she knows that I meditate; nor do I know really what she means by that term. But I know that our house is perfumed by more than Simple Green when she leaves. I also have the honor of friendship with a young woman who runs errands for me two or three hours every week. She is estranged from the religion of her youth but a fantastic (if underemployed) jazz singer.[47] Both of these women radiate a kind of super-natural kindness that would make them excellent candidates for the "compassion studies" scientists are now undertaking. They are reminders that goodness and compassion flow wherever they will, with little regard for traditional religious practice or even the rudiments of belief. Technique is evidently inessential to the nurture of compassion. And yet a few words on what contemplatives have said about their practice can be helpful.

Because contemplation is understood as relationship with the Divine under the direction of the Holy Spirit, Christianity offers relatively little emphasis on method or technique.[48] The persecution of many of its noblest practitioners no doubt undermined the preservation of a sustained tradition articulating techniques of meditation. In this Christianity differs from other traditions. Yoga and Buddhism, for example, preserve an enormous wealth of teachings concerning methods for harnessing the body, breath, voice, the imagination, the senses, discursive reasoning, nondiscursive awareness, devotion, intellect, emotion, and sexual energy for contemplation.

It is odd that a tradition whose central revelation is the incarnation of Divine Wisdom has been so slow to incorporate the body in contemplative practice. Restricting practice to mental practices, even wonderful ones like centering prayer, fails to include the transformative power of the body in the work of divinization. The hesychasts are somewhat of an exception to this rule. Their enthusiasm for the divine light suggests how powerful attention to breath and body can be.[49]

---

47. Her name is Nicole Chillemi and her music is available on her Web site.

48. Pierre Hadot points out that "no systematic treatise codifying the instructions and techniques for spiritual exercises has come down to us." There appears to have been a well-known oral tradition that was never written down (*Philosophy as a Way of Life*, 83, 84). The anonymously written *Cloud of Unknowing* provides some recommendations for practice, and Gregory Palamas in *Triads* brings together negative theology and bodily practices, such as attention to the breath. There are other Christians that discuss technique and methods of prayer, but these writers are far from the mainstream of Christian thought and even of more familiar "mystical" writings. Basil Pennington dedicates the third chapter of *Centering Prayer* to an excavation of some of these writers: Evagrius Ponticus, John Climacus, Gregory of Sinai, Necephorus, as well as Teresa of Avila and her spiritual brother St. John of the Cross.

49. Both feminist and queer theologies have been focused on rethinking the role of the body in theology. Carter Heyward's *Touching Our Strength: The Erotic as Power and the Love of God* was an

An increasing number of Christians and post-Christian practitioners draw on the expertise and wisdom of other traditions to aid their practice. Ruben Habito describes the significance of the Zen practice of watching the breath: "Coming to Zen practice—being told to do away with all such conceptualizing and mental effort and to just sit with my breathing—opened the windows of my being, letting wonderfully fresh air come in. This was for me the living Breath of God, which recreates the earth and makes all things new."[50] Cynthia Bourgeault provides teaching on chanting, which she describes as Christian yoga because of its bodily qualities; and Father Thomas Ryan has developed yoga into a form of embodied Christian practice.[51] Diana Eck quotes Father Raguin as saying that there is no "Christian" prayer, and so Zen and other forms of meditation can be completely consonant with the attention that is necessary to contemplative practice. "The proof is in the practice."[52] Vipassana or Zen meditation, yoga, Tibetan visualization or deity yoga, and Sufi poetry are examples of traditions that can enrich Christian contemplative practice. In addition to anchoring contemplation in a rich complex of bodily and mental practices, dialogue with other traditions helps to deepen a sense of the inadequacy of names and the desirability of hundreds of names for the Beloved.

Even without much attention to bodily practice or meditation techniques, the contemporary Christian tradition does provide clues about how to engage a contemplative practice. Father Pennington uses the analogy of a trellis to explain why method is useful: "It is of the very nature of a climbing rose to reach up toward the sun and blossom forth. But without a trellis it keeps falling back on itself, and soon we have a large knotted mass that does not rise very high and gives birth to very few blooms. But if the climbing rose is given the support of a trellis, it can reach up and up toward the sun."[53] Awareness of some of the literature providing guidance for meditation is helpful. But each person is different, so even the most general discussions of technique are secondary to the process of discernment appropriate to one's own situation.

There are a variety of approaches to contemplative prayer: centering prayer, watching the breath, mindfulness practice, mantra recitation, the Jesus prayer, chanting.[54] The Center for Contemplative Mind in Society draws a tree of

---

early example of this rethinking. *Queer Theology: Rethinking the Western Body,* ed. Gerard Laughlin, and *Toward a Theology of Eros: Transfiguring Passion at the Limits of Discipline,* ed. Virginia Burrus and Catherine Keller, provide anthologies of more recent reflections in this direction. See also, among others, Daniel T. Spencer, *Gay and Gaia: Ethics, Ecology, and the Erotic;* Eugene Rogers, *Sexuality and the Christian Body.*

50. Habito, *Living Zen, Loving God,* 5.

51. Father Ryan has books and a DVD: "Yoga Prayer: An Embodied Christian Spiritual Practice." See also Bourgeault's *Chanting the Psalms: A Practical Guide with Instructional CD.*

52. See Eck, *Encountering God: A Spiritual Journey from Bozeman to Banaras,* 163.

53. Pennington, *Centering Prayer,* 74.

54. There are countless resources for introducing the theory and practice of meditation, including: James Finley's books, e.g., *Christian Meditation: Experiencing the Presence of God,* and audio CDs, e.g., "Christian Meditation: Entering the Mind of Christ"; Keating, *Open Heart, Open Mind;*

practice on its Web site that includes a variety of practices on the tree of contemplation: stillness practices (e.g., centering prayer, insight meditation), activism (e.g., pilgrimage or volunteering), generative practices (loving-kindness meditation, *lectio divina*, visualization), movement (yoga, tai chi, walking meditation), creativity (singing, chant, calligraphy, journaling), among others.[55] Different people find different approaches to meditation useful. Some prefer methods that integrate bodily movement into prayer. In this case, yoga, pranayama, or chanting are helpful because the body itself becomes the focusing device for prayer. For others, visualizations or single-pointed concentration may be most helpful. The gentleness of centering prayer makes it attractive. Jon Kabat-Zinn translated Buddhist meditation into a secular mindfulness practice to help patients struggling with ongoing pain. Many studies have supported its effectiveness in clinical contexts. The tradition-neutral structure makes mindfulness practice useful for people for whom Christianity has become too toxic as a context for spiritual practice.[56] The Buddhist kindness meditation focuses on the generation of compassion, a practice that can be usefully combined with intercessory prayer.[57] It is not so important that one finds the right method as that one finds a good fit between one's own predilections and one's practice. This might have as much to do with the community or teacher that is available as anything else. Meditation is not like a new car; one does not need the latest, flashiest model. One needs only to find an approach that suits one's situation.

Many teachers of contemplative methods recommend that one find twenty minutes twice a day to practice. Indeed, some teachers are adamant about this commitment. Even these relatively short blocks of time can stabilize one's practice and integrate it deeply and naturally into one's life. On the other hand, I am a mother of three children as well as a professor. Traumatic stress disorder shredded my ability to concentrate. These experiences make me less confident that the twenty-minute requirement is necessary to define a minimum practice.

Pennington, *Centering Prayer*; Bourgeault, *Centering Prayer and Inner Awakening* and *Chanting the Psalms;* John Main, *Word into Silence: A Manual for Christian Meditation*; Swami Amaldas, *Christian Yogic Meditation*; Joseph Chu-Cong, *The Contemplative Experience: Erotic Love and Spiritual Union*; Meadow et al., *Christian Insight Meditation*; Habito, *Living Zen, Loving God*; Carlo Carretto, *Letters from the Desert*. One could add to these books on yoga: Indra Devi, *Yoga for You*, or T. K. V. Desikachar, *Health, Healing and Beyond: Yoga and the Living Tradition of Krishnamacharya*; secularized forms of meditation such as that developed by Jon Kabat-Zinn; countless books on Buddhist meditation, such as the Dalai Lama, *How to Practice: The Way to a Meaningful Life*, or Wallace, *Mind in the Balance*. In addition there are many helpful Web sites, including those of World Community for Christian Meditation, Center for Contemplative Mind and Society, Contemplative Outreach. This list is arbitrary and limited but hopefully suggests some avenues of introduction to methods of contemplative prayer.

55. Center for Contemplative Mind in Society, www.contemplativemind.org.

56. Jon Kabat-Zinn has written a number of books on this subject. He also has a CD describing the techniques, "Mindfulness for Beginners."

57. Sharon Salzberg, cofounder of the Barre Center for Buddhist Studies and Insight Meditation, introduces this practice in *The Force of Kindness*, which includes a CD of guided meditations. Pema Chodron, an American Tibetan nun, also has produced a number of guided meditations on CD, including "Awakening Compassion."

Father Pennington quotes Dom Chapman: "Pray as you can. Don't pray as you can't."[58]

Structured descriptions of what contemplative practice should include can be helpful as one develops a practice. They provide some framework for thinking about how to begin working with one's mind and reorienting one's time. But any requirement or model that sets the bar of practice too high may prevent someone from practicing the way they can. For many of us, twenty minutes once a day is too high a bar. It is like learning that one must know calculus before signing up for marine biology. For some of us, that meant that marine biology was simply not going to be an option. But all one needs for contemplative practice is a mind. Most of contemplation is simply working with the particular mind that we have, in its particular circumstances as they unfold and change over time. Even more than a spouse, we have our mind for better and worse, richer and poorer, sickness and health. As long as we have this mind, we have the means to engage contemplative practice. The question is how to work with our mind in the particular circumstances we are in right now. "Pray as you can. Don't pray as you can't."

What different methods have in common is that they suggest ways to focus the mind, to gather it in one place when it is tempted to scatter. It is the nature of mind to constantly produce thoughts. Mind is a factory of memories, images, emotions, and anticipations. This busyness of the surface of the mind is quite useful for getting us through each day, but the constant noisiness of the mind obscures the silence that is the first language of the Divine. In order for the mind to become more receptive to the Beloved's presence, we need some device to calm it. One watches the breath, focusing the mind simply on the breath itself as it is inhaled and exhaled. Or one places one's mind on a visual object, such as a candle flame or an icon or, alternatively, on a sacred word as a resource for drawing the mind back from its wanderings. Techniques are ways to help the mind focus on one thing so that restless leaping from thought to thought can be stilled. This does not mean that thoughts themselves stop arising or that we do not follow them, but these devices give us something to focus on when the mind wanders. A more focused mind allows those parts of awareness that are not governed by words and images to rise closer to the surface and to become more integrated into our stream of consciousness.

Like the game Go, contemplative techniques are simple enough to be described in under five minutes, but they open up the infinite permutations of mind that emerge through the persistent practice of contemplation. The practice itself is simply using a device to recall the mind from its distractions. It must be admitted that it can be frustrating to find how unwilling the mind is to be tethered to any single object. We might have sought peace and serenity, the calm that we imagine is going on inside the heads of all of the other meditators in the

---

58. Pennington, *Centering Prayer*, 45.

world. Instead, we are confronted with endlessly noisy chatter, as if were trapped in an elevator with Shrek's donkey, who blathers on and on about nothing.

A second-order practice for contemplation prayer is gentleness. As one uses the word or breath or asana to return focus, do so gently, tenderly. Resist the temptation to scorn poor donkey mind that finds it impossible to calm itself. Frustration, irritation, judgment, condemnation, and envy of those who (one imagines) are placidly concentrating are common emotional detritus that arises along with the mental busyness of the mind. In the reassertion of attention, practice nonjudgment. Of course the mind produces thoughts. That is its job and its habit. Calming the mind allows things to rise to awareness that the mind has been working hard to keep at bay. The threat of this will provoke the mind into even more frantic efforts to distract awareness. Silence, serenity, peace, joy are all somewhat alien modes, and the mind will need to chatter a great deal about them. It will need to comment on them, evaluate them, puffing up like a peacock when they appear, stomping in aggravation and self-abuse when they evaporate. Be gentle and patient. This kind of metapractice of gentleness and compassion for one's own mind can be as useful as the method of meditation itself.

In any case, method is less important than the intention to practice. Contemplative practice may seem impossible to anyone busy with work, exhausted from parenting, struggling with depression, preoccupied with a party scene, frenzied by the preoccupations of modern life, overcommitted to obligations that seem infinitely more pressing than a few minutes of private silence. The first practice is not finding the magical extra twenty or forty minutes in each day to struggle with the noisiness of mind. The first practice is to desire practice—even if this seems impossible, absurd, and contrary to one's identity and lifestyle. For three seconds a day or a week, one can remember that desire. One might imagine that, if one had five minutes—or a more focused mind, or greater discipline, or freedom from pain, or less of a hangover, or a quieter environment, or fewer obligations—one would enter for one minute or twenty into the delicious silence of the Beloved. This intention is itself a reconnection with the mysterious, apophatic dimension of faith.

Techniques of attention are only to support the intention to open oneself to the Divine. The primary energy is not to discipline the mind to stay in one place but to release the effort of mind altogether so it can rest more easily in the Divine. The ego is not in charge of the world, and its control over itself and its surroundings is frighteningly small. Contemplation releases the ego from the illusion of control so we might be held, nourished, and cherished. Some other part of ourselves opens up, like a pool hidden under the floor. Even while the mind chatters on, we can sink into this pool that is always there but not available to our conscious awareness.

It is surprisingly difficult to surrender the expectation that we must do something to transform our mind, to draw down a contemplative "experience." This sense that we should be "doing" something is not necessarily the prideful insistence that we control everything. It might reflect our healthy desire for a calmer spirit and a more compassionate heart. This sometimes shades over into the overwhelming sense of responsibility that has transposed the good news of divine grace into another obligation. If somehow we prayed "right," various good things would happen. We would become "better" people. But the practice of contemplation moves in the opposite direction.

The effort of prayer is simply the intention to rest in love that is always already there. It is like an adopted child who spent many months in an orphanage and then finds herself in the home of loving parents. It can take a long time for the child to be able to rest in her parents' arms, to gradually release and relax and let her parents hold her. This is natural. She spent many months in a place where crying did her little or no good, where there was no one to come to her when she was hungry or lonely or afraid. She learned to comfort herself and to expect the world to be unreliable. It would be silly to expect her to fall into the arms of her new parents with perfect trust. But over time, she can learn that they really are reliable. They do provide for her needs. They want to comfort her. She does not need to be in charge of everything. In contemplation we gradually learn to release into a love that we do not have to generate by proper technique or earn by perfecting our virtues. There is some effort in gently asserting focused attention into the confusion of thoughts during a period of meditative prayer. But the deeper effort is this sacrifice of effort that lets us drop into the womb of God and be nurtured there.

DARK NIGHT

Over time, practice can have a self-reinforcing quality. One wants to take a few minutes in silence each day or several days a week and misses it when the schedule is interrupted. Thoughts may or may not calm, but the practice becomes more familiar. This is true even if the practice is wishing one might want to practice for ten seconds each week. What happens during any period of prayer or period of one's life will be particular to the practitioner. The most predictable aspect of contemplative practice is that whatever one imagined would happen is the least likely thing to actually occur. But there are common patterns that often accompany contemplative practice. Some awareness of difficulties that often arise can make it easier when we encounter problems on the path.

Few guides of the contemplative way neglect to mention some version of what St. John of the Cross calls "the dark night of the soul."[59] Whether viewed psychologically or theologically, the exposure of the heart in prayer challenges our beliefs and our experience. That classical writers like Teresa of Avila, St. John of the Cross, and Ignatius of Loyola dedicate significant effort to the process of

59. In addition to St. John's own poignant and helpful description in *The Dark Night of the Soul*, Keating describes the dark night in more contemporary terms in *Invitation to Love*. Lanzetta describes a feminist version of the dark night in *Radical Wisdom*.

discernment of spirits suggests that contemplation can surface unpleasant emotions. St. John provides clues to distinguish depression ("melancholy") from the darkness that accompanies progress in prayer. Ignatius spells out how to deal with the oscillation between consolation and desolation.[60] From a theological point of view, darkness is "both the anguishing confrontation with the roots of the soul's inordinate passions, and the glad and lovely night in which lover and beloved are united."[61] Our minds and hearts are habituated to patterns that may have been useful for navigating the world as we understand it, but that are obstacles to the deeper flow of love. The dismantling of these obstacles is ultimately freeing, but the process can be painful and disorienting.

The darkness that emerges in the spiritual life of women, queer people, and the afflicted includes a specific dark night in which the soul's internalization of the church's misogyny, homophobia, racism, and other degradations are purged. Beverly Lanzetta gives the example of St. Teresa, whose reformation of the Carmelite convents pitted her against the Spanish Inquisition and its teachings on the dangers of uppity women and private prayer. The church backed its insistence on the inferiority of women with secular and monastic arrangements that seared that inferiority into women's psyches. For someone like Teresa that meant that "just being a woman is enough to have my wings fall off—how much more being a woman and wretched as well."[62]

Part of the particular poignancy of the dark night from the "underside" is that the church is both the context in which faith is nourished and one of the primary mediators of the self-hatred and guilt that must be purged by divine love. The institution is an abusive parent poisoning one with self-abasement and yet also the reliquary of symbols, songs, images, prayers, beliefs, traditions, communities, and practices that nourish mature faith. The interior riptides by which one's self-identity and images for God are dismantled can be excruciating. It is disorienting to discover that the church has taught one deeply distorted untruths about oneself and about the divine nature. Surrendering one's faith in the reliability of the church may be a relief but it is painful.

More difficult yet is untangling the knot of habituated illusions that have served as a core of identity. Virginia Ramey Mollenkott describes learning to read Scripture "from low and outside." After being told at thirteen that if she continued to love women she was "'without God in my mind' and 'worthy of death,'" she came to identify with Hagar, Sarah, and Ruth rather than Abraham and Boaz. "As I divested myself of the male-identified androcentric and hetero-centric mindset and became woman-identified and queer-identified, I realized

---

60. See Newman, *Disciplines of Attention*, 64–67; "Rules for the Discernment of Spirits," *The Spiritual Exercises of St. Ignatius,* translated by Anthony Mottoloa, with an introduction by Robert W. Gleason, S.J., New York: Doubleday, 1964, Image Edition, 1989, 129–34.

61. *Radical Wisdom*, 121.

62. Lanzetta, *Radical Wisdom*, 128, quoting Teresa of Avila, *Life* 10.8. Reading Teresa's account of her own struggle to fulfill her vocation in a dangerous and misogynist environment can be encouraging to contemporary people facing similar hostility from the church.

that the God of scripture lifts up the lowly and brings the outsider into the community."[63]

Mollenkott is an example of those who find their way to a life-giving identity by wrestling with Scripture and authority. But in the midst of this process, one can feel without resources if the church had in the past served as the place through which religious identity and understanding were formed. If it loses this role, it can seem as if there is no place to turn. This is a normal aspect of contemplative practice. One reason authoritarian forms of Christianity have been troubled by contemplation is that it recognizes the limits of human constructions and institutions. But the struggle with religious identity delivered by the church is only intensified when we have internalized doctrines proclaiming the inferiority of women, that our desires make us "worthy of death," or that oppression and violence are part of God's will for us. In these situations the dark night will mean that our relationship to the church must be reforged along with our identity and our faith.

If our ideas of God are too closely tethered to church teachings, this process of renegotiation can make it appear as if all is lost. Because one is seeking the Beloved in ways that are alien to what the church has taught, it can seem as if God no longer exists or that a recovery of healthy self-respect requires a complete rejection of the church, perhaps even religion itself. To make matters more complex, women and sexual minorities are often put at odds with their secular communities who cannot imagine why a healthy person could stay in such a repressive and humiliating institution.

But from a contemplative point of view the disintegration of these markers of identity, of community, and of doctrine is not the loss of faith but the loss of one's fantasies about oneself and God. Horace Griffin describes this arc in his challenge to the black church, concluding: "Our acceptance and celebration of lesbians and gays . . . will allow us to appreciate the beauty of God's diverse creation. In doing this, in affirming the erotic in all of us, we will proclaim a true black liberation theology and in so doing, we will honor God."[64] But giving up fantasies is often at the cost of participation in the community that formed them.

Saint John of the Cross argued that the painfulness of the dark night reflects nothing in God but only the difficulty the soul experiences as it is prepared to receive God more fully. In the case of those on the church's margins, exposing ourselves to divine love requires the exposure of the raw and tender wounds inflicted by the church. The orphan who gradually allows herself to be loved must let go of the self she had constructed, the self that enabled her to survive the orphanage. To do this she has to in some sense, even if only unconsciously, integrate the experiences of being afraid, forlorn, and loveless. This unloved self

63. Mollenkott, "Reading the Bible from Low and Outside," in *Take Back the Word*, ed. Goss and West, 14.

64. Griffin, *Their Own Receive Them Not: African American Lesbian and Gays in Black Churches*, 225.

must become integrated so that another self, one that is cherished and adored, can take its place. Depending on each person's life experiences, this unloved self might include things we feel guilty about, behaviors we are ashamed of, violence we endured, or oppression to which we were subjected. Allowing this unloved self to be integrated can be dark and painful.

But working with the mind in this way brings the constructed qualities of identity into clearer focus. Aspects of identity that might have seemed fixed become more flexible. Contemplation releases attachment to both the good and bad aspects of self-identity. We are not destined to the stain of worthlessness that had come to seem an essential part of us. The good in us is not dependent on an infinitely receding horizon of achievement. Neither the seeming intransigence of emotion nor the determinations of identity are absolute. We can work with our minds and hearts in more open ways.

For those on the underside, this flexibility of identity, this lack of essence, can contribute to a freedom from the constraints of a reified identity. It means a freedom from demeaning stereotypes but also agility in the use of cultural constructions so they become more life-giving.[65] Elizabeth Stuart argues that baptism places all cultural identities "under eschatological erasure." Sexuality and gender "are not of absolute importance, they are not determinative in God's eyes and in so far as any of us have behaved . . . as if they are grounds upon which to exclude people from the glorious liberty of the children of God we are guilty of profanity and a fundamental denial of our own baptismal identity, which rests in being bound together with others not of our choosing by an act of sheer grace."[66] The dark night changes the way we experience identity formation. Translating the dialectic of naming and negation into the dark night, we might say that falling into the apophatic no-self loosens the fixity of identity construction while enabling us to use names in truer and more beautiful ways. We do not lose the concreteness of who we are but become more limber in inhabiting identity. The dark night burns and illuminates.

SINGING THE BELOVED'S SONG IN A STRANGE LAND

It is natural to expect prayer to accomplish the wonderful goal of union with God, submerging us in an outflowing of peace and love. The difficulties of life will dissolve, our choices become clear, and our decisions unambiguous. These hopes reflect our natural desire for God and the restlessness that haunts the human heart. They also reflect the desire for the ego-mind to find a way of life that will relieve it of suffering. Contemplative prayer is not necessarily especially

---

65. Judith Butler's work on the construction of gender as well as the use of parody in gay communities may suggest potentials for this kind of agility in identity formation.
66. Stuart, *Gay and Lesbian Theologies*, 107.

satisfying to this part of our minds. Attachment to goals, spiritual or otherwise, is still attachment and it is still goal-oriented.

Contemplation can actually increase some forms of suffering. It can erode our defenses that make it possible to deceive ourselves about our situation or ourselves. Difficult parts of our personality can be unmasked. The muffling of our own pain or the pain of others can be reduced. We might feel the suffering of those around us and in the world itself more acutely. Or we might be disappointed to find we are basically just as anxious and selfish as ever. We might realize that the tyranny of the ego, its pains and pleasures, its petty vices and self-righteousness and fears, erode more slowly than we had hoped. It is helpful, as Father Pennington says, to be encouraged by the witness of others who have gone before us. But it is important to understand that we are working with our own minds, in the concrete situation we find ourselves. This is not a fantasy self or an idealized path. It is the reality of all of the layers of who we are as they become integrated into the stream of our life through the gracious and healing power of the Divine Lover. But whether this integration is difficult or pleasant matters only a little bit. We are already in the womb of Love and nothing we do can change that.

Contemplative practice weaves together our apophatic depth with the particular and unique qualities of individual personhood. For Christians, the decisive exemplar of the unity of divine depths and unique personhood is Christ. This long detour through negative theology and contemplative practice will, I hope, allow us to conceive of incarnation of Divinity as the illumination of humanity rather than the juxtaposition of two alien substances. The nonduality of the Divine Eros is not alien to human nature: it is its most natural desire and home. The next section turns (finally!) to a reflection on the incarnation of the Divine Eros in Wisdom, in creation, in gospel, and in humanity.

Chapter 5

"Breath of the Power of God"

The Emanation of Wisdom

For she is a breath of the power of God, and a pure emanation of the glory of the Almighty; therefore nothing defiled gains entrance into her. For she is a reflection of eternal light, a spotless mirror of the working of God, and an image of his goodness. Although she is but one, she can do all things, and while remaining in herself, she renews all things; in every generation she passes into holy souls and makes them friends of God, and prophets.

Wisdom of Solomon 7:25–27

He is the image of the invisible God. . . . In him all the fullness of God was pleased to dwell, and through him God was pleased to reconcile to himself all things.

Colossians 1:15, 19–20

Contemplative prayer and the apophatic tradition carry us into the Erotic Abyss, beyond light and dark, beyond naming and negation. This imageless womb nourishes the divine emptiness that lies in our own depths, and it reminds us that no name is adequate to this great, healing mystery. But from this fathomless depth proceeds Wisdom, the "only begotten, God the Word";[1] Christ, the Beloved; the Rose of Sharon; Morning Star; Fairest Lord Jesus; Jesus, lover of my soul. Jesus opens the path of Bhakti yoga for Christians, evoking devotion, longing, and participation in the Divine Eros. Those who walk this particular

---

1. This is from the Chalcedonian Creed, which can be found in its entirety at earlychurch texts.com.

way find in Christ a door to the Divine, an image that makes the imageless depths accessible to our human way of understanding.

We have taken what may seem like a long detour. A book that is supposedly about the incarnation is only now, five chapters in, taking up its subject matter. But the incarnation is an element of Trinitarian theology. It is thinkable, as much as possible, in light of the Christian understanding of the Divine. The idea of the Trinity protects us from conceiving of Divinity as a kind of Zeus who clothes himself in human form and strolls around heaven and earth causing whatever mayhem that occurs to him.[2] Divinity is uncreated, apophatic, infinitely mysterious, beyond being, beyond names. YHWH is a collection of letters that cannot be spoken because there is no name for the Holy One of Israel. The discipline and joy of the way of negation combined with contemplative practice are ways Christians have tried to remain faithful to this essential wisdom.

The relentless paradox of the Christian way is that it combines this understanding of Divinity, which it shares with the other religions of the world, with the intuition that Divinity has been made present in history through the body and the event of Jesus of Nazareth. It is nonsensical to think that a human body can manifest Beyond Being. It is like imagining the inexhaustible brilliance of the sun as a cave-dwelling fish. Not only is it too small, it is the wrong sort of thing. The idea of divine reality as Trinitarian in nature is a way of holding fast to these paradoxical truths: the nonduality of Divinity and the salvation available through Christ. The incarnation is about Christ but it is also about the second person of the Trinity.

Christians understand this second person to be really and truly God: God from God, Light from Light, True God from True God, Begotten, not made, of one being with the groundlessness of true Divinity. Yet this second person is thinkable. The second person—Wisdom or Logos—is not yet Jesus of Nazareth but it is an initial manifestation of nondual goodness. Christians say that God is Love but the root metaphor for this beginningless expression or self-manifestation of *Ungrund* is Wisdom. Wisdom is the hinge between the fathomless depths of the Divine Eros and the utter concreteness and uniqueness of a human body. Wisdom renders the Abyss into concrete form. It is the principle of mind and of order: thinkability at its most general and comprehensive. It is the principle of understanding that allows us to contemplate Divinity and it is the principle of order that transforms chaos into cosmos. This is a form of concreteness that vivifies everything that exists in any way whatsoever. It is the creativity of Divinity imagined through an intellectual or psychological metaphor.

Wisdom is the movement of pure Divinity into action so that something other than nondual infinity might take shape. It is that by which Divinity creates. As the mediation between nonduality and concrete existence, it is also that

---

2. My father, Edward Farley, pointed out the unnuanced version of "Zeus" I present here. I am thinking of, for example, the Zeus of *Prometheus Bound* or "Lyda and the Swan." There is in Greek philosophy and poetry much richer versions of the symbol of Zeus than these.

by which Divinity can be said to become incarnate in a human being. Human beings are bodies that clothe Divinity. Wisdom is the metaphor, present in many of the world's religions, for our power to participate in Divinity. The human form is perfected precisely in its approximation to wisdom. Incarnation in Christ is an example of this approximation in a perfected form. This chapter will reflect on Wisdom as the first emanation of Divinity from the Good Beyond Being. Wisdom breathes Divinity into existence eternally as the second person and in time through creation.

GOD FROM GOD: WISDOM AS PERFECT MIRROR

The various interwoven threads that give shape to the idea of the Trinity shared the insight that mind was both a metaphor for ultimate reality and also a medium through which humanity participates in Divinity. For Platonists, *Nous* (from which our word *knowledge* evolved) was a word for the Good or the One as it manifested itself in being. It uses the metaphor for self-reflection as one of the most fitting to express reality as both unknowable and yet known. The human mind has a capacity for awareness of both aspects of reality. It can move into nonconceptual reality and it can talk about this, think about this, refine under-standing, and deepen participation by working with the mind's capacity for conceptual thinking. The human mind mirrors reality, just as *Nous* mirrors the Good. It is the medium by which human beings are transformed, divinized. It is also a metaphor to express Divinity in conceptual form: the Good Beyond Being is manifest as Wisdom.

The Hebraic tradition also used the mind as a primary metaphor for and medium of participation in Divinity. Wisdom (translated to Greek as *Sophia*) is the mirror of God. "She is a reflection of eternal light, a spotless mirror of the working of God, and an image of his goodness" (Wisdom 7:26). While she remains herself, that is, a perfect image of God, she moves outward to create and she does so by and through beauty. She is the power of the Divine expressed as creativity. "She reaches mightily from one end of the earth to the other, and she orders all things well. . . . If understanding is effective, who more than she is fash-ioner of what exists?" (Wisdom 8:1, 6). Wisdom is the first principle and beauty of the Divine and as such she is creator. By using the metaphor of Wisdom to express divine creativity, the Hebraic tradition says that creation is ordered well, even beautifully. The beauty of the earth manifests an eternal truth about the divine nature. But wisdom is a metaphor drawn from the human mind. It is the medium by which human beings befriend God, that is, participate in the divine nature. In a macrocosmic sense, Wisdom expresses the beauty and order of the cosmos. In a microcosmic sense, it suggests that mind links human nature to the divine nature.

It is for modern people a little more difficult to consider mind as a metaphor and medium of Divinity because we associate mind with a particularly narrow and reductive function of reason. We often think of the sapient aspect of Homo sapiens as our ability to perform calculations, to correctly organize and interpret data, to get our facts right. Science is the paradigm of reasoning, and even science is often conceived of in terms that occlude the imaginative and synthetic powers of thought that are at the root of great scientific insights. If we think of mind as a really good data collector, it does not make intuitive sense to think of it as a divine quality or as that part of us that connects us to the Divine Eros.

Imprisoned in this somewhat distorted view of the human mind, we might think of religion as an imitation of science: faith is correct belief and accurate facts. Or we think of religion as having nothing to do with reason at all, a matter of the heart or emotion or social justice. The ancient understanding of Wisdom challenges us to enrich our understanding of mind. It is a matter of the heart: it is delight in beauty and longing for justice. But it is the heart as the locus of mind: our capacity for truth is a matter of the heart. Mind is what orients us to reality, it is the truth-bearing aspect of human beings. But truth is not correct data. Truth is reality in all of its dimensions. By using the metaphor of mind to express the creative and ordering dimensions of ultimate reality, ancient writers emphasize that what we call religion is not a matter of merely subjective feeling. Just as gravity draws objects to the earth, ultimate reality draws the heart-mind to truth. Mind is luminous with the Divine especially in its longing for Wisdom.

Wisdom expresses the capacity of the mind for immediate awareness. Wisdom, even in ordinary human life, is more spontaneous than deductive. When a mother knows, immediately, nondeductively, something about her child we can say that she is manifesting a kind of maternal wisdom. We sometimes use the term *intuition* for these leaps of insight and responsiveness that are spontaneously in tune with a situation. But *wisdom* would be the older word for this. We call it intuition because it bypasses the more obvious functions of deliberation; it is not step-by-step or inductive or deductive. It has an immediacy about it that seems to modern people "irrational," and yet it seems right somehow, so we call it intuition.

Wisdom is an older word for the human mind's capacity for immediate awareness. Wisdom mediates between this awareness and concrete action. Through wisdom action becomes more balanced, courageous, and attentive to what is really going on. Wisdom has an element of nonduality to it: it is an immediate grasp of something. But it also has an element of self-reflection. We can be consciously aware of what is happening and how we are responding. This liminal capacity stands at the threshold between nondual, immediate awareness and conceptual thought and action. If a mother has preconscious, intuitive awareness that her child is not simply misbehaving but is actually sick, she might act on this awareness. But if she cannot call this assessment to conscious awareness, there may be a muddiness to her actions. They will seem irrational or unjustified. She may not trust her intuition and so fail to act on it. More fully realized wisdom sees reality with directness and immediacy but translates it into conceptual, self-aware thought and action.

Wisdom is a metaphor for the Divine as this dual movement: looking backward to an immediate awareness of nonduality and looking forward to concrete expression. Wisdom is thus a perfect mirror. It is a *mirror*, begotten, the second person because it is not unbroken nonduality. It is the manifestation of nonduality in the form of duality and plurality. Through creation, Wisdom is the beauty of a world that is constituted of beings different from one another, a world made up of same and different. Wisdom is the duality of language: pure intuition arising in conceptual thought and translated into words and language. Divine Wisdom is a *perfect* mirror because it inhabits the full truth of nonduality. It is not separate from nonduality. Its being, if we can use that word, is fully constituted by the Divine Eros, with no gap or alienation or obscuration. There is nothing about Wisdom that is not fully and perfectly united with the ungrounded depth of Divinity. It is Divinity. But it is Divinity as it moves (so to speak) from undifferentiated unity to self-manifestation.

Wisdom is like the movement from a yogini's direct perception of reality to manifestation in words and action. Words and action are not nondual concentration but they are imbued with it; they manifest this wisdom in the world so it can be seen and shared, so it becomes efficacious. Without participation in ultimate reality, thought and action are imperfect. They arise from error and untruth. But without Wisdom, nonduality remains in a sense impotent or unrealized.[3] It does not make sense to imagine Divinity as barren or merely potential. Wisdom is True God from True God as an essential expression of the divine depths. Yet these depths eternally resist translation into order and number and rationality. This is not a chronological or even metaphysical sequence in which One is superior to the Plurality that expresses it. Nonduality is not One, though One is sometimes a metaphor for it. Nonduality and Wisdom are eternally locked in a loving embrace, God from God, Light from Light. Their interdependence is the timeless interplay between Abyss and Being. Divinity does not resolve into unity. The idea of Trinity expresses this eternal fecundity that is the inessential essence of nondual Eros.

Another kind of analogy that might help illuminate the metaphor of Wisdom is orgasm. There is a moment of sexual union when mind ceases to be structured by self-other awareness. The dualities of self and other and of thought itself dissolve in pure experience. This moment is called ecstatic in a double sense. It is, of course, highly pleasurable and ecstasy is associated with supreme bliss or pleasure. But *ec-stasis* also has the literal meaning of standing outside oneself. In this most embodied of experiences, mind loses its egocentric structure and stands outside itself in pure immediacy.

It is significant that these two meanings of ecstasy intertwine. It is precisely

---

3. Catherine Keller's brilliant reflection on plurality as a root of Divinity and divine creativity in *Face of the Deep* expresses the primordiality of plurality somewhat differently. But I would like to indicate a deep sympathy and resonance here with her work by insisting that plurality, depth, and beautiful messiness are eternal and essential dimensions of Divinity.

when we stand outside ourselves in a connection of pure immediacy that abolishes our normal subject-object way of experiencing the world that we are most blissful. Yet the love relationship does not dwell in this site of pure immediacy forever. It passes back into relation. Love is the delight of having another person on whom to lavish affection. Sexual intimacy is this passing back and forth between unmediated, ecstatic union and a relationship between two persons who cannot literally become one another. We can think of Wisdom as this double awareness between ecstatic union and differentiation. A significant disanalogy between orgasm and Wisdom is that this doubleness is eternal rather than chronological. Wisdom eternally dwells in perfect, ecstatic union with the Divine Eros and at the same time eternally manifests in the duality of cosmos, consciousness, and conceptuality. Wisdom is True God from True God, begotten not made: a perfect mirror.

The *Secret Revelation of John* combines Platonic and Hebraic elements, preserving the ineffable quality of Divinity, while personifying the creative, merciful, and salvific powers of the Divine manifest in *Pronoia* (which means something like providence or forethought). Pronoia is the perfect image of the all-giving immeasurable light. "And Its thinking become a thing. She appeared. She stood in Its presence in the brilliance of the light; she is the power which is before the All. It is she who appeared, she who is the perfect Pronoia of the All, the light, the likeness of the light, the image of the Invisible, she who is the perfect power."[4] Like the *Nous* of Platonism, Pronoia is the first thought of a reality that is beyond conceptuality. But like Wisdom of the Hebraic tradition, she is both creator and savior: "Every act of salvation and all the savior figures in the work are directly identified with her."[5] The Great Mother describes herself as "the Pronoia of the pure light; I am the thought of the virginal Spirit, the one who raises you to the place of honor. Arise and remember that you are the one who has heard, and follow your root, which is I, the compassionate."[6]

This emphasis on compassion adds an important element to Wisdom. Platonism is particularly clear and beautiful in its evocation of *Nous* as the intersection between nonconceptual and conceptual reality, and between human and divine natures. It is the background of much of Christian theology.[7] Hebraic Wisdom texts personify the creative and ordering power of this perfect mirror of

---

4. *Secret Revelation of John*, Berlin Codex, 5.13–20, in Karen King, *The Secret Revelation of John*, 32.

5. King, *Secret Revelation of John*, 226–27. She tracks parallels between Wisdom and Pronoia. She is cocreator (Proverbs 8:22, 27a, 30), a teacher of life (Proverbs 8:33–36), teacher and savior of humanity (Wisdom 9:10–18), and she gives immortality (Wisdom 8:17). See ibid., 227–28.

6. *Secret Revelation of John*, Nag Hammadi Codex II, 26.26–28, in King, *Secret Revelation of John*, 79.

7. Plotinus is the great figure here. His biography describes a man who embodies superlative wisdom and goodness. The fifth Ennead in particular describes his understanding of the ways in which the Three Hypostases are related to one another. Pierre Hadot's *Philosophy as a Way of Life* is a particularly useful reminder that Platonism and other ancient philosophies were primarily religious in their function, providing a pathway for transformation, wisdom, and divinization.

the Divine in feminine form. But they also add a loving quality to Wisdom that is at best implicit in Platonism. Wisdom seeks out humanity to protect it from harm and to guide it on the path of virtue and happiness. Wisdom expresses God's care for humanity. The *Secret Revelation of John* continues this theme, emphasizing the compassionate and merciful nature of the Divine, especially as these are enacted through the interventions of Pronoia. We participate in the goodness of Wisdom through divinization, which awakens us to truth but enlivens us with compassion.

WISDOM AND WORD

The Wisdom tradition personified the creative and redeeming aspects of Divinity and conceived of this power as intimate to history. The Synoptic Gospels tend to use the imagery of Spirit and Wisdom to express the presence of God in Christ. The Epistles and Gospel of John identify love as the essence of the Divine, the power that unites the Son to the Father and to the faithful, and through which human beings relate to one another. But it was the Logos Christology so lyrically expressed in the prologue to John's Gospel that came to dominate the Christian imagination: a Word (*Logos*) that was with God and was God, a Word that became flesh to dwell among us.[8] "Logos" has similar connotations to *Nous* and Wisdom: it is a metaphor drawn from mind and language. Logos is the ordering of things by language. But it loses some of the tenderness of Wisdom and the integration of mind and heart that is inherent in Wisdom. It also amputates the feminine from our understanding of the Divine, which has been a catastrophic social and spiritual loss.

Long before Elizabeth Johnson reminded us of the deeper roots of the Wisdom tradition, ancient Christians integrated Word and Wisdom for a richer conception of the way the Divine is present in Christ. Origen was among those who wove them together in his understanding of the incarnation: "in the same manner also must wisdom be understood to be the Word of God. For wisdom opens to all other beings, that is, to the whole creation, the meaning of the mysteries and secrets which are contained within the wisdom of God, and so she is called the Word, because she is as it were an interpreter of the mind's secrets."[9] Like Johnson and Origen, we might understand Wisdom and Word as interdependent and complementary images of Trinity and incarnation. The Logos theology of John moves our understanding of the second person of the Trinity from a mirror of Eros to an emphasis on the divine creativity. "Word" expresses the inexpressible *Ungrund* but does so as creativity.

John's prologue sings of a Word that conflates two relations that coexist at the

---

8. Roger Haight notes these different christologies in the New Testament in *The Future of Christology*, 161, 175.

9. Origen, *On First Principles* 1.2.3 (p. 16).

center of Divinity: the Word is one with the Father in eternity and one flesh with humanity in Jesus Christ in time. First the unity of the Godhead splinters into a Trinity: "In the beginning was the Word, and the Word was with God, and the Word was God" (John 1:1). What a complex and mind-bending assertion! Divinity, which Hebrew Scripture as well as Greek philosophy conceives of as unity, as One, as a one beyond all oneness and unity, is also the Word that was *with* God and *was* God. "With" implies relationship, alterity within the Godhead itself. "Was" implies unity, sameness, differentiation without difference. This is the impossible koan councils and creeds tried desperately to translate into clear and precise verbal formulations. God from God, Light from Light, Begotten not made, one in being: all terms that both defy and assert the contradiction between sameness and difference, between simple unity and relationship.

John Scotus Eriugena wrestles with this in his homily on John's prologue. He argues that "in the beginning" refers to substance rather than chronology. "The Son subsists in the Father. . . . That is to say, 'The Son subsists with the Father in unity of essence and distinction of substance.'"[10] But all of these words—in the beginning, subsists with, distinction of substance—imply two entities, one subordinate to the other. To correct against any hint that the Word is not truly, fully, and eternally God, we are reminded that the Word *was* God. This complex and in its way unthinkable relationship of unity and distinction "may be understood to state more clearly than if it had been said in broad daylight, 'This God-Word, who is with God, is the same of whom I [the evangelist] say, 'In the beginning was the Word.'"[11]

Origen, too, struggles with the timeless beginning that marks the flow of God to God. Jesus is the Wisdom of God, "the brightness of the eternal light. . . . If this point is fully understood, it is a clear proof that the Son's existence springs from the Father himself, yet not in time, nor from any other beginning except, as we have said, from God himself."[12] Or again, "Wisdom, therefore, must be believed to have been begotten beyond the limits of any beginning that we can speak of or understand. And because in this very subsistence of wisdom there was implicit every capacity and form of the creation that was to be, . . . she contains within herself both the beginnings and causes and species of the whole creation."[13]

Doctrines attempt to capture the relationship between the Word and the Godhead, but this effort should not deter us from acknowledging the deeply mysterious character of these relationships. Origen, passionate lover and brilliant philosopher, reminds us: "to utter these things in human ears and to explain them by words far exceeds the powers we possess either in our moral worth or

---

10. John Scotus Eriugena, "Homily on the Prologue to the Gospel of St. John" 6, in *Voice of the Eagle*, 78.
11. Ibid., 79.
12. Origen, *On First Principles* 1.2.11 (p. 26).
13. Ibid., 1.2.2 (p. 16).

in mind and speech."[14] In our devotion we try to find words, but they are love letters, not mathematical formulas. They allow our minds to follow our hearts deeper into the mystery without ever exhausting it.

Meditation on Divinity must open us to the apophatic depth of mystery, the incomprehensible and unthinkable abyss into which reason and experience and language fall in the unknowing of the Divine Eros. Without this memory of mystery our religions become idolatrous and our faith becomes a consoling fiction. This dark radiance nourishes our own apophatic depths. It is the emptiness from which the dizzying display of the cosmos erupts. The Cause of the vast diversities of creation is not itself like anything in creation. It could not engender limitless fecundity if it were limited to some particular kind of being. The first person of the Trinity plunges us into the great Emptiness of Divinity. But if Divinity were "only" this, there would be no creation. The Great Mother is the abysmal womb from which everything is born. The self-manifestation of the Abyss is the coming forth into concreteness of that great energy of love and life. The Good Beyond Being is not only beyond being but also good. It is the nature of the Good to express itself, to be self-disclosing. The first self-disclosure is concreteness itself, the Wisdom that presents a perfect mirror to the Divine Abyss so that mystery takes form, provides itself with an image—a Word that is with God and also God. As intuition rises to thought, and thought enables the intuition to disclose itself to consciousness—the Abyss discloses itself to itself in its own Word.

The Abyss is not a fruitless abstraction, a rarefied thought. It is Eros. The self-disclosure of Divinity in Wisdom eternally enacts the fecundity of this Erotic Abyss. Wisdom does not reflect solitary radiance but creative abundance. Wisdom discloses fathomless Eros to itself as delight in the cosmos. The first relationship between Wisdom and Abyss establishes the creativity of Divinity. Nondual, apophatic mystery becomes active in a "beginning" in which time and eternity mix as paradoxically as unity and distinction. "He was in the beginning with God. All things came into being through him, and without him not one thing came into being" (John 1:2–3). John Scotus Eriugena struggles with this moving image of eternity: "Hear then the divine and ineffable paradox—the unopenable secret, the invisible depth, the incomprehensible mystery! Through him, who was not made but begotten, all things were made but not begotten. . . . The substance of those things, which are made by him, began in him before all the ages of the world, not in time but with times. Time, indeed, is made with all things that are made. It is neither made before them, nor is it preferable to them, but it is co-created with them":[15] time and timelessness, beginnings begun in eternity, timeless because the category of time is inapplicable to it.

From this atemporal depth spins everything that is. Whatever exists in any way whatsoever erupts from this uncreated Wisdom. Word sings into material

---

14. Ibid., 2.6.3 (p. 110).
15. "Homily on the Prologue to the Gospel of St. John" 7, in *Voice of the Eagle,* 80–81.

existence the imageless and wordless beauty of the Mother, manifesting Divinity's Erotic Abyss as fecundity. Perhaps because it is easy to accept in some pale, generic sense that God created the world and yet to remain existentially committed to the view that only our corner of the world is in any meaningful way related to the divine care, John Scotus Eriugena is at pains to emphasize the total dependence of all that is on this Word. His emphasis on utter dependence reminds us that the Word concerns not only the patch of history that arose from the environs of the Mediterranean over the last two thousand years. The Word concerns all of creation. There is "nothing whatsoever that is not made in and through him." Or as "Solomon" puts it, Wisdom "reaches mightily from one end of the earth to the other, and she orders all things well" (Wisdom 8:1). Behind the concreteness of incarnation in Christ is the omnipresence of Word and Wisdom as the universal potency of the Divine, the fathomless generosity that swells from groundless eternity to grant existence to everything that exists.

WISDOM AS PURE ACT: CREATION

Thomas Aquinas describes Divinity as both immutable and as pure act. If we are tempted to think of changelessness as static, boring, and unrelated, the idea of pure act reminds us of the unimaginable energy of Divinity. We humans and everything that lives combine passivity and activity. We come into existence, live a while, and then pass into the utter passivity of death. We imagine God as something that acts, doing whatever God does before time and then getting busy making a world. The idea of pure act corrects this anthropomorphic image. Divinity *is* action, energy. The great luminosity of Eros eternally births beauty in and beyond time.

Wisdom interpenetrates the cosmos, scattering Divinity through everything that is. John Scotus Eriugena invites us to meditate with him on the divine backlighting of creation:

> Consider the infinite, multiple power of the seed—how many grasses, fruits, and animals are contained in each kind of seed; and how there surges forth from each a beautiful, innumerable multiplicity of forms. . . . From the contemplation of such as these, raised above all things by the wings of natural contemplation, illuminated and supported by divine grace, you will be able to penetrate by the keenness of your mind the secrets of the Word and, to the extent that it is granted to the human being who seeks signs of God, you will see how all things made by the Word live in the Word and are life: "For in him," as the Sacred Scripture says, "We live and move and have our being." Truly as the great Dionysius the Areopagite says, "The being of all things is their superessential divinity."[16]

---

16. Ibid., 10, in *Voice of the Eagle*, 87.

The cosmos comes to be in the Word; the Word is the light and life of the world (John 1:4). This image of the Word permits us to imagine separation, distance. Word represents the duality and nonimmediacy of language. By contrast, images of light and life evoke ways in which the cosmos is caressed by Wisdom as light infuses air and life surges through cells, bodies, and ecosystems. Speaking implies a separation, but light and life imply immediate connection. Creation is not divine in the same sense that the Trinity is and yet neither is it separate from its divine source as one object is separate from another object. Divinity bodies forth in creation.[17] John Scotus Eriugena notes that what is illuminated by this light is not other than the Word itself: "And now you [the evangelist] call him 'light' and 'life,' because this same Son, who is the Word, is the life and light of all things that are made through him. And what does he light? Not other than himself and his Father. The light, therefore is, and illuminates itself. . . . Observe the forms and beauties of sensible things and comprehend the Word of God in them. If you do so, the truth will reveal to you in all such things only he who made them, outside of whom you have nothing to contemplate, for he himself is all things. For whatever truly is, in all things that are, is he."[18] Pantheism, panentheism, absolute qualitative distinction: all true—and all inadequate to the infiltration of the cosmos by Divinity.

WISDOM AND NATURE

Meditation on the creativity of Wisdom invites us to revisit our relationship to nature and to the cosmic dimensions of faith. Father Pierre Teilhard de Chardin was a geologist and priest, an apostle of the cosmic Christ. J. Philip Newell reminds of Teilhard de Chardin's insistence that "the incarnation reveals to us that we 'can be saved only by becoming one with the universe.'"[19] Wisdom stretches between Erotic Abyss and cosmos because, poetically speaking, it is the natural desire of the Divine to be in love. Being in love requires another, something to love. The integration of the doctrine of the Trinity and the revelation of the incarnation occurs here. Perichoresis, the lubrication of love within the Godhead, is recapitulated in the wild creativity of Wisdom throughout the cosmos. Unmastered and unknowable depths articulate themselves through relationship, first by the impossible simultaneity of unity and diversity between Wisdom and

17. Grace Jantzen's early and late work develops this panentheistic parable of creation as God's body in interesting ways: *God's World, God's Body* and *Becoming Divine: Toward a Feminist Philosophy of Religion*. Much of Sally McFague's work also discusses the world as God's body.

18. John Scotus Eriugena, "Homily on the Prologue to the Gospel of St. John" 11, in *Voice of the Eagle*, 88, 89. John Scotus is among those who anticipate a process philosophy of beginning and panentheistic theology. Schleiermacher's theology of "utter dependence" resonates with this sensibility. Catherine Keller and Grace Jantzen are among contemporary (feminist) philosophical theologians who retrieve and reshape this lineage for our own time.

19. J. Philip Newell, *Christ of the Celts: Healing Creation*, 116.

Eros, and second in the radiation of light and life in creation. Wisdom lays bare the created world to the Divine, dependent on the Divine as cause. Buoyant with Wisdom, it bears the infinite beauty of the Divine in material form; though, as Catherine Keller points out, this is a "wild aesthetic, a beauty neither classical nor stylish."[20]

The cosmos is the illuminated presence of Wisdom, manifest according to the infinitely diverse forms of beauty, of existence. Ian McFarland reminds us of this cosmic dimension of Wisdom in his retrieval of the work of Maximus the Confessor. He argues that true knowledge of the world is dependent on knowledge of the Logos. "The epistemological priority of the divine Logos is crucial: we cannot regard the many creaturely *logoi* as a basis from which to ascend gradually to the one Logos of God. Instead, we must have first encountered the Logos for us to see the *logoi* in their relation to God. But neither does the revelation of the Logos mean that we can simply leave the many *logoi* behind. On the contrary, the experience of Christ as creator points us to particular creatures as those objects of God's providential care without which our understanding of the divine identity is impoverished."[21]

In order to know the world properly and well, in its irreplaceable, nonutilitarian dignity, it is necessary to come to awareness of the Logos of Wisdom as the source of the world. At the same time, contemplation of the Logos does not raise us out of creation but drives us more deeply into it. Appropriate knowledge of Christ teaches us about the world. Yet, for whatever complex reasons, Western Christianity became tone-deaf to the manifestation of Wisdom in nature. One finds traces of this awareness here and there, but Christianity for the most part forgot the divinity of nature. The cost of that forgetfulness is now taking on a terribly destructive form as the slow agony of nature writes itself in bold letters.

Not long before his death, Teilhard de Chardin wrote in defiant hope of "a new Charity in which all the Earth's dynamic passions combine as they are divinized: it is this, I now see with a vision that will never leave me, that the World is desperately in need of at this very moment, if it is not to collapse."[22] He envisioned the cosmic Christ, ever more completely incarnate, "Christianity re-incarnated for the second time (Christianity, we might say, squared) in the spiritual energies of Matter. It is precisely the 'ultra-Christianity' we need here and now to meet the ever more urgent demands of the 'ultra-human.'"[23] Here we see the intimacy of Christ from the opposite perspective. Christic energy perfumes throughout the cosmos, exploding in red dwarfs, dumbly mourning in the eyes of orphaned creatures, glittering as sun on the waves.

---

20. Keller, *Face of the Deep*, 231.
21. McFarland, *The Divine Image: Envisioning the Invisible God*, 43–44.
22. Pierre Teilhard de Chardin, *The Heart of Matter*, 53.
23. Ibid., 96. Father Pierre explains what he means by "ultra-human" later: "Everywhere on Earth, at this moment, in the new spiritual atmosphere created by the idea of evolution, there float, in a state of extreme mutual sensitivity, love of God and faith in the world: the two essential components of the Ultra-human" (102).

To express this wild divine creativity, Nicholas of Cusa uses the metaphor of a painter who requires a vast plurality of images that only together can represent her vision: "if they [created beings] were not innumerable, you, O infinite God, could not be known in the best possible way. . . . Therefore, by your gift, my God, I possess this whole visible world and all of Scripture and all the ministering spirits in support of my advancing knowledge of you. All things rouse me to turn toward you."[24] Everything is news of Wisdom Christ. All creation points toward its erotic source.

Daniel Spencer draws attention to the links between eros and ecology. He argues that the denigration of the body and sexuality contribute to the twin evils of consumerism and environmental degradation. That is, having lost a way of honoring and delighting in bodies and the earth's body, we are cut off from an intuitive awareness of the sacred in nature. He insists that response to the earth's crisis cannot succeed through a series of crisis management steps but requires a conversion to the earth: a "mutual recovery of the erotic and the ecological, a rediscovery and reappreciation of the interweaving of the spiritual and the material. Conversion to the earth as a positive, energizing, joyful moral response comes in part, at least, through linking the joy and intimacy of the erotic in our lives with the earth, intimacy and joy that comes from reconnecting with the wider web of life."[25] Wisdom is the divine ground of creation and its impulses toward joyous embrace. Love of the earth and of our bodily nature is rooted in love of incarnate Wisdom.

Mary Elizabeth Moore also invites us to a conversion to the earth. Combining theology and practices, she points out some of the challenges we face: "the need to balance appreciation for oneself with walking gently on the earth; the importance of living with paradox, the need to respect the human body and the earth, recognizing their deep interconnection; the need to relate with painful realities as well as joy; the need to seek illumination from the worldviews and spiritual practices of many peoples—East and West, North and South, past and present, many races and many faiths . . . The most fundamental challenge is *to live as if all in creation are our brothers and sisters.*"[26] Wisdom as the ground of creation invites us to recognize not only our interdependence but our family relation to all of humanity and all the earth.

Philip Newell connects this reconversion to nature with a reconversion to Christ. As someone who spends a good deal of time on the island of Iona, he has been formed by Celtic Christianity, which "views Christ as coming from the heart of creation rather than from beyond creation. And it celebrates him as

---

24. Nicholas of Cusa, "On the Vision of God" 117, 119 (*Selected Spiritual Writings*, 288). This point is echoed by Porete: because God is in all things, the soul finds God everywhere (*Mirror of Simple Souls*, chap. 30).

25. Spencer, *Gay and Gaia*, 364.

26. Mary Elizabeth Moore, *Ministering with the Earth*, 47.

reconnecting us to our true nature instead of saving us from our nature."[27] He describes his discovery of the ancient prayers collected in the *Carmina Gadelica* (Songs of the Gaels), which were chanted over centuries "at the rising of the sun and the setting of the sun, invocations for blessing at the birth of a child or the death of a loved one, rhythms of praise for the tides and the turning of seasons, and songs of thanks for planting and harvesting earth's fruits. These were different prayers from the prayers I had grown up with in my Western Christian inheritance. The context was creation rather than church. Love of Christ and love of the earth were woven inseparably together. And I saw in them hidden gems for the journey of the human soul today."[28]

We cannot go back to a mythological Celtic past, but Spencer, Moore, and Newell are among those who remind us that a spirituality of nature can be inherent in our understanding of Christ. The hunger of our hearts for deeper connections with one another and with the earth is a footprint of the Divine Eros who infinitely embodies herself in Wisdom and through her in the earth. This is a hunger to heal what has been broken not only for the pragmatic purpose of avoiding death in massive environmental upheavals. It is a hunger for the truth of our participation in the beauty of creation. This desire for the healing of creation is itself a prayer. When we reconnect with this desire "we will find ourselves hearing again the deepest harmonies of the universe. Heart of Jesus, Heart of Creation, unite us to yourself."[29]

Fierce, sometimes violent beauty is the witness to the divine incarnation in the cosmos. Teilhard de Chardin describes this divine beauty in the synthesis of his vocations: "This is what I have learnt from my contact with the earth—the diaphany of the divine at the heart of a glowing universe, the divine radiating from the depths of matter—a-flame."[30] The unleashing of apophatic depth in the mystery of creativity enacts the metaphysical and moral primacy of relation. The flaming embodiment of Christ is possible because the cosmos is constituted by mutual interdependence with no breach or gap that would separate beings. There is no split between God and creation or between any being or system of beings and another. There is no separation anywhere. This vast web of mutually inhering relations is the enfolding of what we misleadingly distinguish as mind and body: "Matter and spirit, then, as we know them in our universe, are not two separate substances, set side by side and differing in nature. They are two distinct aspects of one single cosmic stuff and there is between them no conflict to baffle our intelligence."[31] The cosmos is by its nature a spiritual entity, imbued with divinity. Or, to put it the other way, the creation of the cosmos by Erotic

27. Newell, *Christ of the Celts*, 127.
28. Ibid., 123–24.
29. Ibid., 122.
30. Teilhard de Chardin, *Letters from a Traveller*, 16.
31. Ibid., 24; cf. idem, *Heart of Matter* 35, 47.

Wisdom saturates it with a spiritual dimension. Devotion to the Word, to Christ, requires veneration of her body in creation.

THE UNIVERSALITY OF WISDOM

The Wisdom of creative nonduality is not a person or a thing but the ground of reality. It is inconceivable that this ground is present in one place and not another. In this sense, the ultimate reality to which Christians try to remain faithful is universal. Wisdom "does all things while remaining in herself," and through the Word all things are made. In Wisdom Christ we have a revelation of the deep and abiding truth of divine omnipresence. The special revelation in the Gospels confirms the nature of this presence as healing and loving. Salvation history tells the story of the utter faithfulness of divine love.

It is therefore painful to contemplate how commonplace it is for Christians to horrifically distort this revelation of omnipresent Wisdom. Instead of conveying the message that God is love, Jesus becomes more tyrannical than the most violent and jealous tribal deity. The great cosmic play of divine creativity is funneled through him alone. The relationship of Wisdom to the Divine Eros collapses into the relationship of the Word to Jesus. Christians, of course, affirm a distinctive revelation in Jesus of Nazareth. There are many senses in which this affirmation of uniqueness makes sense. This corner of history has its own shape and determinateness. The presence of the Divine in Jesus is like a snowflake or fingerprint, unlike anything else in history. It bears a particular wisdom and genius that is irreducible to the wisdom of other religious traditions. But the claim that this uniqueness requires that all humanity be "saved" by Jesus is pernicious and utterly alien to everything else we affirm about the Divine. If the Divine is creator of the cosmos, it makes no sense to limit its efficacy to the lines of history that produced our own past. If the Christian gospel is a revelation of the radical nature of divine love, it is impossible to imagine that the masses of humanity untouched by the story of Jesus are of no importance.

If we affirm the incarnation described in the prologue of the Gospel of John, we cannot imagine that the Word is absent from or alien to the wisdom of other cultures or religions. "In the beginning was the Word, and the Word was with God, and the Word was God. He was in the beginning with God; *all things came into being through him, and without him not one thing came into being*. . . . In him was life, and the life was the light *of all people*" (John 1:1–5). Our devotion to the heartbreaking sweetness of this life and light in Jesus does not require us to harden our hearts against Wisdom's infinite generosity throughout creation and in every human form. To the contrary, our enormous gratitude for the revelation of Wisdom in Christ requires us to be grateful also for all the other ways in which humanity is inflamed with compassion and wisdom. "Those who are not against us are for us."

Just as the immense plenitude of nature is necessary but not sufficient to express the great beauty of Divinity, all the wisdom of the world's religions is necessary but insufficient to refract the unplumbed depths of Divine Wisdom. This omnipresence of the Divine Wisdom runs up against the created and therefore flawed and limited character of everything human. We can find oppressions, failures of imagination, overemphasis on particular insights—not to mention misogyny, violence, cruelty, and ignorance in every tradition and culture. Christianity is not protected from any of these failings. For such a blood-soaked tradition to claim an exclusive access to salvation is not only arrogant and hard-hearted—it is truly shocking. Christian exclusivism ignores its own massive and perennial failures and idolatries even as it demonizes Wisdom's beauty in other times and places.

If Wisdom is divine, she will speak of Divinity in every language—not only French and Sanskrit and Navaho but also Buddhism, Sufism, and Yoruba. One language is not privileged as the more perfect mode through which reason, emotion, and relationship are communicated. We learn one another's languages and in doing so stretch our understanding beyond what might have been thought in our own alone. Yet there is a certain untranslatability from one language to another. It is possible to say certain things in one language easily that can be said only with great difficulty or not at all in another. How could the Erotic Abyss say everything it contains in a single language? How could one religion—even in its own interior plurality and complexity—stand in for the immeasurable mystery of divine reality? Why would we demand of our faith not only confidence in the goodness of God and certainty of our healing but total and exclusive knowledge of ultimate reality?

Marguerite Porete speaks for many other theologians when she says: "For everything one can say or write about God or think about Him, God who is greater than what is ever said, [everything] is thus more like lying than speaking the truth."[32] She acknowledges that Jesus Christ has bound Christians to himself "through His death, and through His Gospels, and through His Scriptures where laboring folk are guided to the right way." But she asks if the grace in Christianity exhausts Divinity: "Has He now set end and limit to the gifts of His goodness? . . . Grasp through love, Love prays you, that Love has so much to give, and so she sets no limit to it."[33] Porete loves God through Christian faith but refuses to subject the unfathomable God to the church. Instead she adores "Him in all places . . . I find Him everywhere, says this Soul, and He is there. He is One Deity, One sole God in Three Persons, and this God is everywhere. There, I find him."[34] If God *is* Love, it does not make sense to imagine that God *has* a certain amount of grace or love to dispense and chooses to spread some here and withhold it elsewhere. It is not the nature of Love to withhold itself any more than it is the nature of the sun to arbitrarily refuse its rays to some parts of the earth.[35]

---

32. Porete, *Mirror of Simple Souls*, 194–95.
33. Ibid., 151.
34. Ibid., 144–45.
35. A somewhat parallel point is made by Joy McDougal in her analysis of Moltmann's criticism

Because our faith opens onto ultimate reality, we too often commit an intellectual sleight of hand in which our faith alone has access to this reality. The inflation of our particular faith by the fullness of divine presence seems to imply that it cannot be elsewhere. To counter this impulse, Nicholas of Cusa suggests a practice through which the universality and particularity of divine grace might be better understood. Nicholas sent to the monks for whom he wrote "On the Vision of God" a painting of "the all-seeing image, which I call an icon of God."[36] He asked them to put up the painting in the chapel. A monk was to walk from one side of the chapel to the other, noticing that the eyes of the icon seem to remain on him wherever he is. Then two monks were to walk, from opposite sides of the chapel at the same time, noticing that the eyes of the icon remain on them, even though they are moving in opposite directions. In performing this exercise, the monks saw that the face moves east and west, north and south, remaining in a single place and beholding all the movements simultaneously. "And while the brother observes how this gaze deserts no one, he will see that it takes diligent care of each, just as if it cared only for the one on whom its gaze seems to rest and for no other, and to such an extent that the one whom it regards cannot conceive that it should care for another. He will also see that it has the same very diligent concern for the least creature as for the greatest, and for the whole universe."[37] Nicholas's devotional exercise is a concrete representation of how the divine face is devotedly fixed on each individual without diminishing its devotion to every other creature throughout the entire cosmos. It is a practice that invites us to rest in perfect confidence that divine love can be utterly devoted to us and our tradition and yet equally present elsewhere. This is a training in Christianity that challenges the egocentric logic that makes of love a zero-sum game and invites us instead to celebrate the universal quality of Divine Wisdom.

Much more can and has been said about the uniqueness of Christ and the plurality of world religions. But for our purposes, it will have to suffice to note that if we make loving-kindness our practice, then it becomes increasingly unbearable to imagine that even a blade of grass, let alone whole continents or epochs, might exist outside the Beloved's tender mercy.

INCARNATION: WISDOM BECOMES FLESH

Wisdom hinges between the ineffable, nonconceptual Good and creation, mediating divine love to the world.[38] For Christians this Eros is encountered

---

of Barth. Instead of the quasi-nominalism of Barth and its privilege of power and sovereignty over love, Moltmann argues that the divine freedom is not free choice but freedom for the good: "divine freedom rests not in absolute power but in the self-communication of the good" (*Pilgrimage of Love*, 77).

36. Nicholas of Cusa, "On the Vision of God" Preface 2 (*Selected Spiritual Writings*, 235).
37. Ibid., Preface 4 (*Selected Spiritual Writings*, 236–37).
38. Cf. McDougal, *Pilgrimage of Love*, 3.

through the incarnation in Jesus of Nazareth. Jesus, the Christ, is a "coincidence of opposites," as Nicholas of Cusa might say. Christ is the place where the utter concreteness, uniqueness, and vulnerability of a particular human body intersects with Erotic Wisdom. This is possible because it is proper to the nature of the Divine Eros to seek union with creatures and with creation. It is possible also because it is proper to human beings to embody nondual reality in and through their flesh, blood, heart, and mind.

Marilyn McCord Adams argues that unitive desire is the essential movement of Divinity, and the incarnation expresses the paradoxical requirements of radical love: "God's passion for material creation expresses itself in a Divine desire to unite with it, not only to enter into personal intimacy, but to 'go all the way' and share its nature in hypostatic union."[39] The desire to communicate itself is the "pure act" of Divinity that finds perfect if not exclusive expression in Christ.

This point is echoed by Friedrich Schleiermacher, who argues that love can be the root symbol for God because union is the fundamental divine teleology. "The Supreme Being imparts Himself, and . . . this constitutes the very essence of divine love."[40] Love generates difference and plurality in an act of self-othering. At the same time, Eros surges toward union with the beloved. These are eternal dimensions of love, interdependent rather than hierarchical or sequential. Love requires difference but longs for union; the instability and delight of Eros is the impulse toward creation and incarnation. Incarnation exemplifies this double movement. It is a place where self-differentiation flows toward the counterflow of union. Incarnate Wisdom is the tidal wave of these countermovements. Its beauty arises from the perfect balance between difference and union, a kind of orgasm of divine love that bodies forth and crashes into the mind and flesh of Christ. Facing one way, Wisdom is a perfect mirror of the Divine Eros. Facing the other way, Christ is the perfect mirror of humanity. Wisdom is this hinge between divinity and humanity; Wisdom is the point of contact that allows human nature to bear the divine nature with such perfect beauty.

The great mystery of human experience is that though we are created in the divine image and placed in a well-ordered and beautiful world, our lot is one of suffering. Looking into our own hearts and at the long sadness of history, we do not discover a method for breaking free from the tyranny that dominates us. It is with enormous gratitude that we conceive of the Divine Eros as incarnating herself not only in Wisdom and in creation but in a human form. She comes among us in a way we can see and touch. We behold her glory walking among us with tender mercy and a courageous heart. She shows us who we are by appearing as one like us. She redeems us from the tyranny of suffering by entering into the darkness with us. The next three chapters will meditate on the healing, saving efficacy of this embodiment of Wisdom in human form.

39. Adams, *Christ and Horrors*, 39.
40. Schleiermacher, *Christian Faith*, §166.1 (p. 727).

Chapter 6

"But Who Do You Say That I Am?"

Union of Humanity and Divinity

*He asked them, "But who do you say that I am?" . . . Then he began to teach
them that the Son of Man must undergo great suffering, and be rejected by
the elders, the chief priests, and the scribes, and be killed, and after three
days rise again.*

Mark 8:29, 31

*He said to them, "Come away to a deserted place all by yourselves and rest
a while."*

Mark 6:31

*For the salvation of every creature is nothing other than the understanding
of the goodness of God.*[1]

Wisdom, the Great Mother, expresses the ordering and creative principle of
Divinity. She is the cosmic Christ, whose power draws beauty from chaotic nothingness and breathes life in the tiniest weed. It was for her that the morning stars
sang together and all the children of the earth shouted for joy (Job 38:7). Christians often forget her in their rush toward devotion to Jesus. But without her, there
would be no Christ, for she is the Divinity in Christ. She is why Jesus is a Savior
and not merely another murdered wisdom teacher. In these last chapters, we consider the incarnation in its human form, as Savior and teacher, Jesus Christ.

---

1. Porete, *Mirror of Simple Souls*, 187.

133

One must acknowledge that though the incarnation is the most distinctive aspect of the Christian tradition, it has not been central to feminist and queer theology. He is a male savior, tortured by an abusive father. He is a wandering Aramean whose miracles embarrass educated people. He upholds patriarchy and racism. He hates fags and Jews. His social gospel redeems him for liberation theologians, but he remains a problem for many who have a troubled relationship with the church.

I rediscovered Christ after I met His Holiness, the Dalai Lama. Like Thomas, I had to see to believe. A human body can contain and radiate the Divine. Such a body heals minds and bodies and relationships. It embodies compassion and good humor. It is exactly fitted to whatever situation in which it finds itself without wavering from its unique fingerprint of personality. Perhaps this is what Irenaeus had in mind when he said that the glory of God is a human being fully alive.[2] I had never seen or really believed in incarnation: human being fully lit by an unwavering divine presence. After that, I found myself falling in love with Christ, entirely against my will and confounded by my intellectual and spiritual formation.

I am trained as a theologian and have read what Augustine and Anselm, Thomas Aquinas, Luther, Calvin, and the rest have said about Christ. I know a little about the christological controversies of the various centuries: the precise relationship between the Father and the Son and the exact way the two natures (human and divine) of Christ relate to one another. But goodbye to all that. May others preserve and revive the wisdom of those traditions. I have found myself surrounded by other companions: the marginalized, afflicted, and disgraced, the contemplative and joyful. Spending time in their company reminds me that great compassion and infinite joy are the footprints by which we know the Divine was incarnate in the Christ.

Between the stultifying debates about Christology that constitute so much of official theology and the passionate attacks on its violence and misogyny, I find it impossible simply to pick up a reflection on Christ as if everything were in order. Theology makes sense only if it speaks to real experience. I start here with voices from outside mainstream theology to remind us of the experiential roots that vivify the meaning of incarnation. We are all made to be divine. We turn to witnesses to that truth.

CAN I GET A WITNESS?

Carter Heyward begins her collection of essays by arguing that traditional christological approaches have ceased to be useful and indeed are "a distraction from the daily praxis of liberation, which is the root and purpose of Christian faith."[3]

---

2. Irenaeus, *Against Heresies* 4.20.8.
3. Heyward, *Speaking of Christ*, 13.

Kelly Brown Douglas is also skeptical that the tradition of Nicaea and Chalcedon is relevant to the intimacy with Jesus experienced by black women. "Womanist understandings of Christ emerge out of the Black Christian tradition. This is a tradition in which Black women and men confessed Jesus as Christ because of what he did during his time as well as in their own lives. They did not make this confession because of his metaphysical make-up."[4] She sees in her grandmother an example of the importance of Jesus to the life of black Christians in ways that are not really captured by doctrinal debates. Her grandmother "trusted that the Christ she prayed to had a special appreciation of her condition. This was a Christ who seemingly identified with a poor Black woman in her day-to-day struggle just to make it. Mama was certain that this Christ cared about the trials and tribulations of an ordinary Black woman. Christ empowered her to get through each day with dignity."[5] Mercy Oduyoye points out that "the word 'Christology' is not in the vocabulary of African Christian women unless they have had some formal theological education; but they all talk about Jesus, believe in Jesus, relate closely to Jesus the son of Mary and testify to what Jesus has done for them."[6] "Christology" may not be important to these writers but companionship with the Divine abiding in Jesus certainly is.

I begin with witness because it is important to remember that people do not talk about Christ because there is a history of doctrine and creed to which we must attend. From testimonies of comfort, liberation, and transformation we are drawn inward, upward toward the divine cause. We affirm the union of the Divine and human in Christ not merely because of quasi-authoritative creeds or theological traditions. We affirm the incarnation because it expresses something that occurs in the concrete experience of peoples from many cultures and kinds of life experience: second-century peasants, medieval contemplatives, African village women, educated white men. We affirm it because it allows us to move through various dimensions of salvation. The incarnation is a way of understanding the dignity and resilience of a poor black woman. Through Jesus, "Mama" is connected to Divinity, the source of courage and dignity in a social world that provides neither. Meditation on incarnation is also a gate through which we enter into the union of Divinity and humanity that is the deep truth of every human being. The face of Christ, "the fairest in heaven," is our face. It is a face sorrowful and acquainted with grief, yet shining with the fullness of erotic, ungrounded Love: our face, humanity's face, Christ's face—divine and human.

Certainly it is easy for academics to efface the vitality of salvation with obscure debates about doctrine, just as it has been easy for institutions to reinforce their power by demanding assent to certain beliefs. Yet the idea of incarnation provides a unifying language that connects Christians across space and time in a common proclamation of a faith. Though I reject the idea that there are truths

---

4. Douglas, *Black Christ*, 111.
5. Ibid., 2.
6. Oduyoye, *Introducing African Women's Theology*, 51.

about Divinity that could be cast in authoritative language, I am nonetheless drawn to the majestic poetry that extols the impenetrable mystery of the Trinity, eternally perfect in love, breaking into and broken by cosmos and history: God from God, Light from Light, Begotten, not made; descended into hell; raised on the third day. The ancient creedal paeans to the paradox of union between uncreated Eros and humanity haunts these reflections, like the music that accompanies the women's narratives in Schleiermacher's Christmas Eve dialogue.[7]

The doctrine of the incarnation has often tempted Christians to commit the common human folly of thinking of our own corner of the universe as the only one that has any real significance or meaning. But we can honor the Divine in Christ without insisting the rest of history and the cosmos is denuded of Wisdom. The incarnation shows us that Wisdom falls from the womb of eternity into the womb of Mary, accompanies us to hell and draws us back to our divine source. The name of Christ bears the power of compassionate and joyous transformation. It is a name that gives us back our own name. It is not the only one that can do that, but it is one. In gratitude, Christians sing many kinds of love songs to the Beloved. We begin here with voices testifying to some of the masks Wisdom wears as she walks among us, consoling us, empowering us, and showing us who we really are.

LOVE SONGS

Serene Jones lamented the absence of God and the failure of her tradition when her friend Wendy (a different Wendy) showed up at her door, undone by a recent miscarriage. The male- and sin-dominated liturgies of the church offered nothing to this woman in her anguish and need. Yet Serene somehow jerry-rigged a ritual out of bottles of wine, soup, burying, anointing, weeping for a lost baby, and tears for the betrayals of a body that failed to carry her. Christ and his atoning death were irrelevant to this common but commonly invisible grief. But "looking back on that ceremony now, six years later, I realize I wasn't as alone as I felt that day. I had a church that had taught me to grieve with God, and a community of lovers who had taught me how to say, 'I know,' and a heart softened by grace that was supple enough to take the weight of her body as it leaned into me. And most of all I had Wendy, a sister who would go with me to the grave. Two women. A tomb. And there with us, the most blessed gift of all, the dark, miscarrying, aching Trinity that held us."[8] Mother Christ ministers here in this most female

---

7. In Schleiermacher's *Christmas Eve* each of the women at the party tells a story capturing an element of the life of Christ as it intersected with their own struggles and sufferings. A fourth woman improvises on the piano as they talk (p. 57). This combination of story and music resonates with Schleiermacher's view that the incarnation cannot be expressed directly as theological doctrine but is best told by the women in story, music, and song.

8. Jones, "Rupture," in *Hope Deferred*, 65.

tragedy, using wine, soup, tears, and the wisdom of a theology professor to open to her presence.

Womanists, feminists, queers, and divine lovers emphasize that it is awareness of what Jesus has done that generates "vital fellowship with Christ."[9] Music is one place where the testimony of faithful outsiders finds a public voice. Evidently, we are far from councils and creeds here, but beginning with images from the marginal voices of folk traditions opens a path for thinking about what we might mean when we attribute divinity to Jesus of Nazareth.

One theme that is common in religious folk music is that Jesus invites us to lay down the heavy weight of condemnation and judgment. Ethics is, of course, an important and useful—essential in its way—dimension of human life. Yet it, like everything human, can become an obstacle rather than a path. It can block us when we feel ourselves too unworthy or stained to lift our heads even to pray for mercy. It can also block us by encouraging us to despise people who we consider moral failures. The radical grace Christianity preaches is, perhaps paradoxically, sometimes more vividly captured in folk music. One traditional song provides a portrait of a man who is a drunk and a gambler; his failures have lost him his wife and family. The song pleads with its listeners to:

> Lend a hand and do not fail to show him pity
> Always lift him up and never knock him down. . . .
> Remember that he is a mother's precious child
> Always lift him up and never knock him down.[10]

In caressing tones, Ry Cooder shows us the pathos of a man we might despise if we encountered him on the street. Transubstantiated by music, he is no longer a drunk gambling away his money. He is a "mother's precious child," and we are called on to encourage him and sympathize with him. More recently Bruce Springsteen has sung of a train that carries all kinds of riffraff among the lost and brokenhearted, and Brad Paisley and Alison Krauss have sung a "whiskey lullaby" about star-crossed lovers who drink themselves to death.[11] Dervish tells the story of a camp follower, now a broken-down alcoholic who, when she can "with two hands hold a glass steady," still "drinks a toast to fair soldier laddie."[12] These songs are only indirectly religious, but they capture an aspect of the good news that troubles middle-class morality. The melodies and voices unveil the raw

9. This phrase is from Schleiermacher, perhaps an honorary woman and queer because of his "impossible wish" to be a woman.

10. "Always Lift Him Up/Kanaka Wai Wai," traditional, sung by Ry Cooder.

11. Bruce Springsteen, "Land of Hope and Dreams"; Brad Paisley and Alison Krauss, "Whiskey Lullaby."

12. This practice of telling the stories of the reviled and despised by society is common in folk music. "Louise" (sung by Bonnie Raitt), "Soldier Laddie" (sung by Dervish), and "Tecumseh Valley" (Nanci Griffith) tell the stories of prostitutes; the list would be endless of songs depicting the poignancy of the lives of black-lung victims, drunkards, wounded soldiers, and so on. Flannery O'Connor's short story "Revelation" is another example of a narrative assault on the moralism that structures much Christian piety (reprint in O'Connor, *The Complete Stories*, 488–509).

sorrow of the human lot, the fragility of our lives, and the waywardness of fortune that lands many of us in destitute and despised situations.

At one level judgment makes sense. One does not hope and pray one's beloved daughter grows up to be a prostitute. It can be easier to sympathize with a woman whose children were held hostage to the alcoholism of their father than with a drunk gambling away the family's grocery money. But here we are invited into the stories behind an unattractive appearance; in seeing the face of the downcast through compassionate rather than judgmental eyes the poignancy of life can become more vivid and the habit of judgment or disgust somewhat eased. Salvation is universally present to every being. In our destitution we are still recognized as precious and beautiful. Laying down the burden of stale moralism, we startle as we recognize the divine image in every face.

Sinead O'Connor, bad girl of Irish music, expands this gentle graciousness into an image of Mother Christ, a mother whose love makes her indifferent to morality.[13] For the Great Mother Christ all pain is in a sense one. Nonjudgmental kisses relieve all forms of unhappiness, violence undergone and violence committed alike. Ethics, appropriately, draws distinctions among these things. But here is an order in which wounds simply require healing, wherever they come from. Much of Christianity places great emphasis on the importance of moral action. Our fate depends on it. But in this music from the displaced of the world, we see visions of another order. Where condemnation creates an illusion of separation, compassion dismantles boundaries that divide us from one another and separate us from redemption. Mothers, ideal ones at least, cherish their little ones and ache for their pains and separation. As Whitehead says, love is "a little oblivious as to morals."[14]

In addition to the generosity and gentleness of this love, Sinead O'Connor also emphasizes that this love is always already there. Even if we do not see it, this Mother Love sees us. There has never been separation between us, only the inability to see the tender arms always surrounding us, cherishing us. Julian of Norwich's parable of the lord and the servant also envisions humanity as always already beloved of God. In her vision, she sees humanity personified as a servant who has fallen into a ditch while running to do the Lord's bidding. He is injured and moaning and cannot rise to help himself. "And of all this, the greatest hurt which I saw him in was lack of consolation, for he could not turn his face to look on his loving lord, who was very close to him, in whom is all consolation."[15] The human race suffers as one fallen in a ditch, not seeing the arms that so tenderly hold us. Sinead O'Connor, Bruce Springsteen, Ry Cooder, Dervish, and Julian

---

13. I was not able to get permission to quote this song but you can see a video of O'Connor singing this on YouTube: http://www.youtube.com/watch?v=IdeMkywlS54. You can also read the lyrics, among other places, at http://www.sing365.com/music/lyric.nsf/This-Is-To-Mother-You -lyrics-Sinead-O'Connor/E66A42F493CB5C6D48256897000C280B.

14. Alfred North Whitehead, *Process and Reality: An Essay in Cosmology*, 342.

15. Julian of Norwich, *Showings*, chap. 51 (p. 267).

of Norwich are among those who witness to a gracious compassion, whose indifference to ethical transgression is balm to the afflicted.

Another image of Christ comes from Arkansas songwriter Jimmy Driftwood when he speaks of moonlight shining in on his pillow and he sees a man "a-walking" with a long chain on. The chain is welded to his body, dragging on the ground, and yet he does not look like a robber or a thief, so the narrator sets out food for him. Though famished, a bright light came upon him, he bowed his head, and said a beautiful grace. Struck by the beauty and suffering of the strange man, the narrator offers to get his chisel and set him free, but the man simply says, "I guess we had best let it be." After his supper, the man thanked him and though the years passed, the man still sees him dragging his long chain.

Christ wanders in solidarity with our bondage. Hungry, tired, dragging a mournful chain, he wanders among us, making visible the chains that bind us. It is like a dream image. It does not matter what the chains represent: guilt, suffering, grief, oppression, or any of the indignities with which life afflicts us. This weary man drags his chain with us—but his face is graceful, hauntingly beautiful. When Odetta weaves this song together with "Another Man Done Gone," the lynching of African Americans and the sufferings of Christ converge.[16] Christ is present in outrage, the union of divine and human in moments that have become hopeless.

Marcella Altaus-Reid describes a similar parallel between the murder of an Argentinian transvestite and the crucifixion of Christ. A transvestite is found along the side of a road, broken and dirty, lying in mud and blood. "Perlongher's narrative on the death of an innocent transvestite forms a close parallel to the scene of the crucifixion of Christ described in Mark 15. Jesus' clothes become the centre of attention. This is Jesus in drag, dressed in a royal purple cloak with a crown of thorns. He is the subject of laughter and derision, just as the transvestite of the Panamerican highway in Buenos Aires or in the Brazilian slums attracts laughter and derision for her gender-fucking, that is, for crossing borders of dress codes and dislocating identities. And there are also Jesus' own torn clothes, muddy clothes that are taken by the soldiers. . . . And people will tremble sensing the mystery of Queer holiness."[17] The union between Christ's suffering and human suffering grants a dignity that suffering itself strips away. Wearing a long chain or the torn clothes of a transvestite, Divinity appears in a degraded and even shocking form. The divine incognito illuminates human degradation; at our most desperate moments we are still backlit by Divinity.

Mechthild of Magdeburg also saw an image of Christ bound to the distress of his people and sharing their imprisonment. When the community in which she

---

16. Kelly Brown Douglas is among those who see in slave songs the convergence of Jesus' suffering with that of the slaves (*Black Christ*, 20–24). See also *Cut Loose Your Stammering Tongue: Black Theology in Slave Narrative*, ed. Dwight Hopkins and George C. L. Cummings; and David Emmanuel Goatley, *Were You There: Godforsakenness in African American Spirituals*.

17. Althaus-Reid, *From Feminist Theology to Indecent Theology*, 168.

lived was persecuted by church authorities, she spoke to Christ in the solitude of her heart: "'Lord, how do you like this prison?' And our Lord said: 'I am held captive in it.'"[18] We may wish for one who delivers us from our chains, but these are witnesses to solidarity that dignifies bondage that is, for the time at least, inescapable. In his Letter to the Philippians, Paul wrote that Christ emptied himself of Divinity and took the form of a servant. The man "with a long chain on" points to this emptying not only as a moment in ancient Galilee but as the perennial state of the moon-drenched Wisdom who wanders among us as in chains. We find her still incarnate in the cast-off body of a murdered transvestite and in the "strange fruit" that hung from southern trees. Following her gives us eyes to see her in the sufferings of "the least of these."

Consolation and solidarity open up the space of compassion, but another kind of witness is more sanguine about the social causes of suffering. Woody Guthrie sees an analogy between Jesus' ministry to the poor and the working class of his own day. Then as now the poor are exploited by institutions of wealth and religion. It is the alliance between these interests and military and political ones that lead to Jesus' crucifixion. Should Jesus return in the flesh, this would be as true today as it was two thousand years ago.[19]

Richard Cleaver is among those who extend the analogy between Jesus' ministry and contemporary injustice into gay and lesbian experience. "If Jesus, in his passion and death, freely chose to become a victim of injustice, his sharing of our oppression entitles those of us who are still victims of injustice to demand that any pronouncement of scripture or ecclesiastical authority be judged by whether it helps or hinders our liberation, our becoming subjects of history, not victims only."[20] Liberation means that redemption is not only individual or "spiritual": "The resurrection has to have a social dimension among us too. We cannot limit ourselves to preaching personal salvation. To make this dimension of the resurrection real in our own lives, we have to put it in terms of our own social situations, in all their pain and in all their richness."[21] The ministry and passion of Jesus do not secure us escape from deserved punishment but rather reveal to us the injustice of our situation and empower us for resistance.

Womanists are also among those for whom the salvation of Christ is never separate from the struggles for liberation. Monica Coleman notes that the divine power to "make a way out of no way" includes "a challenge to the existing

---

18. Mechthild of Magdeburg, *Flowing Light of the Godhead* 7.53 (pp. 321–22). Schleiermacher argues that the condition upon which all of Christ's actions depends is his "sympathy with the condition of men" (*Christian Faith*, §97.3 [p. 407]).

19. In a somewhat hilarious irony, Woody Guthrie's estate wanted to charge me $500 to quote two lines from this song. I encourage you to find the lyrics yourself and read them. One place they are available is at http://www.sing365.com/music/lyric.nsf/Jesus-Christ-lyrics-Woody-Guthrie/0A1 66013798EFE3B4825708B0007F701.

20. Cleaver, *Know My Name*, 17.

21. Ibid., 19.

order."[22] Emilie Townes emphasizes that this includes grassroots activism and economic analysis but it is rooted in spirituality: "This blaze of glory is found, in part, in the lives and commitments of children, men, and women of faith who seek to live their spirituality as social witness."[23] Spirituality, compassion, and justice cannot be isolated from one another. If one is concerned about suffering, one must be concerned about its causes.

Liberation synthesizes dimensions that are often kept separate: interior experience and external conditions, salvation and liberation, spirituality and politics. Seeing analogies between Jesus' ministry and the injustices of contemporary oppression make it possible to refuse both the cultural construction of one's identity and the social conditions that produce it. Mercy Oduyoye expresses the unity of compassion and justice as they are experienced by African women: "Jesus' outrage against oppressive culture encourages women not to condone oppression. Jesus lived by the future of God articulated in the Magnificat, the hymn attributed to his mother. The caring compassionate healer is another strong face of Jesus that women appropriate. The lives they live need this Jesus who can exorcise the evil that torments Africa and gnaws at the womb of her daughters. Steeped in African Religion and believing in Jesus, women are able to proclaim the Jesus who breaks the chains of evil. Jesus feeds the hungry and sets free the victims of patriarchy."[24]

If we limit ourselves to traditional preoccupation with correctly establishing the relationship between Divinity and humanity or allow denominational structures to constrain our encounter with Christ, we may miss the voices of Irish lesbians, slaves and their descendants, wandering white folksingers, and anomalous contemplative women who write love songs to an intimate who remains near to them in their suffering. This nearness grants dignity to those the world despises and refreshment in situations where there is little relief. This Jesus defuses judgment even as his presence generates a spirituality of justice. He wanders among us, sharing a pan of cold biscuits. In his presence, we refuse the identity poverty, patriarchy, racism, or homophobia would impose on us and challenge the structures that justify these degradations.

The effect of affliction tends toward destruction. It deadens us to the divine image in ourselves and others and tempts us to participate in the mutual predation we humans visit on one another and on the earth itself. These songs testify to the intimacy of Jesus in the ordinary degradations of life. Companionship consoles and empowers. But the underlying story is of something that pierces the destructive power of suffering. The humanity of Jesus makes him a soul friend, an intimate who understands. But it is the divinity of a tender mother or a man with a long chain that pierces suffering with a luminous beauty. These love songs

---

22. Coleman, *Making a Way Out of No Way*, 33. See also Katie Canon, "Racism and Economics: The Perspective of Oliver C. Cox," *Katie's Canon*, 149–60.

23. Townes, *In a Blaze of Glory*, 139.

24. Oduyoye, *Introducing African Women's Theology*, 64.

testify to consolation and resistance. But the consolation is so potent because it is Divinity dwelling there. Another kind of love song tracks this consoling Mother, this soul friend back to its divine source.

THE EMBODIMENT OF WISDOM: EROS AND KENOSIS

Through whatever images we try to conceive the unimaginable unity and differentiation between Good Beyond Being and Wisdom, our minds reel again when we imagine the inflation of a human form with Divinity as fully as it is in Christ. Wisdom is present everywhere, throughout the earth, the cosmos, and beyond. The divinity of nature is its beauty; our obligations to it are spiritual and not merely pragmatic. Yet humanity has called forth the incarnation in a more specific sense. Christianity knows the eternal and infinite Good through the form of a particular human being.

The embodiment of Wisdom is possible in part because something about human nature makes it a home for Wisdom. The prophets, mystics, yoginis, arhats, bodhisattvas, avatars, and adepts of many ages testify in various ways to this possibility. But Christian narrative expresses ways in which humanity is estranged from its divine source. This is not the place to rehearse the story of the fall or to try to untangle even a few of its meanings. For the purposes of this analysis, it must suffice to simply acknowledge the tragedy that we humans seem to have lost our way. We do not recognize the divine in one another. We are torn by large and small sufferings. Our history is laced with disasters and cruelties. The claim that we are bearers of the divine image is counterintuitive and countercultural. Suffering tyrannizes us, often compelling us to act in ways that betray our beauty. Few of us extend to the utmost our full reach as God-bearers. From a Christian point of view, a Savior comes to us because we cannot tolerate our suffering and because our divinity lies dormant in us, it has ceased to burn. Wisdom comes to us in intimate, familiar form to heal us and to inflame us with divine life. But in what sense does it make sense to say that Wisdom took a human form or that Jesus was divine?

In his Letter to the Philippians, Paul describes Jesus as emptying himself of the form of God in order to be born in the form of a human being (2:5–7). But in an odd way it was just this emptying that opened a space to display divinity. Wisdom empties herself of divinity and takes on humanity but this is precisely what makes known divinity (John 1:18). Wisdom's "desire was by means of this very emptying to display to us the fulness of the godhead."[25] While creation is good, we humans suffer an estrangement from our divine source. It is part of the great beauty of the Christian faith that it envisions our Beloved as being unable to tolerate this estrangement. As Mechthild of Magdeburg puts it, the Beloved

---

25. Origen, *On First Principles* 1.2.8 (p. 21).

is "powerless, for I cannot restrain myself as to my gifts."[26] Wisdom is powerless to withhold her desire for humanity: she empties herself so she can come near those for whom she longs. The impulse of Eros is *kenosis:* longing that is fulfilled by emptying; emptying gushing with the fullness of divine presence.

WISDOM IS JUSTIFIED BY HER CHILDREN

Wisdom literature is a source for conceiving of the Second Person of the Trinity as a manifestation of divinity in creation. Elizabeth Johnson is among those who reminds us that much of the imagery of incarnation is also drawn from Wisdom literature.[27] Wisdom is the main character of Proverbs, Sirach, and the Wisdom of Solomon. Protestants came to exclude the last two from their canon and in doing so obscured much of the scriptural justification for associating Wisdom with Jesus. In Proverbs Wisdom is a personification of transcendent power who comes to aid humanity. Like Jesus, she "cries out in the street; in the squares she raises her voice. At the busiest corner she cries out; at the entrance of the city gates she speaks," calling people back to the life-giving way of God (Proverbs 1:20–21). She is present before the beginning and through her God creates the world. Wisdom and the Lord delight in one another and in the humanity they have created (chap. 8). Also like Jesus, she invites the lost to her table: "Come, eat of my bread and drink the wine I have mixed. Lay aside immaturity, and live, and walk in the way of insight" (9:5–6). The book of Sirach identifies Wisdom as present in the eternity before creation and poured out on all of creation (Sirach 1, 24). Wisdom asks why people thirst when they can receive what they need from her without money. She promises they will find rest if they place her yoke upon them (51:24–27). Wisdom, though eternal, is commanded by the Creator to set up her tent in Israel (24:8). Wisdom protected Adam and "delivered him from his transgression." She preserves, rescues, and shelters those who need her. "When a righteous man was sold, wisdom did not desert him, but delivered him from sin. She descended with him into the dungeon, and when he was in prison she did not leave him." She "delivered [a holy people] from a nation of oppressors. She entered the soul of a servant of the Lord, and withstood dread kings with wonders and signs." She was a guide, a shelter, a starry flame. She "opened the mouths of those who were mute, and made the tongues of infants speak clearly" (Wisdom 10:1, 13–14, 15–16, 21).

It is easy to see resonances between these images and those the Gospel writers used for Jesus. His yoke is easy and his burden light. He delivers us from sin and oppression. He opened the mouths of the dumb. He took the form of a servant

---

26. Mechthild of Magdeburg, *Flowing Light of the Godhead,* 1.1 (p. 39).

27. Elizabeth Johnson, *She Who Is.* She points out the role of Wisdom literature in chap. 5, especially pp. 86–100, and then develops a Trinitarian theology on the basis of Sophia in chaps. 7–10. We can only be grateful for this wonderful contribution to our understanding.

and remains with us in our servitude. He has come to the lost. We eat his bread and drink his wine. In some unfathomable way, he exists at the intersection of time and eternity and manifests the creative and redemptive powers of Divinity throughout the cosmos.

Elizabeth Johnson argues that Wisdom-Sophia is a "female personification of God's own being in creative and saving involvement with the world."[28] When early Christians sought language to express the salvation they were experiencing through the good news of Jesus Christ, the Wisdom tradition was ready-to-hand. Like Wisdom, Jesus was sent by God to Jerusalem. "The words, functions, and characteristics of Sophia were now associated with the human being Jesus. . . . Jesus was so closely associated with Sophia that by the end of the first century he is presented not only as a wisdom teacher, not only as a child and envoy of Sophia, but ultimately even as an embodiment of Sophia herself."[29] Even before Matthew appropriated the images of Sophia for Jesus (23:37–39; cf. 11:28–30), Paul describes Jesus as "the power of God and the wisdom [Sophia] of God" (1 Corinthians 1:24). "Here is the transvaluation of values so connected with the ministry, death, and resurrection of Jesus: divine Sophia is here manifest not in glorious deeds or esoteric doctrine, but in God's solidarity with the one who suffers. While seeming to be weak and defeated, the personal Wisdom of God is in fact the source of life."[30] John's Gospel is soaked in images drawn from the Wisdom tradition. He represents the Word as in eternal beginning with God and in a sense as God. Like Wisdom, he sets up his tent among our tents ("lived among us"). He is rejected by some, yet a radiant light that darkness cannot overcome. "As with Sophia, whoever loves Jesus is beloved by God (14:23) and enters into a mutuality so profound that they may be called friends (15:15)."[31]

Paul Knitter also appeals to the Wisdom tradition as one background of the idea of incarnation. He reminds us that it is one of the oldest images of Jesus: "Here Jesus was seen and felt to be the embodiment, and therefore, the supreme Teacher, of God's Wisdom—or in Hebrew, God's '*Hokma*,' which was translated into the Greek '*Sophia*' (both, by the way, female!). And the reason why he was so filled with God's Wisdom was because he was so filled with God's *Spirit*. . . . His spirit and the Divine Spirit, though different, were indistinguishable. To meet Jesus was to meet and feel God's Spirit. This, mainly this, is what Christians were trying to say when they later called Jesus the Son of God. . . . To be with this Jesus was, somehow, to be with God, to feel the presence of the Divine. Here was a human being so filled with and tuned to what they called the Spirit of God that they realized that to know him was to know God."[32] The association

---

28. Elizabeth Johnson, *She Who Is,* 91.
29. Ibid., 94–95.
30. Ibid., 95.
31. Ibid., 97.
32. Knitter, *Without Buddha,* 115.

of Christ with Sophia faded in part because of the increasing misogyny of the ecclesial tradition. But as we consider the light that flows from Abyss to incarnation, we can continue to cherish this boldly feminine persona of the Divine who blew through canonical and extracanonical Scriptures and also through the wandering Galilean who is still a "starry flame" at the intersection between time and eternity, between divinity and humanity.

ABIDING IN THE DIVINE

Meditating on the begetting of Christ by Wisdom follows out one lineage of her presence in the human world. If we are saying that in having to do with Christ we have something to do with Divinity, then we are saying something remarkable and wonderful about the Divine Abyss, known and adored by so many names. We are bearing witness to the divine desire to set up her tent among our tents. We are martyrs to the intoxicating truth that humanity has a capacity to bear the flame of this presence. If these are truths revealed to us by the "glory as of the only Son from the Father" (John 1:14 RSV), we are given a capacity to rejoice in the *logoi* of all beings and traditions as signs of the omnipresent, incarnating Wisdom of our Beloved.

This intersection of Divinity and humanity so vividly enacted in the enfleshing of Wisdom might imply a synthesis or union of two diametrically opposed substances. Specifying how these different qualities coinhere has been the work of many councils. To fully embrace an expression of the coming together of humanity and Divinity in Christ we would have to have full or total understanding of what constituted human and divine natures. I suspect this is not possible.

The way of negation reminds us that we work with metaphors and concepts, all of which can have misleading implications. But the testimony of the woe-be-gone, the despised, the justice seekers connects us to the ancient need to affirm that Jesus the human being somehow embodies and mediates Divinity. The urge to find a way to express this has produced a variety of ways of representing incarnation.

John is one Gospel writer for whom it became important to insist that in Christ we behold the glory of God (John 1:14). Jesus is not simply a teacher of wisdom, not even the ultimate teacher of wisdom—he is the embodiment of Wisdom. But John also specifies the medium of embodiment as love. In the farewell speech to his disciples, Jesus reflects on how the Divine can be made present through a human body. The one who sees Jesus sees the Father, but the medium and content of this seeing and dwelling is love: "those who love me will be loved by my Father, and I will love them and reveal myself to them" (14:21). He describes the mutual indwelling of Christ in those who love him. This love allows them to abide in the Father. It is by this love, this mutual abiding, that the Father is glorified.

The farewell speech (John 13–16) is an attempt to draw two connections that the Gospel writer apparently felt were most urgent. In seeing Jesus we see Divinity.

When Philip asks to be shown the Father, Jesus describes being infiltrated by the Divine: "Do you not believe that I am in the Father and the Father is in me? . . . Believe me that I am in the Father and the Father is in me; but if you do not, then believe me because of the works themselves" (14:10, 11). But in case Philip and the other disciples are confused about what exactly constitutes the Divinity that is revealed in Jesus or what works testify to who he is, he speaks at length about love. Several times in the course of these few chapters Jesus repeats to the disciples that the commandment they must keep is love and that it is love through which he abides in the Father and they abide in him. John is the Gospel writer through whom the idea of incarnation is expressed and also through whom an account of the medium of incarnation is placed in the Savior's mouth.

The Word is manifest as the force of creation in light and life; it is manifest in human form as love. It is love that connects the human Jesus to the divine Word and it is love that connects his disciples to their teacher and through him to Divinity. In seeing this love we see Mother-Father God. In this sense Jesus is "the way, and the truth, and the life" (John 14:6). No one comes to Divinity except through love and as love. As Marguerite Porete says, quoting the twin love commandment: "These commands are of necessity for salvation for all: nobody can have grace with a lesser way."[33] Incarnation means the embodiment of the power of love.

The Creed of Chalcedon, adopted in 451, transfers John's incarnation of love into the language of metaphysics. It is indebted to Greek words and concepts such as *ousia* (substance), *physis* (nature, of sorts), *hypostasis*, *prosopon* (person). All of these words have difficult shades of meaning and become even more difficult when they are translated from one language to another. But we can evade being tangled in these complexities by taking a more minimalist view of the creed. The Council of Chalcedon wanted to affirm that Jesus was fully human and fully divine and that neither of these "natures" eclipsed the other.[34] This should not be taken to mean that two utterly unlike substances somehow mix in the person of Jesus, infinity and finitude somehow lapping around each other inside Jesus' head like oil and water.

We attribute to Divinity qualities that are the opposite of those we attribute to human beings: infinity, simplicity, unity, transcendence, immutability, omniscience, and so on. We cannot really bring to mind a human person who is also infinite and simple, transcendent, immutable, and omniscient. It would be like trying to think of a square circle. But it is a mistake to think of the Divine as a kind of thing that has certain attributes and then trying to imagine how these attributes apply to Jesus. The Eternal Eros is not a kind of thing and it does not have attributes. We use attributes to discipline our minds in such a way that we are able to contemplate nonconceptual, nondual reality.

---

33. Porete, *Mirror of Simple Souls*, chap. 3 (p. 81).
34. Translations of the Chalcedonian Creed can be found in many places, including Wikipedia and earlychurchtexts.com.

Jesus was fully human, as the Chalcedon Creed says: he was really and truly a person in all of the senses we mean by that term. We say he is also "fully divine" in the sense that he was completely infused by nonduality. His body-mind-spirit was absorbed into nonduality. The incarnation is possible because it is proper to the human person to open onto the sphere of nonduality. Christians, following various New Testament writings, interpret this nonduality to be primarily or most perfectly expressed as love. That is, the name we give to something that evades all names is love. If we keep in mind the indwelling by love described in the Gospel of John we might say that we see in the human Jesus the indwelling of a shaft of Divinity. The name Christians prefer for nonduality as it moves into a dimension of conceptuality is love. Or put another way, the consequence of dwelling in nonduality is an ever more perfect embodiment of love. This is not the awkward and paradoxical juxtaposition of two unlike, even opposite, substances. It is the natural capacity of nonduality to manifest through a human consciousness and of human consciousness to be a site of this manifestation. Nonduality and a human personality become "one taste." The unbelievable potency of this integration is such that now, two thousand years later, we still feel the intensity of love vibrating in this coincidence of opposites: Divine in the human person, nonduality in a human body.

This phrase, "coincidence of opposites," preserves the sense that there are important distinctions between human and Divine; yet, on the other side of the wall of reason where paradise lies, we see that these are not opposites. "Rahner reminded us that to say that Jesus was truly divine was another way of saying that he was fully human."[35] It is the truth of human nature that it bears the Divine. Jesus reveals this to us in an astonishingly potent way. But this does not contract Divinity, the Eternal Eros, into the body of Jesus of Nazareth so the rest of creation and human history is emptied of it. As Schleiermacher puts it, flesh is "finite, limited, sensible . . . and the Word's becoming flesh is therefore the appearing of this original and divine wisdom in that form."[36] But what we see in Jesus is this form transposed by Divinity "whereby nothing lives in him but devotion and love."[37] We see Divinity refracted through the concreteness and limitation of a human form. We see also what humanity looks like when it is infused as completely as possible by the Divine Wisdom.

Nicholas of Cusa affirms that the human being can be united with the divine nature "and that a person, in receiving you, the God who can be received, crosses over into a bond with you so close that it can be named 'filiation.'"[38] Through this *theosis* or divinization, "all children will attain to final happiness

---

35. Knitter, *Without Buddha*, 116. Karl Rahner's Christology is developed in various places. A somewhat succinct version of it is in *Foundations of Christian Faith*, especially chaps. 1, 2, 4, and 6.
36. Schleiermacher, *Christmas Eve*, 82.
37. Ibid., 84.
38. Nicholas of Cusa, "On the Vision of God" 18.82 (*Selected Spiritual Writings*, 272).

and perfection."[39] But there remains a difference between the divinization of human beings and that of Jesus. "In this highest Son filiation is as art in a master or as light in the sun, but in the other children, it is as art in disciples or as light in the stars."[40]

The councils of Nicaea and Chalcedon affirm the Trinitarian quality of Divinity, which cautions against the error of thinking of Jesus as identical with God. Jesus incarnates the Divine but does not exhaustively transform the invisible Godhead into a visible man as if there were no Divinity except what is manifest in Jesus of Nazareth. There remains, after all, the first and third persons of the Trinity as well as the eternal form of the second person of the Trinity. At the same time, the "two-nature" Christology affirms that the divinity of Christ does not abolish the human form of the incarnation. As Nicholas of Cusa puts it: "You show me, O never-failing Light, that the maximum union by which in my Jesus human nature is united to your divine nature is in no way similar to infinite union. For the union by which you God the Father are united to God the Son is God the Holy Spirit, and therefore it is an infinite union, for it attains absolute and essential identity. It is not so where human nature is united to the divine." In Jesus "the attraction of the human nature to the divine" is achieved in the highest degree possible. "The union, therefore, of the human nature of Jesus, as human, to the divine is maximum, because it is unable to be greater, but it is not simply maximum and infinite as is the divine union." We see in the human nature of Jesus the divine nature existing "in a human way."[41]

Nothing finite or created is adequate to the infinite depths of Divinity. What we see in Christ is humanity maximally transparent to Divinity. To the extent that humanity is capable of the indwelling of Divinity, we see this in complete, maximum, perfected form in Christ. We see Divinity in its human form, Divinity revealed through the refraction of human nature. This may help us navigate the conceptual difficulty of the double begetting of Christ: once, according to the Godhead, in the eternity beyond time, consubstantial with the first principle of Divinity but in some sense differentiated from it; a second time according to the human body of Jesus, who is born at a particular time and place. Because of the apophatic depth of the human being, because humanity is created in the divine image, it can bear the Divine in a particular way. Deep calls unto deep. Yet this proximity so intimate it becomes incarnation does not render the Erotic Abyss of Divinity naked to vision. Such an indiscretion is unnecessary; it would only speak to our perception, to our cognition. It would not enter into the darkened bridal chamber where we meet the Beloved most intimately.

39. Ibid.
40. Ibid. A somewhat similar point is made by Schleiermacher: "during the union the Divine Essence in Christ retained its identity, only becoming active in temporal fashion, and that only that side of this activity is temporal which had already become human and passed over into the sphere of outward appearance" (*Christian Faith*, §97.3 [p. 408]).
41. Nicholas of Cusa, "On the Vision of God" 20.87, 88 (*Selected Spiritual Writings*, 275).

HONEY IN THE ROCK

The union between Christ and the Godhead, the intimacy that emerged between humanity and Divinity in the incarnation, is not the juxtaposition of substances but a union in love that makes them "one taste." Origen uses the image of fire to describe this union. Through love, Christ becomes fire, and in him "we discern nothing else . . . except fire. . . . And while, indeed, some warmth of the Word of God must be thought to have reached all the saints, in this soul we must believe that the divine fire itself essentially rested, and that it is from this that some warmth has come to all others."[42]

Christ is fire but also, like Wisdom, Christ is an "unspotted mirror of the energy or working of God" because "there is absolutely no dissimilarity between the Son and the Father."[43] These images of fire, mirror, bridal chambers, of filiation and starlight attempt to draw into the misleading specificity of word and concept the existential vividness of God-with-us. This nearness is honey in our mouths. In the midst of our own exile we find relief and succor. We describe it as a man in a long chain or as a mother kissing away our pain. Analogies with Jesus' ministry allow us to pierce collective self-deception and decry injustice. For theists, the name for the always astonishing piercing of the veil of suffering and deception by a healing and illuminating force is God. As womanist theologians argue, we testify to what is done in our lives, and incarnation is a way of saying that what is done reflects the transparency of our ordinary lives to Divinity. Creeds and their contemporary interpreters celebrate the capacities of discursive reasoning to follow out the logic of incarnation. These various love songs, which savor the impenetrable mystery of the incarnation in such different ways, may help us to sympathize with Teilhard de Chardin: "I believe that the Church is still a child. Christ, by whom she lives, is immeasurably greater than she imagines. And yet, when thousands of years have gone by and Christ's true countenance is a little more plainly seen, the Christians of those days will still, without any reservations, recite the Apostles' Creed."[44]

42. Origen, *On First Principles* 2.6.6 (p. 113).
43. Ibid., 1.2.12 (p. 26).
44. Teilhard de Chardin, *Heart of Matter*, 118.

Chapter 7

"Every Spiritual Blessing"
The Passion of Christ

Blessed be to the Good and Mother of our Beloved Jesus Christ, who has blessed us in Christ with every spiritual blessing.

Ephesians 1:3 (my paraphrase)

And so Jesus is our true Mother in nature by our first creation, and he is our true Mother in grace by his taking our created nature. All the lovely works and all the sweet loving offices of beloved motherhood are appropriated to the second person, for in him we have this godly will, whole and safe forever, both in nature and in grace, from his own goodness proper to him.

. . . And in that, by the same grace, everything is penetrated, in length and in breadth, in height and in depth without end; and it is all one love.[1]

But will the Queer Jesus resurrect? I belong to a community of people who think that yes, the resurrection of the Queer God is not only possible, but already a reality. The Queer God is present in every group or individual who still dares to believe that God is fully present among the marginalized, exceeding the narrow confines of sexual and political ideologies. . . . In fact, in every community of excluded people and in every inch of the struggle for sexual and economic justice, the Queer God manifests Godself with full glory, power, and grace.[2]

---

1. Julian of Norwich, *Showings*, chap. 59 (pp. 296–97).
2. Marcella Althaus-Reid, *From Feminist Theology to Indecent Theology*, 176.

Love is the medium through which the Good Beyond Being manifests as Wisdom and, through Wisdom, becomes incarnate in human form. The purpose of the incarnation can be conceived of in relationship to the two great tragedies of human existence: suffering and ignorance of our true nature. The passion speaks to the intimacy of Christ in our suffering, and the incarnation speaks to Christ's intimacy with us as we rise to awareness of our spiritual nature. Salvation includes both of these elements: compassionate presence and divinization. For many, particularly in early Christianity, the saving event is the incarnation itself, in which the divinization of humanity is so vividly accomplished. The passion is another site of particular potency. These two chapters reflect on how Christ "saves" us from our tragedies—in this chapter, the tragedy of suffering, in the next chapter, the tragedy of self-forgetfulness.

I have been at some pains to reincorporate feminine imagery of the Divine in meditating on the incarnation. But in turning more concretely to the Savior, Jesus of Nazareth, I would be remiss if I ignored entirely the difficulties raised by the maleness of Jesus. So we will begin with that issue, if only briefly, before returning to incarnate Wisdom, who brings us "every spiritual blessing."

MALE AND FEMALE HE (!) CREATED THEM

I am grateful that feminist theologians raise the issue of whether a male savior can save women. An easy answer is yes: if he is God, and can walk on water and whatnot, he can save women too. Problems remain. One problem is the shameful idolatry of the church, which conflates maleness with Divinity. This is a theological problem and harms every Christian. Idolatry is not good for anyone, perhaps least good for its ostensible beneficiaries. The spiritual harm done when someone lives by lies and oppression, by mendacious scriptural appeals and childish reasoning, is probably more violent than what is done to women themselves. But women are harmed. The journey toward self-recognition as a God-bearer is made more difficult when the imagery for this is almost exclusively male. One has to translate, to work in spaces of invisibility, to implicitly visualize oneself as male, to tacitly accept that one is less than fully human, small, inferior, secondary, limited. There is no door for us to enter the divine order.

Many Christians understand Jesus as the one who alone is able to accomplish the salvation of humanity. So concentrating divine healing into the body of Jesus has had devastating effects on our ability to conceive of love as universal in scope. This general problem is intensified when the maleness of Jesus' body becomes essential to his saving power and to his ability to incarnate the Divine. It is this patriarchal emphasis that has been deadly to women. God is in some more or less literal sense male, and it is the privilege of the male body alone to be fully open to Divinity. It is necessary to acknowledge the problem here so we can better identify the patriarchal character of so much of our tradition and to see how deeply it shapes our consciousness. Luce Irigaray points out that there is no God as far as the feminine gender is concerned: "no female trinity: mother, daughter, spirit."[3] Women are forced to imagine their perfection as becoming a man, imagining a male God. "If she is to become woman, if she is to accomplish her female subjectivity, woman needs a god who is a figure for the perfection of *her* subjectivity."[4] I think this is true. It is very difficult to reconnect with our divine nature if we have to first convert our femaleness to male.

Missionary Christianity perceived the divinity of Jesus' body not only as male but as European as well. The cultures, sometimes even the language, of missionized peoples were demonized and destroyed so that salvation could take hold. Irish Christianity had to be Romanized. First Nations peoples had to convert to European culture before they could be beloved by God. Africans and their descendants in diaspora must worship a white man with a long beard and eschew everything African. Queer men and women must destroy their sexual identity to come before the Redeemer. Christianity has been in the habit of conflating a dominant image of humanity—a straight, white, European, cultured male—with Divinity. It has insisted that only this subjectivity can represent or become divine. In order to be divine, everyone else must, *per impossibile*, take on an entirely different form of the human. This deadly way of thinking belies the great beauty inherent in plurality and the common estrangement we all, even cultured European men, suffer.

Estrangement from the Divine is not because we are women or queer or non-European. Neither is reconciliation accomplished by being male or white or Palestinian. But it is common to the human condition to find ourselves fallen away from our divinity, tyrannized by suffering. It is our common destiny to make our way back to our Beloved. Shawn Copeland is among those who remind us that it is precisely as beautifully diverse bodies that we share divinity. "The sacramental aesthetics of Eucharist, the thankful living manifestation of God's image through particularly marked flesh, demand the vigorous display of difference in race and culture and tongue, gender and sex and sexuality."[5] We do not need to be saved from the form of human we embody. This is how Divinity plays itself: in the infinite plurality of particular forms.

Any manifestation of Divinity can save. In this sense, we could become enlightened by looking on the Beloved anywhere, for that is where the Beloved is: in any person or religion, in nature, yogic discipline, in art or scholarship. We have clouds of women who witness to Christ's intimacy to women empowered in vision or social action or healing to embody Christ for their community: Wisdom permeating their wisdom. The slave woman Blandina was Christ for her fellow martyrs at Lyon.[6] The Most Reverend Katherine Jefferts Schori presides over the Episcopal Church.

---

3. Irigaray, "Divine Women," in *Sexes and Genealogies*, 62.
4. Ibid., 64.
5. Copeland, *Enfleshing Freedom*, 82.
6. Blandina's story is told in various places, including Elaine Pagels, *Gnostic Gospels*, 85–86.

A male savior can save women. But when Christianity creates the additional obstacle of denigrating the feminine or withholding feminine imagery from the Divine, it is more difficult for an image of a male incarnation to offer healing to women—and also to men. Men and women alike suffer truncated and distorted self-understanding when the feminine is not part of our imaginative constructions of Divinity. When we lack feminine symbols, images, and names of the Beloved, our own femininity—whether we are male or female or transgendered—is wounded. What is not assumed is not saved. Humanity merges with Divinity only when the fullness of humanity is present, male, female, and transgendered.

Is there a special reason that the incarnation took on a male form? It is hard to credit the view that men more easily represent the Divine in light of a long history of male violence and ignorance. It might have made more sense for Wisdom to embody herself as a woman, since women share more directly her creative power, her synthetic form of knowing, her maternal care. Women disciples in both canonical and noncanonical scriptures understand Jesus better than the male disciples do. They are more steadfast when he was arrested. They were the first witnesses to his resurrection. Jesus himself was in many ways more feminine than masculine—an honorary woman because of his tender heart, his fierce love, his repudiation of patriarchal privilege, his particular ease and friendship with (other) women. He did what women do: he healed and fed people, he enjoyed the flowers, he was courageous when his love was met by violence.

There is nonetheless a reason we recognize the Divine in a male savior. We murder or ignore women saviors. The idea that there is only one divine being is itself an artifact of an exclusive orthodoxy, blind to the holy persons through whom Wisdom illuminates her lost children: Buddha, the Dalai Lama, Yeshe Tsegyel, saints and yogis. Christ's closest spiritual friend was demoted by the tradition from apostle to a penitent prostitute. The greatest Christian yogini, Marguerite Porete, was burned as a heretic in a Paris square in 1310. If we cannot bear to accept women apostles recommended to us by Christ and we commit to the fire her greatest teachers, we are unlikely to recognize Wisdom Christ in a female form.

The Great Mother is skillful in the means she uses to come near to us, to heal us. She took the body of a man in Palestine so Gentiles could be saved by a Jew, the wealthy could be saved by a poor person, white-skinned northerners and black skinned southerners could be saved by a brown-skinned Mediterranean, women saved by a man, and men saved by a victim of torture. But because the image of a male savior reinforces patriarchal privilege, it is all the more important to break the hold of the idolatry of the masculine by reincorporating other images for the Divine.

The Bible itself uses a great deal of female imagery.[7] Is it not disrespectful to

---

7. Virginia Mollenkott's book *Divine Feminine: The Biblical Imagery of God as Female* is one

Scripture to so thoroughly ignore the revelation of the feminine Divine within it? Perhaps if we recognized the feminine power within Divinity more openly we might find the male body of Jesus less confining. If we were more creative in augmenting our imagination, we might find our pluriform humanity refreshed and expanded. If we recognized the presence of Wisdom in the wisdom of mothers of revolution, in the fight against injustice, in ordinary and extraordinary courage and compassion, we might find that the Paraclete has been among us but we did not recognize her. If we acknowledge that salvation has been lavished on all the peoples of the world and is available in countless forms, the maleness of Jesus may shrink in importance.

WISDOM AGONISTES

The incarnation is the astonishing claim that Divinity takes on a human form. This claim becomes even more absurd—if that is possible—in the way this human form is depicted. Jesus does not show Divinity as the inbreaking of longed-for power to bring justice to a history of persecution and oppression: a mighty king, a conquering emperor, a wish-fulfilling jewel. Instead of these useful powers, we are shown only an itinerant teacher wandering through a conquered country, himself hardly better than a peasant, he preaches that Divinity is as near and tender as a parent and that we dwell there by dwelling in love.

Other religious traditions share the view that awakening to ultimate reality is the proper destiny of humanity and that love is the most natural consequence of such an awakening. But Christianity's distinctive genius was to display the unity of the Divine and human not in meditative equipoise but as a participant in the anguish of human suffering. The distinctive wisdom Christianity offers the world is that the Beloved does not take on the human condition in a general sense. Our condition is one of suffering and affliction, of sin and the perception of God-forsakenness. Mother Christ meets us by coming to us in our extremity. The Beloved seeks us in our destitution where we have been divested of the beauty of spiritual beings. Or to put this another way, it is as creatures destitute and suffering that we bear the divine nature.

The cross is very ugly but it is a door to Christ. As my colleague Noel Erskine reminds us: no one wants to walk through that door. No one wants to accept affliction as the door to Christ. We do not have to walk through that door because God wants us to suffer in imitation of Christ. We are standing in that door every day. Our body is stretched on the cross in refugee camps, in hunger, in greed and violence, in self-hatred and paralysis, in illness that opens up only on more pain, in prisons and the terror of dangerous homes, in the emptiness of

particularly rich recovering of feminine imagery in Scripture. If one added noncanonical texts such as the *Secret Revelation of John* (to use only one example) the imagery would be even more widely expanded.

luxury and meaningless work. Christ does not invite us through this door so we can be like him. He stands at this door so he can be like us.

When we see that Christ's blood flows with our own, that the hand that caresses our wounds is itself wounded, our cross is knit with his and we walk through the door to Divinity. In the story of Cinderella, the prince looks for his beloved princess all through the villages and even in the home of her stepmother. But she is hidden from him, locked away and disguised in cinders and ashes. He must seek out her hiding place and recognize her soot-smeared face. Christ is wise enough not to be fooled by our masks. He seeks the hidden places where despair or delusion would conceal us. He sets his tent among our tents, even if we are encamped at Golgotha. He comes all the way to where we are so that we might be restored to ourselves.

The cross is, even among religious symbols, excruciatingly potent. It does not reside in the safe space of intellectual discourse or the consoling space of contemplation. It enters full on into the horrific unmaking of violence. This makes it supremely healing and also supremely dangerous. Suffering is poisonous. There is something humiliating about suffering. However innocently we suffer, suffering is woven together with degradation and guilt. "Evil dwells in the heart of the criminal without being felt there. It is felt in the heart of the [person] who is afflicted and innocent. Everything happens as though the state of soul suitable for criminals had been separated from crime and attached to affliction; and it even seems to be in proportion to the innocence of those who are afflicted."[8] Because of this mysterious transference of the experience of stain onto affliction, theological doctrines that emphasize our worthlessness make a great deal of existential sense.

Because our minds are contorted by suffering, the idea that we all fell in the garden of Eden and were sinful from before our birth is easy to believe. Our worthlessness is so deep that the few years of our life are insufficient to contain it. Tracing it back through a primordial past expresses the metaphysical and essential nature of our worthlessness. That God is angry with us makes sense: of course God is enraged, he has every right to be. If only eternity could be made longer, if only the sublime tortures of hell could be made more horrible, then perhaps they might be suitable to our crime. That the Father would require infinite satisfaction from us and extract it from the finite body of his incarnate Son is natural. It makes possible a moral universe in which guilt is punished and punishment fits the crime.

A cross on which the infinity of God resides in the limitation of the Son's body seems a barely adequate recompense for the intolerable offense of which affliction is the sign. For suffering humanity, original sin and the atoning death of the Son at the hands of his Father makes sense in the same way abuse makes sense in the pathetic confusions of children. They must be guilty if their par-

---

8. Simone Weil, "The Love of God and Affliction," in *Waiting for God*, 121.

ent is hurting them so badly. When British oppressions escalated into "ethnic cleansing," the traumatized Irish pathologized their faith, making of guilt itself a religion. The bloody crosses of Latin America speak to a brutalized people. Suffering is somehow welded to feelings of degradation and worthlessness. From this perspective the cross makes sense of our guilt, justifies our torment, and makes of God a righteously enraged prosecutor who upholds a moral universe. Yet in the midst of all of this is a tender and loving brother. We get news of love in the form traumatized humanity can understand it. The doctrine of atonement is so resilient because it is psychologically compelling.

Job is the spokesperson for those who refuse this identification of suffering and guilt. Insisting on his innocence, he rejects the solace offered by his friends: accept that you are guilty, repent and ask forgiveness, and God will be reconciled to you. The basic structure of much Christian liturgy reflects the theology of Job's comforters. But Job, ally of all the afflicted, rejects this theology:

> I know that my redeemer lives,
> and that at the last he will stand upon the earth;
> and after my skin has been thus destroyed,
> then in my flesh I shall see God,
> whom I shall see on my side,
> and my eyes shall behold, and not another.
>   Job 19:25–27

Against the evidence of affliction and loss, against the evidence of the comforters' tried and true theology, Job sees something else: a redeemer who will not accuse but justify him. Even if he is utterly destroyed by affliction and his skin is rotted from his cold, dead body, he will still expect to see his redeemer. Death, suffering, humiliation, loss of family, and alienation from friends will not quell his heartbroken confidence that God will be revealed on *his side*. His eyes will behold *this* face of Divinity and no other. He will not curse God and die but persist in his rebel faith. There are biblical and liturgical images of God that resonate with the comforters' theology. Such a god would naturally require the sacrifice of his son in order to reconcile with fallen humanity. But the Voice in the Whirlwind scolds the comforters: "My wrath is kindled against you and against your two friends; for you have not spoken of me what is right, as my servant Job has" (Job 42:7).

Following the example of Job we see that the task of speaking what is right requires that we resist stories about the Beloved that vilify our divine Mother and betray her loving desires for us. "Any way of telling the story that does not take us more deeply into the freeing and empowering love of God and impel us to radiate that to others is not an adequate version of the story. Nor is it an adequate version if it ignores, trivializes, or increases the sufferings of real women and men, particularly those who suffer most in our world."[9] I will not rehearse but

9. Barbara E. Reid, *Taking Up the Cross: New Testament Interpretations through Latina and Feminist Eyes*, 182–83.

presuppose the many voices who have pointed out the toxicity that seeps from the theology of atonement.[10] To glorify the atonement "is to glorify suffering and to render their [black women] exploitation sacred. To do so is to glorify the sin of defilement."[11] Progressive male theologians as well as feminist, womanist, and Latina theologians decry the valorization of suffering.

Just as in Julian of Norwich's parable of the Lord and Servant, we are most hurt by our sense of alienation and fear.[12] The Beloved is right there, filled with love. But the condition of the ditch is such that the servant cannot see the lord. He thinks that the fall has separated him from the lord when in fact it has only hidden the divine love that is always flowing toward him. Because of the ditch, he cannot see that his actual relationship is one of love and redemption. He experiences only alienation and anger.

The doctrine of atonement reinforces the power of suffering to make us feel alienated, worthless, and alone. It creates an entire theology representing the perspective of the servant in the ditch. It conspires with suffering to hide Mother Christ so we do not see how near our Beloved is to us and how sweetly we are cherished. Our deep affliction expresses itself in every cruelty and indifference, in every injustice elevated to social or religious necessity, in every act unworthy of God-bearers. The logic of atonement exacerbates these debilitating, poisonous illusions: not only are we evil but we are also despised. In the doctrine of atonement, our amnesia in which we have forgotten ourselves and our Beloved is elevated to dogmatics.

At the same time, we might appreciate ways in which the logic of atonement genuinely speaks to a psychological predicament. I do not believe it is true that God is angry or that humanity is hopelessly, hideously defaced by sin, or that a tortured body somehow rectifies this situation. But perhaps this teaching is a way of bringing a healing word to spiritual pathology. Speaking the language of delusion, atonement also carries the news that one is loved. In the film *Lars and the Real Girl*, Lars suffers the delusion that his life-size doll is his girlfriend. The people in his community, relatives, neighbors, and coworkers conspire in this pretense and ultimately enable him to abandon his imaginary girlfriend in favor of a real one. Perhaps the idea of atonement, as well as serving to justify suffering and uphold patriarchal power structures, also speaks to the delusions

---

10. Many versions of this criticism exist; I will list only a few by way of example: Rita Nakashima Brock, *Journeys by Heart: A Christology of Erotic Power*; Brock and Rebecca Ann Parker, *Saving Paradise: How Christianity Traded Love of This World for Crucifixion and Empire*; Adams, *Christ and Horrors*; Delores S. Williams, *Sisters in the Wilderness: The Challenge of Womanist God-Talk*; Darby Ray, *Deceiving the Devil: Atonement, Abuse, and Ransom*. Feminists and womanists were not the first to deplore the idea of atonement. In a long history of countervoices, we find examples such as Schleiermacher, who considers it a manifestation of sin in *Christian Faith*, §§ 101 and 109; and Edward Farley, *Divine Empathy*, chap. 18.

11. Delores Williams, *Sisters in the Wilderness*, 167. Williams does not distinguish between theologies of atonement and other possible meanings of the cross. She instead emphasizes the importance of Jesus' ministry of word, touch, and prayer.

12. Julian of Norwich, *Showings*, chap. 51 (p. 267).

of guilt and punishment in ways that bring news of a gracious love. We might cling to this imaginary love until we are strong enough to accept the reality of an infinite tenderness that had never let us go. But it is important to remember that it is unnecessary to imagine that the cross has anything to do with satisfactions or substitutions, with divine rage or punishment. These are merely bad dreams troubling restless sleepers.

"NOT BY VIOLENT MEANS"

Substitutionary atonement became very influential but it was not the first or only way Christians symbolized the meaning of the passion. Many early Christians, including Irenaeus, having been close witnesses to some of the most sadistic outrages of Roman tyranny, refused to image God as merely a more potent emperor. The ethical or spiritual contrast between early Christians and Rome had in part to do with fundamentally opposed views about power and violence. Irenaeus had reason to feel the full horror of imperial terror and knew better than to fantasize about a deity whose own terror and might would simply reverse the winners and losers of history. But how does one imagine a power dedicated to conferring upon humanity the blessings of salvation that is entirely different from the power that controls history? Irenaeus knew the destructiveness of tyranny, symbolized by Satan, realized in history by Rome. His beloved teacher had been martyred and his community in Lyon had been savaged by an unbelievably violent unleashing of torture against Christians.

His dilemma—the difficulty we all face—is to imagine how to interrupt this kind of power. Tyranny terrorizes. It does not play by rules. It is ruthless, baffling, and intent on victory at any price. How does anything compete with that? For Irenaeus, the incarnation interrupts tyranny not only by defeating it but by deploying a counterpower, a counterstrategy. If one defeats the enemy by using the very means that make him an enemy, one has become (rather than overcome) the enemy. Someone like Irenaeus can help us imagine the passion as a paradigmatic expression of this renunciation of the methods of terror. The images through which Christians imagined the meaning of the passion are highly symbolic, even mythological. The meaning of the passion cannot be expressed directly, in the precise concepts of Hegelian philosophy. But wandering around in this symbolic universe is a way of conceiving of the power displayed on the cross.

The first problem, as many early Christians saw it, was that Satan had taken possession of the human race and God wanted to free us. There is a basic amorality at the root of the divine desire: there is no reason why God should want to free us since we had in effect gone over to the dark side more or less of our own free will. According to the reasoning of law and morality, we got what we deserved. The distinctive character of divine goodness is displayed in the desire to violate these decent, reasonable rules by liberating us.

A second problem was that God cannot simply deploy superior force, Rambo-like, to spring us free. God's hands are tied: God cannot invade history with Archangel Michael at the lead to defeat Satan and his evil minions. This warrior god would simply be a more powerful Satan. It is not that God has an angelic army but decides not to use it. It is rather that if God had an angelic army to send against his enemy he would not be God. This would be the universe where mighty cosmic tyrants fought one another, Zeus versus Prometheus. This apotheosis of violence and might is precisely the spiritual world that early Christians rejected.

There is a moral order here in which evil receives evil in return: the law of karma, symbolized by Satan's right to sinful humanity. God cannot magically change the rules of the game like a dictator for life and suddenly say some people are free and others are in jail. But this just-deserts morality, however reasonable, does not express the radical nature of divine love. God is powerless to restrain God's love, so even though human beings must be liberated the moral order cannot be overturned by force. The process of freeing humanity is a somewhat delicate one because we are in a sense legitimate slaves of evil. God, therefore,

> gave Himself as a redemption for those who had been led into captivity. And since the apostasy [Satan] tyrannized over us unjustly, and, though we were by nature the property of the omnipotent God, alienated us contrary to nature, rendering us its own disciples, the Word of God, powerful in all things, and not defective with regard to His own justice, did righteously turn against that apostasy, and redeem from it His own property, *not by violent means*, as the apostasy had obtained dominion over us at the beginning, when it insatiably snatched away what was not its own, but by means of persuasion, as became a God of counsel, *who does not use violent means to obtain what he desires.*[13]

For Irenaeus, tyranny is the primary mark of evil. This tyranny is insatiable, achieving dominion unjustly and enslaving those who do not by nature belong to it. This portrait of satanic evil is at the same time a portrait of Rome, which enslaves and brutalizes people in violation of their deeper nature as bearers of the divine image and yet in accord with Roman law. The power of evil, in Satan or in Rome, is insatiable and cruel—creating its own laws. By contrast, God is omnipotent but is less of a rule follower. God plays with the law and, against all (ordinary) reason, eschews violence to obtain what he desires. God does not tyrannize even over Satan but joins Godself with the victims of tyranny. God is something of a trickster. God is clever about bending the rules to get what God wants and generous enough to put Godself on the line to work God's game.

This theme is echoed by Gregory of Nyssa, who also identifies evil with tyranny: "the love of rule, the primary and fundamental cause of propension to the

---

13. Irenaeus, *Against Heresies* 5.1.1.

bad and the mother, so to speak, of all the wickedness that follows."[14] In a lengthy account of how and why God ransoms us from our enslavement to evil, Gregory emphasizes that both the desire to free us and the method for doing so reflect the distinctive quality of divine goodness: "As good, then, the Deity entertains pity for fallen [humanity]; as wise He is not ignorant of the means for [humanity's] recovery; while a just decision must also form part of that wisdom; for no one would ascribe that genuine justice to the absence of wisdom."[15] Gregory likens our condition to a person of noble birth who bartered away his freedom. The slave legally belongs to the master, and it would be unjust to violently free the slave. God abhors slavery but must acknowledge its legality.

The method of liberation must accomplish the desired end but do so non-violently: "It is the not exercising any arbitrary sway over him who has us in his power, nor, by tearing us away by a violent exercise of force from his hold."[16] He describes in eloquent detail the power of Jesus to heal, restore the dead to life, absolve the damned, feed the hungry, and so on.[17] But these miracles are little compared to the incarnation itself. The power of Divinity is especially revealed in "the Gospel mystery, where that Power conjoined with Love is more especially exhibited. In the first place, then, that the omnipotence of the Divine nature should have had strength to descend to the humiliation of humanity, furnishes a clearer proof of that omnipotence than even the greatness and supernatural character of the miracles. . . . His descent to the humility of man is a kind of superabundant exercise of power."[18] This is a completely countercultural view of power. It is not when Jesus works miracles that Divinity is most characteristically revealed but when Divinity becomes embodied in humanity, weaving together the unique goodness of divine love and wisdom with the humiliated human form. This, not in the great tyrants of history, is where power is definitively displayed.

These ancient texts, like contemporary feminist and queer ones, eschew violence as a name of divine power. They eschew also the slavery and degradation that seem inherent in the human condition. They reject a legality that would prop up or justify the suffering of humanity, however supposedly well deserved. The universe these ancient writers inhabit is one in which slavery is a constant threat and tyranny knows no constraints. But it is one infiltrated by another, paradoxically impotent and omnipotent reality in which compassion, wisdom, and love conspire to disarm tyranny and free those in a bondage that seemed beyond repair.

---

14. Gregory of Nyssa, *Great Catechism* 23 (p. 493). Darby Ray provides a very fine reflection on these ancient texts in the context of feminist and liberation theology in *Deceiving the Devil*, 122–24.

15. Gregory of Nyssa, *Great Catechism* 21 (p. 492).

16. Ibid., 22 (p. 492).

17. Ibid., 23 (pp. 493–94).

18. Ibid., 24 (p. 494).

"FOR IN HIM IS FOUND NO WRATH"[19]

The Divine Mother, apophatically hidden in darkness and light, does not substitute her child for sinful humanity. By knitting divinity to tortured humanity, she abolishes the bondage to guilt that suffering creates. She does so by using innocence and impotence to defeat evil. She disarms the connection between guilt and suffering and at the same time reveals her adamant rejection of tyranny, slavery, and violence. In the cross we see who we are and who she is. When we see an innocent man on the cross, we are invited to recognize that there is no logical or necessary connection between guilt and suffering. Even the eternally sinless Christ suffers the torments of hell. So much more should we, enchained to our mortality, expect to find ourselves in situations of suffering and affliction. But suffering is in itself innocent. It is simply suffering.

Suffering becomes more toxic when it is shot through with feelings of stain, shame, and humiliation. Suffering has the power to denude us of our humanity and our dignity. It destroys us as spiritual beings. It makes us aware that we are nothing. But when we see Christ on the cross we receive a sign that this link we have made between suffering and shame is an illusion. Our sense that if we suffer we must deserve punishment is challenged. As Schleiermacher argues, the cross represents the forgiveness of sins *in the sense that* through it the "consciousness of deserving punishment" disappears.[20] The experience of suffering as a sign that we deserve punishment is pierced when we enter into "vital fellowship" with Christ, in whom there was no connection between suffering and punishment. The habit of mind that tempts us to despise the unfortunate is confounded when we see the icon of innocent suffering on the cross. Forgiveness in this sense remains a kind of miracle. It is not simply cognitive assent to a theological doctrine. It unlocks a deep spiritual habit in which affliction and just deserts have become soldered together.

In persons and communities that have experienced afflictive suffering, this habit can be so deep that it seems irredeemable. For many gay, lesbian, and transgendered people the stain of self-loathing cannot be washed out even if we leave the church. At some level, many victims of rape or violence feel their suffering is justified by their unworthiness. Racist or sexist images too often become metabolized as if they were true. The unworthiness is multilayered: it arises out of the strange dynamics of suffering itself: suffering makes us feel guilty. Our sense of disgust compels us, like an evil tyrant, to act in depraved and humiliating ways. Self-hatred is reinforced by theologies of sin and atone-

---

19. Julian of Norwich, *Showings*, chap. 49 (p. 265).

20. Schleiermacher, *Christian Faith*, §101.2 (p. 433). Schleiermacher is unusual, to say the least, in identifying this association of suffering and guilt as a primary form of sin that is broken by the passion of Christ. But he finds support for his position in his close readings of the New Testament, citing, for example, Romans 8:1 ("There is therefore no condemnation for those who are in Christ Jesus").

ment that drug us with images of an angry and hateful god, a divine father who beats or rapes or impoverishes us, enslaves or imprisons us, and demands we praise him for his justice. Our sense of unworthiness is intensified yet again by church moral teachings that denigrate sexuality or collude with violence and oppression. The very place we should be able to go to be reminded of our precious beauty is likely to humiliate us even more. In these situations the balm of gospel compassion is displaced by harsh social teachings and demeaning theology.

Unseating the "consciousness of deserving punishment" is aided by things like a feminist critique of atonement theology. But the problem is not primarily cognitive; it is existential and spiritual. It requires the inbreaking of a power sufficient to "put off the old man and put on the new." For Schleiermacher this kind of forgiveness effects a death of the former personality. That is, the identity shaped by stain and degradation dies. Self-identity is reformed and arises as a new way of experiencing one's personhood.[21] Forgiveness in this sense is not an extrinsic juridical act that reconciles individuals to a righteous Divinity. It is the re-creation of the living principle of personhood so that the self-loathing that had blocked a full and healthy God-consciousness withers. In its place is the equanimity and compassion that perfumes off those who are alive to a sense of divine worth. For Schleiermacher, this is the primary significance of the cross. It is the vocation of the church to mediate this power to its community.

It is because the cross accomplishes salvation, not extrinsically but experientially, that we say that it was Divinity itself that suffered in Jesus' passion. In a sense, it was necessary to create the doctrine of the Trinity in order to express this. It does not make sense to say that the apophatic mystery of Beyond Being suffers. Suffering requires bodies, nerve endings, a psyche, a spirit. None of these things can be attributed to the Erotic Abyss in any meaningful way. On the other hand, we experience in the cross the healing, compassionate love so powerful that it breaks the chains of evil. This potency witnesses to the fullness of divine presence. Christians have attended to this quandary by saying that Christ is the intersection between humanity and Divinity through which suffering passes into the Godhead and healing passes back to humanity. Beyond Being does not suffer but divine power is drawn into suffering.

In Christ we see the fullness of Divinity in human form. This means that Jesus experienced bodily sensations, pain, even agony. He experienced the emotional battering of loneliness, betrayal, and humiliation. As a hinge between humanity and Divinity, the cross displays the full paroxysm of suffering inflected by Divinity. Divinity did not prevent Jesus from undergoing the full force of afflictive suffering, neither did it save him from the terror of imperial power. But in imagining that these things occurred to the incarnate Divinity, Christians are

---

21. Schleiermacher, *Christian Faith*, §101.2 (p. 433).

also saying that these things did not have the power to sabotage the unity with Divinity that constituted the foundation of his being. If suffering testifies to the humanity of Jesus, the persistence of the divine light on the cross testifies to the incarnation. In seeing and feeling this, we are given to understand that the divine light in us is not destroyed by suffering or sin. Like the servant in the ditch, we experience God-forsakenness, but the passion brings us the news that we are not forsaken. Suffering tells us we are unredeemable. The passion tells us that we are saved and that we always were and always will be.

This impermeability of the Divine to destruction by suffering invites us into a paradox. The most destructive aspect of suffering is its ability to destroy the spiritual beauty of human beings: to defraud us of hope and life, to destroy in us a capacity for empathy, to make faith turn to dust. It is sometimes possible to endure suffering with a kind of stoicism, but stoicism cannot face down the afflictions that occur on this blasted heath where humanity has been cast. Our unmaking goes all the way down.

Marilyn McCord Adams gives the example of the "psychic wasteland of Holocaust survivors surrounded by new families, professional success and personal luxury. Despite the strength of their survival instinct and their own resourceful ingenuity, the concentration camps had crippled their capacity for making meaningful connections with other people, had violated their sense of personal worth too deeply for ordinary created goods to reverse the trauma of their lives. Their horror-participation had thus stumped their efforts to make positive sense of their lives, because none of the many and impressive things they could conceive of and carry out added up."[22] Affliction destroyed the present in the camps and the future when the camps no longer existed.

Adams continues her appalling litany of the randomness of horrendous evil: "a moment's inattention behind the wheel can turn a star athlete into a paraplegic, a brilliant mathematician into a brain-damaged vegetable." She notes that perpetration of horrors reflects in part a psychic incapacity to cognize the suffering caused: "seventeen-year-old male soldiers lack the empathetic capacity to experience anything like enough to match the mother's anguish as her baby is bounced on sharp bayonets." She presses us to acknowledge the casual and universal perpetration of suffering by every member of the human race: "few individuals would deliberately starve a child into mental retardation. But this happens even in the United States, because of the economic and social systems we collectively allow to persist and from which most of us profit."[23] If we cannot imagine the passion entering into these places of total desolation and utter depravity, then we cannot imagine that humanity has a Savior adequate to its needs.

---

22. Adams, *Christ and Horrors*, 46–47. Adams is a rare theologian who insists Christology must be conceived primarily in terms of the ability of God to defeat the horrors of soul-destroying suffering.
23. Ibid., 35–36.

THE MOST BEAUTIFUL FACE IN THE WORLD[24]

Suffering causes and reflects God-forsakenness. If we are to understand that "we do not have a high priest who is unable to sympathize with our weaknesses, but we have one who in every respect has been tested as we are" (Hebrews 4:15), then we must imagine the impossible paradox of Divinity entering into the condition of God-forsakenness. Or put another way, if the cross is to save us then even God-forsakenness cannot dissolve the unity between humanity and Divinity. Indeed, since this is the place of deepest destruction and woundedness, it is precisely here that Wisdom must descend. As Athanasius and other early Christians put it, What is not assumed is not saved.

Paradoxically, mysteriously, even the cry of dereliction, the human experience of abandonment, did not sever the human nature of Jesus from Divinity. We understand that Jesus suffered innocently, "without sin," but also as a condemned criminal. The crucifixion makes him proximate to the innocence of suffering and the wasteland of a criminal's despair at the same time. The persistence of Divinity on the cross is not stoicism. The extreme vulnerability of human being to destitution and unmaking enters into the Godhead. He enters hell with us. In the midnight of the heart when faith is lost and when nothing but bitter blackness remains, when suffering has unmade who we were and who we might have become, when nothing is left upon which we might rebuild our psyche, our community, or our hope, here too we find traces that the Beloved has preceded us.

Paradoxically, mysteriously, to taste the nearness of the Beloved here would release us, but such tasting is precisely what is not available in hell. Carved on the wall of our inner heart we read the pitiless words: abandon hope all ye who enter here. But next to these words carved in stone is a lamp, a set of matches. We can light it at any time. However long the bitterness gnaws at us, if it follows us into death itself, the lamp remains, the matches remain. We gradually see in the hopeless dark the outline of a face. Like our own it is a face contorted by the ugliness of what we have done and what we have suffered. We realize there is in our destitution a fellow prisoner, as ugly and hopeless as ourselves. Yet "to the Almighty nothing is impossible, nor is anything beyond the reach of cure by its Maker," even if it requires "the lapse of infinite and immeasurable ages."[25] A time will come when we will recognize the face of our companion as "the fairest of heaven."[26] This face, fairest Lord Jesus, is our own. Christ has born this

24. Julian of Norwich describes the beauty of Christ's face on the cross: "Many marvelled how it could be the case that he imprinted this image with his blessed face, which is the fairest of heaven, the flower of earth and the fruit of the virgin's womb. Then how could this image be so discoloured and so far from beauty? . . . But truly I dare to say—and we ought to believe—that there was never so beautiful a man as he, until the time when his lovely complexion was changed by labour and grief, suffering and dying" (*Showings*, 194–95).

25. Origen, *On First Principles* 3.6.5, 6 (p. 251).

26. Julian of Norwich, *Showings*, 194.

face beyond suffering and humiliation into the land of utter despair and hellish destitution that we may recognize ourselves, our pitiable suffering and our luminous beauty. The cry of dereliction of the Incarnate One on the cross inflames history by enacting the deep truth that there is nowhere we could go on earth or in the heavens above the earth or in the deep under the earth and fail to find the Beloved. Nothing severs the unity between Divinity and humanity. Nothing obscures from the Beloved the radiance of our own spiritual beauty.

Joanne Terrell provides a glimpse of why the story of the passion is difficult but sweet. "I cannot gainsay the value of the Christian story for understanding and ordering the early phases of my life and vesting me with power to withstand the storms therein. Although I despised the melodrama captured in the depiction of Jesus crucified, I could not avoid contemplating the suffering God because here was a mirror to my world. Viewing his pathos, I saw my mother's and my own. Secretly I despised Jesus, my mother and myself because I resented what seemed to be needless suffering. And yet I loved us all because I willed it, and because somehow I knew I was loved. It was evident in the Providence I encountered in nature, whom I could not believe sanctioned the suffering brought on by evil human choices."[27] Not only suffering but the despising of our suffering self is brought into the passion and dwells at the intersection between humanity and Divinity.

When we suffer, we see in the gospel our suffering. Our story of suffering is the story of the Divine Eros. Our suffering passes into the womb of the Great Mother. Held there, its toxicity and shame are healed and we begin to remember who we are and that we bear the divine image and that tyranny cannot ever, under any circumstances, change that.

ON THE THIRD DAY: THE KINGDOM OF GOD IS AT HAND

The early Christians were right to perceive in the incarnation and passion of Christ a cosmic event. It is not inspirational like the death of Socrates or of Martin Luther King. It is not a witness to courage like Rosa Parks or a reminder of the cost of challenging injustice like the death of Harvey Milk. It enacts and reveals an eternal metaphysical truth. God is with us in nature, in our humanity, and in our most extreme afflictions and sins. The interruption of history by this truth is like honey from a rock (Psalm 81:16). It releases not only nourishment, but sweetness in what seemed barren. There is nowhere to go where the power of redeeming love cannot find us.

The incarnation did not, unhappily, transform the conditions of human history. It did not even really challenge "the ruler of this world" for possession

---

27. Joanne Marie Terrell, *Power in the Blood? The Cross in African American Experience*, 143.

of history. The Roman Empire continued its predations. The logic of empire infiltrated the church. Jesus did not save us from patriarchy or poverty any more than he saved himself from the cross. The de facto victory of the kingdom of might over the kingdom of God has permitted Christianity to clothe itself in a divine prerogative and to project the significance of the gospel onto a receding eschatology that degenerates into a heavenly reward for the faithful. The ministry of Jesus and his resurrection point to ways in which the honey of salvation remain mixed in the long torment of history. We live in this irritating mix of honey and rock, of wheat and tares, of injustice and transformation. Refusing to release the tension of this is a crucial practice of faith.

Delores Williams points out that we live in a world "where nuclear bombs, defilement of the earth, racism, sexism, dope and economic injustices attest to the presence and power of evil in the world. Perhaps not many people today can believe that evil and sin were overcome by Jesus' death on the cross. . . . Rather, it seems more intelligent and more scriptural to understand that redemption had to do with God, through Jesus, giving humankind new vision to see the resources for positive, abundant relational life. . . . The kingdom of God is a metaphor of hope God gives those attempting to right the relations between self and self, between self and others, between self and God."[28] Like other womanist theologians, she sees in resurrection a call that empowers us to live differently. "The resurrection of Jesus and the kingdom of God theme in Jesus' ministerial vision provide black women with the knowledge that God has, through Jesus, shown humankind how to live peacefully, productively and abundantly in relationship."[29]

Robert Goss also sees in the resurrection a sign of a divine opposition to everything that oppresses and diminishes life. As real as suffering is, in Christ God asserts that "human barbarism, political oppression, and dominating power relations will not triumph."[30] This theological claim helps us to discern where to look for Divinity in the ongoing crucifixion of the world. Through whatever atrocities the world continues to mete out, we have in Jesus a parable that enacts the Beloved's vindication and presence in every suffering. This presence is metaphysical in that it displays our divine origin and the way we are cherished by the Beloved. This presence also carries us into the social and political world to seek justice and to embody compassion in it. The rebirth that is accomplished by "forgiveness" overcomes our paralysis and creates a different way of being in community and creating community.

History and society are always in motion and open to endless novelty. We do not have a static set of rules in the gospel of resurrection but an invitation to walk the "Way of Life." In an earlier century, Christians were called upon to extend the logic of the gospel into the territory of slavery. The gospel made it

28. Delores Williams, *Sisters in the Wilderness*, 165–66.
29. Ibid., 167.
30. Goss, *Queering Jesus*, 160.

possible to recognize the abomination of chattel slavery. *As Christians* some were compelled to seek the abolition of slavery, even if Scripture could be cited to defend it. In our own time, as history continues to move, the gospel of Christ's ministry and resurrection gives us eyes to recognize other ways in which society and religion conspire to defraud human beings of their humanity. "The message of Easter is the hope of God's universal solidarity with the oppressed. The hope of resurrection is the faith that God's power will continue to transform the reality of oppression and death into life and freedom. God's Christ continues to be politically configured in solidarity with the poor and weak, the socially deviant and the outsider. . . . God will remember innocent gay and lesbian people, and Easter justice will triumph."[31] *As Christians* we are called to abolish laws, policies, and attitudes that debase sexual minorities, even if Scripture can be cited to defend these.

The resurrection of Jesus allows us to inhabit the confidence of Job that our redeemer lives and it is *that* face of Divinity we behold. The passion of the Beloved displays the intimacy of the Divine with our suffering. There is light in what we experience as the darkest hell. There is opposition to the prevarications and injustices of history. This is an indelible aspect of reality. Whether we find our way out of hell sooner or later, whether we do so through Christian faith or in some other way, the cross reveals that our Redeemer lives. Christ's incarnation in ministry, passion, and resurrection is a light that "shines in the darkness, and the darkness did not overcome it" (John 1:5). Whether any particular struggle is successful, whether our leaders are murdered or betrayed, the very act of demanding justice defrauds "the ruler of this world" of total mastery. It is a witness that another truth animates humanity and our history.

31. Ibid., 161.

Chapter 8

"The Least of These"

Salvation as Theosis

Truly I tell you, just as you did it to one of the least of these who are members of my family, you did it to me.

Matthew 25:40

I am what I am, says this Soul, by the grace of God. Therefore I am only that which God is in me, and not some other thing. And God is the same thing that He is in me, for nothing is nothing. Thus He is Who is. Therefore I am not, if I am, except what God is, and nothing is beyond God. I do not find anything but God, in whatever part I might find myself, for He is nothing except Himself.[1]

The passion saves us from the destructive effects of suffering, which pin us to deformed understandings of ourselves and others. But release from this tyranny is not the fullness of salvation that early Christians envisioned. Indeed, suffering was likely to increase upon their entrance into Christianity. Irenaeus, whose community was traumatized by persecution, held on to a vision of humanity as full of divine light and presence: "For the glory of God is a humanity fully alive."[2] This fullness of life is participation in the divine life. "For those who see the light are within the light and partake of its brilliancy; even so, those who see God are in God, and receive of His splendor."[3] This participation in the divine life is a paradoxical participation in the apophatic divine mystery that is manifest

---

1. Porete, *Mirror of Simple Souls*, chap. 70 (p. 145).
2. Irenaeus, *Against Heresies* 4.20.7.
3. Ibid., 4.20.5.

as fullness of life: "For as His greatness is past finding out, so also His goodness is beyond expression; by which having been seen, He bestows life upon those who see Him. It is not possible to live apart from life, and the means of life is found in fellowship with God; but fellowship with God is to know God, and to enjoy His goodness."[4] This knowledge is not only cognitive but, like biblical "knowing," deeply intimate. Early Christians, as well as Christians throughout the ages, have conceived salvation to be not only the overcoming of sin or guilt or suffering but as positive and joyous: "I have come to give you life and give it abundantly." Jesus, on the eve of his death, speaks of joy: "I will see you again, and your hearts will rejoice, and no one will take your joy from you" (John 16:22). The Savior not only redeems us from suffering but also invites us to share in the divine life that our joy may be full (John 16:24).

"I DO NOT FIND ANYTHING BUT GOD": INCARNATION AND DIVINIZATION

Incarnation represents the coming of Divinity to humanity even in our deepest suffering, but it also lights the path by which humanity returns to the Divine Eros. The old words for this are divinization or *theosis*. Divinization is a practice of love, an ecstatic fall into the Divine Emptiness. It cherishes high hopes for humanity but casts a critical eye toward political and religious institutions. It is a form of Christian faith that is as old as Christianity itself and that has survived in every age. Retrieval of this Christian ideal is especially important for those who find themselves on the margins of the church: those that the church despises because of their sexual practices, those that the church patronizes because of the supposed inferiority of women, those who are more radically inflamed with concern for social justice, those whose suffering have made the rhetoric of sin and forgiveness feel like yet another violence. Divinization remains unsatisfied with the milk of right belief and decent behavior. It craves the meat that liberates us from whatever is unworthy of our divine selves. It ignites a different desire: why not be flame?[5]

Christians as diverse as Athanasius, Angela of Foligno, and Friedrich Schleiermacher believe the incarnation is a cosmic event through which Divinity became human *so that* humanity could become divine. Christ may not provide exclusive access to our divine nature, but the incarnation is an invitation to awaken to our deepest desires and truest identity. The idea that humanity bears the divine image

---

4. Ibid.

5. An ancient desert ascetic, Abba Lot, asked Abba Joseph what else he should do beside fast, pray and meditate, keep clean thoughts. "Then the old man stood up and stretched out his hands toward heaven, and his fingers became like ten torches of flame. And he said: If you wish, you can become all flame" (*Desert Wisdom: Sayings from the Desert Fathers*, trans. Yushi Nomura, 92).

is not unique to Christianity. It is the common wisdom of the world's religions and is the more original goal of philosophy's love of wisdom.

Plotinus is among those who understood philosophy as the route to rediscover the unity of the soul with the Good. He recognized that we do not all experience ourselves as luminous with divine beauty, but believed that if we doubt that we are "one taste" with the Divine, it is because bad emotional and spiritual habits obscure our reality from us. Plotinus points out that the beauty of the divinized soul cannot be seen without training. He recommended a gradual adjustment to our primordial nature:

> first of all to look at beautiful ways of life: then at beautiful works, not those which the arts produce, but the works of men who have a name for goodness: then look at the souls of the people who produce the beautiful works. . . . If you do not yet see yourself beautiful, then, just as someone making a statue which has to be beautiful cuts away here and polishes there . . . till he has given his statue a beautiful face, so you too must cut away excess and straighten the crooked and clear the dark . . . till the divine glory of virtue shines out on you. . . . If you have become this, and see it, and are at home with yourself in purity . . . then you have become sight; you can trust yourself then; you have already ascended and need no one to show you. . . . This alone is the eye that sees the great beauty. . . . You must first become all godlike and all beautiful if you intend to see God and beauty.[6]

Plotinus's point that it is only by being Godlike that one sees God is echoed centuries later by Marguerite Porete: "The Soul does not see herself. . . . Nor does she see God. . . . But God sees Himself in her by His divine Majesty, who clarifies this Soul with Himself, so that she sees only that there is nothing except God Himself."[7] Many Protestant traditions are suspicious of divinization for various reasons. I would emphasize that it is not a kind of works righteousness that inflicts endless labors or that is necessary to merit salvation. It is the opposite of this. It is the desire to experience more fully what is already the case. It is the process of sanctification for those already justified.

Many early Christians shared the philosophical view that the truest human vocation is deification, the reunion of humanity and Divinity. This divinization is what many early Christians understood themselves to be called to when they became Christians. For them, Christianity was the philosophical life par excellence. These Christians believed that Christ surpassed all other teachers because he not only taught but embodied *theosis*. Christ accomplished the unity between Divinity and humanity in a more decisive way than Western history had seen before. What great sages such as Socrates or Moses taught and to a certain extent witnessed in their lives, Christ manifested as a fully realized human possibility.

---

6. Plotinus, *Ennead* I, 6.9. Cf. Meister Eckhart: "The eye with which I see God is the same with which God sees me. My eye and God's eye is one eye and one sight and one knowledge and one love" (Sermon IV, "True Hearing").

7. Porete, *Mirror of Simple Souls*, 193.

As both the teacher and the embodiment of divinization, Christ provided an accelerated access to our divine source.

For many early Christians, human beings are bearers of divine beauty, which an almighty Goodness would not allow to be lost. Because the incarnation is not only something to be believed but something to be imitated, Christian sages such as Valentinus, Clement, and Origen understood contemplation of God to be the center of the Christian life. Though Athanasius wanted it to be controlled by bishops, he shared the view that Christian life was dedicated to practices of divinization. Moral reformation and purification were preparatory practices that reflected and empowered the confidence that it is proper to human nature to "progress in the divinizing contemplation of God."[8] Practice was the heart of a Christian way of life.

Clement of Alexandria understood this divinization as intimate companionship with Christ, "sharing one house with us, sharing our deepest counsels, speaking within the soul, sitting at table within it, sharing the moral effort of our life."[9] Contemplative practices align us with the divine Logos and allow Christ to teach "us to conduct ourselves to resemble God and to accept the divine plan as the guiding principle of all our education."[10] This intimacy was accomplished through vigilant practice. The lifelong process of formation was understood by someone like Clement to be rigorous but nonviolent. Meticulous, exacting, loving: "It was a polishing away of those ugly excrescences that blurred the true, sharp form of the person. Clement had little doubt that this was an exacting process [yet] . . . Clement's most tender images of the Christian life were images of unswerving, eager activity set loose to love and serve the Lord."[11] Divinization practices are ordinary, everyday practices of moral discipline as well as dedication to the study of Scripture and to prayer and meditation.

In a later century, Gregory Palamas described this process in ecstatic terms: "when the saints contemplate this divine light within themselves, seeing it by the divinising communion of the Spirit, . . . then they behold the garment of their deification, their mind being glorified and filled by the grace of the Word, beautiful beyond measure in His splendour."[12] Contemplative practice reflects this impervious trust that human beings are capable of freedom from everything that impedes the fullness of life. But freedom requires practice; only gradually are the worries and attachments that create misery and inspire oppression neutralized.

The ideal of divinization reminds us of the great beauty that is bestowed on us through our creation. If we find it difficult to see this beauty in us, it is because

---

8. Brakke, *Athanasius*, 145. Aaron Stalnaker's book *Overcoming Our Evil: Human Nature and Spiritual Exercises in Xunzi and Augustine* is an excellent account of the often overlooked role of spiritual practice in Augustine's thought.

9. Clement of Alexandria, *Protrepticus* (*Exhortation to the Greeks*) 4 (59.2), quoted in Brown, *Body and Society*, 128.

10. Hadot, *Philosophy as a Way of Life*, 128.

11. Brown, *Body and Society*, 130.

12. Palamas, *Triads* 1.3.5 (p. 33).

we have developed spiritual habits, individually and collectively, that obscure it. There is a gap between who we really are and our actual experience. Practice is required to bridge the gap, to transform our deluded experience into reality. The incarnation lays out a pathway by which we can remember ourselves.

PRACTICES OF DIVINIZATION

Divinization emancipates us from the obscurations that deny us our true identity. Through increasing intimacy with the Divine we come to the state where we are "incapable of hurting or wounding anyone" and discover psychologically nonviolent ways of relating to those who harm us.[13] Divinization fosters an optimistic view of the human capacity to participate in divine *eros* and *caritas* for the world. But it is also serious about how difficult this reformation of desire is. In recovering the ideal of divinization for a contemporary theology of incarnation, it is important to remember that this difficulty is not supposed to be discouraging. To the contrary, by retaining some image of the luminosity within us, we can understand suffering not only as overt pain or oppression but as spiritual longing for our Beloved.

We are made to eat and drink Divinity, to see in the face of every being the loveliness of the Divine Eros, and to notice ungrounded beauty radiating from the earth itself. Naturally we find our lives restless and difficult when we are uprooted from the divine life. The ideal of divinization encourages us to be gentle with ourselves. It is the Divine in us that enables us to be compassionate to those parts of ourselves we might reject. Estrangement from our divine source may be with us a long time. It is a good practice to be kind rather than judgmental during the time of our exile.

Those parts of Christianity that emphasize the path of divinization make contemplative practice an important part of faith. Physical and emotional discipline is a normal part of life: dieting and exercise to lose weight, eating and not eating certain foods because they are good or bad for us, training for athletic events, caring for a sick child, learning conflict management, acquiring less environmentally destructive habits. But we tend not to associate discipline with spiritual transformation. Asceticism (from the Greek word *askesis*) uses the metaphor of athletic exercise to describe our participation in the process of divinization. Athletics allows us to accomplish a form of excellence and take joy in our physical being. The stronger and better trained the body is, the more fun things it can do. Divinization appropriates the metaphor of athletic training to describe practices that pursue another form of excellence and allow us to take joy in other parts of our being.

Richard Valantasis argues that asceticism "constitutes a human impulse.

---

13. Pelagius, "On the Christian Life" 6 (*Celtic Spirituality*, 386).

Something drives humans to dream of being a better person in a more healthy society and in a cosmos that holds promise of helping them to flourish. In dreaming of that wholesome state for self, society, and the cosmos, humans become dissatisfied with their lives, relationships, and connection to the cosmos. The dissatisfaction births the ascetical impulse."[14] He understands asceticism not simply as physical deprivations, but as the reconstruction of relations to self and others. This reconstruction defies cultural norms.

Pierre Hadot also emphasizes the importance of practice not primarily in the sense of deprivation but as "inner activities of the thought and will."[15] Moral discipline but also what we might call mindfulness or watching the mind reforms negative emotions and reduces mental obscurations. By means of spiritual exercises the individual "raises himself up to the life of the objective Spirit; that is to say, he re-places himself within the perspective of the Whole."[16] For Hadot, *askesis* refers to exercises that align one's entire being with its divine nature.

Various groups experimented with many kinds of practice, but they shared the view that the transformation of mind made possible a joyous and universal compassion that make the pleasures of the body rather dull by comparison. From the perspective of someone like Origen, for example, preoccupation with bodily pleasures allows one to settle for very little—perhaps like drinking beer and watching reruns of old situation comedies all day on a gorgeous, perfect spring day when a sun-dappled garden is singing outside with delight in its own beauty. Whether he was right, I cannot say, but I would suggest that the admonition to limit the domination of bodily pain and pleasure was not so much body-hating as it was spirit-loving. For Origen the body was a reflection of God's skillful means. God gave to each soul the body best suited for the "slow healing of the soul. It was only by pressing against the limitations imposed by a specific material environment that the spirit would learn to recover its earliest yearning to stretch beyond itself, to open itself, 'ever more fully and warmly' to the love of God."[17] Contemplative practice and *askesis* made it easier to cast off obstacles that blocked more deeply life-giving desires.

Origen uses the language of the senses to convey the desirability of these practices: intoxication, wine, kisses, perfume, beauty, pillow talk, sexual dalliance. The scene of lovemaking best conveys the genuine joy possible through contemplative practice. Preparation for this joy is analogous to the way a bride adorns herself in preparation for the delights of the bridal chamber. "Be you of one mind with the Bridegroom, like the Bride, and you will know that thoughts of this kind do inebriate and make the spirit glad. . . . Not with one perfume only does He come anointed, but with all. And if He will condescend to make my soul His Bride too and come to her, how fair must she then be to draw Him down

14. Valantasis, *The Making of the Self: Ancient and Modern Asceticism*, ix.
15. Hadot, *Philosophy as a Way of Life*, 128.
16. Ibid., 83.
17. Brown, *Body and Society*, 165.

from heaven to herself, to cause Him to come down to earth, that He may visit His beloved one! With what beauty must she be adorned, with what love must she burn that He may say to her the things which He said to the perfect Bride."[18] Origen understood the human spirit to be "destined for a moment of startling, unimaginable precise 'knowledge' of Christ, of which the subtle 'knowledge' of a partner gained through physical love was but a blurred and—so Origen was convinced—a distracting and inapposite echo."[19] Not many reading this book are likely to want to embrace Origen's own chastity, but he does invite us to consider what physical, psychological, and spiritual practices might awaken our own spiritual senses.

PRACTICES OF PRAYER AND COMPASSION

When ascetical practices were confined behind the walls of monasteries, integration of asceticism and ordinary family life and of contemplation and activism tended to fray. The incarnation as a sign of the glorious possibilities of human embodiment often gave way to more negative assessments of bodily desires. The story of Macrina, told by her adoring brother, Gregory of Nyssa, illustrates the genius of this young woman as she experimented with a way of life that brought together egalitarian ideals of community, acts of compassion, and dedication to practices of divinization. She did not leave her family but cared for it, gradually drawing her mother and brothers toward a distinctive vision of what Christian life could look like.[20]

As a young, extremely wealthy girl, Macrina was promised to a young man in marriage. When he died before the wedding, she insisted on taking on the status of a widow and refused to be married to anyone else. She trained herself in philosophy, excelling to the point that Gregory of Nyssa identified her as the smart one in a family that included two bishops. She devoted herself to contemplative practices. When the older brother, Basil (later "the Great"), came home from school, she scolded him for his intellectual arrogance and sent him into monastic training. When her father died, she cared for her mother and ran the estate. More provocatively, she took up the practice of making bread with the slaves.

She eventually moved her mother and other members of the household to a community of ascetic women who gathered around her. She advised this community as well as the men's community, run by her brother, across the river. The women chanted psalms, studied Scripture and philosophy, slept on the floor, ate modestly, tended to the sick, succored the poor, aided victims of famine, bought young girls destined for the sex trade, and provided a place of retreat and spiritual

18. Origen, *Song of Songs,* 271–72.
19. Brown, *Body and Society,* 173.
20. Gregory of Nyssa tells Macrina's story in two works: *Life of Macrina* and *The Soul and the Resurrection.*

guidance for laypeople. Macrina's community was egalitarian, open to both the extremely wealthy and to freed slaves. It was dedicated to contemplative practices and compassionate care for anyone who needed it. Gregory describes Macrina's death as a parallel to the death of Socrates told in Plato's *Phaedo*. The dying sage embodies courage and detachment as she teaches her grieving disciples about mortality and resurrection.

Susanna Elm describes Macrina as "a 'manly virgin' . . . She gave away her property, but did not impoverish her community; she was a figure of authority, but not a part of the hierarchy."[21] Excluded from education and the clergy, contemplative practices gave to her an astonishing freedom. Her story remains intriguing because it is a witness to the charisma generated by practices of divinization: compassion, contemplation, study, simplicity, community. As a young woman she managed to fend off the fate proper to her as a medium of wealth transfer. She initiated the monastic career of her brother, who would later be given credit for inventing Eastern monasticism. She exercised remarkable authority in her household and later in the community of fellow practitioners. She healed the sick, freed slaves, and gave counsel to people regardless of their class. At the same time, she took up a practice that would have been demeaning to even its lowliest member: she made bread with her own hands in the company of slaves. Practices of divinization are indifferent to access to social power. Deprived of formal education and excluded from civil and religious authority, Macrina provides an example of human being at full stretch.[22]

In an interview, a conservative Christian rejected the idea that there was no hell: if this were true, why would anyone go to church?[23] Divinization suggests another motivation to follow the Incarnate One. Attachment to the fate of the ego does not express the great beauty of the divine image and its yearning for the Beloved. In his commentary on the Song of Songs, Origen describes a spiritual eros driven by desire rather than fear: "And the soul is moved by heavenly love and longing when, having clearly beheld the beauty and the fairness of the Word of God, it falls deeply in love with His loveliness and receives from the Word Himself a certain dart and wound of love. . . . If, then, a [person] can so extend his [or her] thinking as to ponder and consider the beauty and grace of all the things that have been created in the Word, the very charm of them will so smite him [or her], the grandeur of their brightness will so pierce him [or her] as with a chosen dart—as says the prophet—that he

21. Elm, *Virgins of God*, 223.

22. Over the centuries the authority of figures such as Macrina deteriorated. Elm suggests the tenuousness of the authority Macrina exercised. Legal and doctrinal struggles "directly affected the ways in which women could henceforth realize their ascetic ideals: they would act no longer in concert with their 'brothers in Christ,' and would be less and less involved in charitable works and direct doctrinal conflicts—or so it appears. . . . It is doubtful that all forms of [women's] communal ascetic life, despite the impression generated by our 'orthodox' sources, disappeared entirely" (ibid.).

23. This American Life podcast, "Heretic," http://www.thisamericanlife.org/radio-archives/episode/304/heretics. Originally aired 12/16/05.

[or she] will suffer from the dart Himself a saving wound, and will be kindled with the blessed fire of His love."[24] The dart of love makes us long for the Beloved and also to be charmed by the beauty of the Beloved spread so carelessly throughout the world.

CHRIST ALL IN ALL

Christ is our Savior. But for what are we saved? From the womb of eternity Wisdom bodies forth in creation, an eternal and simultaneous descent and ascent that clothes in time the uncreated truth of incarnation. The incarnation enacts the indissoluble unity between humanity and Divinity—not only in a moment in a barn in Bethlehem but as an ultimate truth about humanity itself. Wisdom descends into a body, carries Divinity into suffering, death, and hell, and ascends again, shining like the sun. The cleavage between humanity and Divinity is folded into the heart of the Trinity. Eternity breaks its fast and eats the cosmos, all the way to hell, and takes it back into itself more deeply than ever. These events unfold in linear time: creation, incarnation, passion, resurrection, ascent. They cycle through liturgical time, a candlelit path that processes through ordinary time: Advent, Christmas, Ash Wednesday, Holy Thursday, Good Friday, Easter Sunday, Pentecost. They wind through history as repetitions and analogies: chattel slaves tell the story of the exodus. Moses returns in Harriet Tubman and Martin Luther King. A South African prison becomes for Allan Boesak a palimpsest of Patmos, and he knows that apartheid, like Rome, is destined to perish. Wisdom eternally falls backward into undifferentiated unity in the Erotic Abyss while ceaselessly emptying herself of imageless perfection so that a beginning can be made—in time, in space, in a cosmos, among human beings. The pulsing of the Divine Eros erupts in the dark beauty of exploding stars and in the tiniest pearl that troubles an anonymous oyster at the bottom of the sea. As on the deep breath of a yogini, the cosmos is exhaled from nothingness and inhaled back into the heart of the Trinity. Our Savior, so tenderly represented in the Pietà and in Rembrandt's *Holy Family*, so familiar to us in our songs and petitions, returns to heaven, where Christ is again God from God, Light from Light, entrained with light as a Divinity should be. Yet do we not long for the nearness of our "courteous" Savior (as Julian would say)?

The humanity and divinity of Christ mirror our own humanity and divinity. Passion defeats the tyranny of suffering, if not suffering itself. Incarnation elevates us to the sweetness of our divine source. Marguerite Porete reflects on the relationship between passion and incarnation. She sees in the passion a revelation of such enormous love it inflames our hearts beyond measure. "It is a greater thing to inflame our hearts in love for you, in pondering only one of the benefits

24. Origen, *Song of Songs*, 29–30.

you have accomplished for our sake, than it would be if the whole world, heaven, and earth were engulfed in fire in order to destroy one body."[25] Such is the power of the humanity of Christ: the love inflamed by this generosity in the heart of a single person is greater than the destruction of the entire earth and heaven by fire. When we ponder this event we see its efficacy igniting all of heaven and earth. Nothing remains exterior to the burning desire of the Divine Eros. It is inconceivable that anything should fall outside the potency of Love. This does not require us to believe that all are saved by faith in Jesus but rather that in the passion we are privileged to witness the good news of universal salvation.

Yet Porete continues. "Then I pondered who it is who will ascend to heaven. And Truth told me that no one will ascend there except the one who descended from there, that is, the Son of God Himself. . . . And thus Jesus Christ Himself said that my brother, my sister, and my mother is the one who does the will of God."[26] The passion saves us from the overwhelmingly destructive power of suffering. But healing—salvation—is transparency to Goodness. The passion witnesses to our release from bondage and to our restoration to divine love. There is nothing to be anxious about. There is no condemnation to fear. But this is for Porete not the best we can hope for. Of course we are reconciled with God—our alienation was only ever on our side. The passion calms our fears and encourages us in the midst of travails. But we can also hope to reconnect with the spotless mirror that is our own soul and that is illuminated by the nondual Good.

> I have said that I will love Him.
> I lie, for I am not.
> It is He alone who loves me:
> He is, and I am not.
> . . . .
> And by this am I impregnated.
> This is the divine seed and Loyal Love.[27]

Porete opens our mind to the deeper truth that suffering and attachment alike can obscure. The incarnate body of Christ is lit with the same eternal luminosity that lights our bodies. Only Christ ascends to heaven. Our humanity craves the relief of heaven, where tears are wiped away; we are consoled with this promise. But our divinity craves only God. If God were hell, our divinity would crave hell. If God were nothingness our divinity would crave nothingness. But this is to speak oxymoronically. It means only that divinity loves the Divine, not as something alien and other, seated far away, "way beyond the blue," but near at hand, closer even than one's own heart or breath. We crave Divinity not only to console us in our misery but because we are light and we long for radiance. Only

---

25. Porete, *Mirror of Simple Souls*, 208–9.
26. Ibid., 209.
27. Ibid., 201.

Christ ascends to heaven because there is nothing but Christ. Light from light, a light that burns within us too.

There is another image, perhaps more familiar, of our redeemed state in which "God is all in all." Matthew 25 invites us to the task of recognizing Christ in one another. Indeed, this parable of the Sheep and Goats demands it of us as the single criterion that separates those destined for heaven from those of us who remain loyal to hell. Prisoners, starving and naked people, the unclean, and the sick do not make for consoling images of Divinity. It is hard to be comforted by a faith that locates divine presence and power, not exclusively but characteristically, among the destitute. To undertake this practice of trying to recognize Christ in the faces around us moves us far beyond charitable giving or platitudes about compassion.

This kind of seeing requires nothing less than a restructuring of our psyche and our spirit. It awakens to the Divine that is waiting for us. "God has nowhere to place His goodness, if He places it not in me, nor has He a dwelling place which might be appropriate for Him . . . if it is not in me."[28] Julian echoes this point, describing God as a man in rags sitting on the ground in the wilderness: "But his sitting on the ground, barren and waste, signifies this: He made man's soul to be his own city and his dwelling place, which is the most pleasing to him of all his works. And when man had fallen into sorrow and pain, he was not wholly proper to serve in that noble office, and therefore our kind Father did not wish to prepare any other place, but sat upon the ground, awaiting . . . until the time when by his grace his beloved Son had brought back his city into its noble place of beauty by his hard labour."[29] When we look with the divine eyes within us, we see that everyone is Christ and then our Beloved sits again on her throne in our heart.

It is unfortunate that Jesus is so often understood as an object of belief. This is probably not an accident. It is not hard to believe things, even impossible and absurd things. But to accept the relentless failure of one's practice of the Way of Life is discouraging. It is yet another absurdity of Christianity to set the bar both impossibly, inhumanly high and at the same time to simply lay the bar on the ground. To see every other being as Christ is impossible. If this is what is required of us, surely we are all goats, sent away and cursed "into the eternal fire prepared for the devil and his angels" (Matthew 25:41).

But Christ insists that his burden is light, his yoke easy. We see the bar as so high "only the most finely tuned spiritual athlete could ever hope to clear it. . . . Then, just as we have become exhausted and spent in our futile efforts to rise above our own limitations, the saving event happens. Compassion steps out and places the bar flat on the ground! Approaching the bar, bewildered by the unthinkable simplicity of the task, we trip over it and fall headlong into God,

28. Ibid., 186.
29. Julian of Norwich, *Showings*, 272.

waiting to reveal to us that we are precious in our frailty and strangely whole in the midst of our fragmentation."[30] This light burden is not a demand that we achieve anything. But as we glimpse the presence of Christ in every face we manifest the Divine in us. The longing to know this, to see this way, is the Divine in us. The wish to long for this even when we do not is Holy Wisdom wishing in the depths of our heart.

We are saved not only for forgiveness, not only for survival. We are saved to see and bear the face of Christ in the world. Nicholas of Cusa's meditation on the face of Christ is one way to consider this interplay of Divinity and humanity as a metaphysical reality and as a daily practice.

THE TRUTH OF ALL FACES

In chapter 5 (p. 131) I described the practice of the all-seeing icon Nicholas of Cusa recommended to his brothers. We return to this practice as a way of contemplating Christ in every face.

After describing this meditation on the visible image of Christ's face in the "all seeing" icon, Nicholas describes the invisible face, the true face that is the face of faces, and he becomes "numb with astonishment." He sees that Christ's face is the "truth of all faces . . . Thus, O Lord, I comprehend that your face precedes every formable face, that it is the exemplar and truth of all faces and that all are images of your face. . . . Every face, therefore, which can behold your face, sees nothing that is other or different from itself, because it sees there its own truth."[31] In meditating on the true face of Christ we encounter our own true face. This face is not different from the face we see in the mirror: it is not a male face, a Palestinian face. It is my face, with the scar down the forehead and the pale gray eyes. This face, this scarred and pale face, is the face of Christ, in which there is nothing other or different from my face but precisely by being my own face it is the face of Christ.

Whatever direction we turn, north, south, east, west, we encounter the face of Christ looking at us, preoccupied with only us. And we know that every other person, whichever direction they move, knows Christ is preoccupied only with them. As we continue to meditate on this exterior face, this icon, we see that this image is not only looking at us but is our own face. Our face shines with the light of this face that is gazing on us so lovingly. Great compassion begins here. It is rooted in this "facial vision" in which the loving gaze of Christ's face becomes indistinguishable from our own face and from every other face. Compassion flows through each face; we are Christ for one another, giving and receiving the tender mercies of Christ.

We recognize the divinity of human faces by ascending to the apophatic

---

30. James Finley, *Christian Meditation*, 282.
31. Nicholas of Cusa, "On the Vision of God" 6.18 (in *Selected Spiritual Writings*, 242).

face of Christ. The face of all faces is the Divine Emptiness: empty of form yet flickering in the form of every face. "Whoever, therefore, undertakes to see your [Christ's] face, so long as one conceives anything, is far removed from your face. For every concept of a face is less than your face, O Lord. And every beauty that can be conceived is less than the beauty of your face. . . . [Your face] is thus absolute beauty itself, which is the form that gives being to every form of beauty. O immeasurably lovely Face, your beauty is such that all things to which are granted to behold it are not sufficient to admire it."[32] The beauty of Christ's face is invisible to the sensible eye because it is not sensible; it has nothing that could be envisioned or thought or imagined. Vision has become a metaphor for seeing that is empty of every sensible or intellectual content.

Desire compels us to seek the absolute beauty of Christ's face. Such seeking abandons light, leaping beyond light into darkness. The denser this darkness, this cloud, the nearer we are coming to uncreated light. "I see, O Lord, that it is only in this way that the inaccessible light, the beauty, and the splendor of your face can be approached without veil."[33] This seeing of what has no sensible form is entirely in the dark.

This ascent into imageless darkness wherein we see the unveiled beauty of Christ's face is what makes it possible for us to recognize Christ in human faces. Ascent to uncreated darkness helps to break the hold of the ego-mind so that we can encounter the unveiled beauty glimmering in the mobile beauty and suffering of every face. The Divine Emptiness is the simultaneity of otherness and sameness. It is always the same as itself, divine, in such a way that it can be manifest only through endless variety. Or rather, itself empty of otherness and sameness it is displayed in the infinite diversity of actual faces.[34]

This fecund emptiness allows each being to see itself in this face of all faces. A young person would see this face as youthful, an older person would see this face withered with age. "In the same manner, if a lion were to attribute a face to you, it would judge it only as a lion's face; if an ox, as an ox's; if an eagle, as an eagle's."[35] The beauty shrouded in imageless dark illuminates every face; yet beings know this only through the contraction of their way of knowing. Young persons naturally conceive of the divine face like their own, just as oxen and eagles do.

We could add: Christians see this face only as Christian, Muslims as Muslim, Sikhs as Sikh. The Divine Emptiness is the truth of every face "in such a way that it is the exemplar of all and of each individually and is so most perfectly the exemplar of each as if it were the exemplar of no other."[36] Christ plays in every face, "lovely in limbs not his."[37] But our vision and our awareness are human.

---

32. Ibid., 6.20 (p. 244).
33. Ibid., 6.21 (p. 245).
34. Ibid., 6.18 (p. 242).
35. Ibid., 6.19 (p. 244).
36. Ibid., 6.20 (p. 244).
37. This is from Gerard Manley Hopkins's poem, "As Kingfishers Catch Fire": "For Christ plays

We see the face of Christ not only in each individual form but *as if* that form were the only one that represented Christ. Christ's face shines in the uniqueness of our own face as if this very face alone, in its peculiarities, bore Christ's own face. We see the eyes of the icon on us wherever we are *as if* those eyes were only on us, devoted exclusively to us. In seeing and knowing this, we can enter into a deeper awareness of the cherishing nearness of Christ—not in a generic sense but for us, precisely as we are. Our ordinary ego-consciousness interprets this to mean that we alone—my people, my religion—bear Christ.

Every being bears the face of Christ as if it were her or his alone, even lions and oxen and eagles. Nicholas provides a way of thinking about a familiar element of Christian worship. We imagine Christ in our own image. Renaissance Mary and Jesus looked very like Italian people. The Jesus hanging in white, middle-class Sunday school classes of the sixties looked familiar to the blue-eyed children who made sock puppets and memorized Bible verses under his mild-mannered gaze. Centuries after Nicholas sent his icon to his brothers, Monica Coleman wrote: "Jesus Christ can be seen as a black woman. . . . The Savior may be a teenager, a person living with disability, a lesbian woman."[38] Kelly Brown Douglas echoes this point: "'Here's the thing,' Christ is inside of my grandmother and other Black women and men as they fight for life and wholeness."[39]

Robert Goss extends this in the direction of homophobic violence: "Three assailants harassed two gay men outside a gay bar and slashed the bar doorman's throat with a knife when he attempted to stop the harassment. Leaving the bar, they approached a gay man waiting for a bus and said to him, 'We're going to teach you faggots a lesson.' They stabbed the victim, puncturing his lung. . . . The Queer Christ is politically identified with all queers—people who have suffered the murders, assaults, hate crime activities, police abuse, ecclesial exclusion, denial of ordination and the blessing of same-sex unions, harassment, discrimination, HIV-related violence, defamation, and denial of civil rights protections."[40]

Marcella Althaus-Reid describes a postcard advertising Absolut vodka she sent to friends that pictured "Christ amongst drunkards sleeping in the street of a city." They wrote back to her, not realizing it was an advertisement, "People feel touched and there has been a conversation in our prayer group of several who, looking at this picture of Christ, felt that for the first time, Christ was speaking to their condition."[41] Edwina Sandys constructed a beautiful, haunting, four-foot-tall sculpture of Christa, a female Christ on the cross, which has been deeply refreshing for some and yet quite controversial.[42] We might add to these crucified faces the

---

in ten thousand places, lovely in limbs, lovely in eyes not his, to the Father through the features of men's faces."

38. Coleman, *Making a Way Out of No Way*, 170.
39. Douglas, *Black Christ*, 117.
40. Goss, *Queer Christ*, 168, quoting *Anti-Gay/Lesbian Violence, Victimization, and Defamation in 1990* (Washington, DC: NGLTFPI, 1991), 13.
41. Althaus-Reid, *Queer God*, 149.
42. One can see this image by Googling Edwina Sandys/Christa.

joyous faces of women dancing together, the tender faces of lesbian mothers with their children, the peaceful faces of friends: two old men, friends of many years, quietly paddling their canoe through the woods. Mechthild of Magdeburg envisions Christ himself insisting on this identification: "Those who know and love the nobility of my liberty cannot bear to love me only for my own sake. They must also love me in creatures. Thus do I remain what is most close to them in their souls."[43]

"Facial vision" is a practice that can begin with what is easy and familiar. Renaissance paintings are unproblematic for participants in the cultures from which these images emerge. Even Gerard Manley Hopkins's beautiful poem (quoted above) is uplifting without being too challenging. But sock puppets and Bible verses did not necessarily prepare us to envision Christ as an African American lesbian teenager, a naked woman on the cross, a bar-hopping victim of homophobic violence, or flopped down among Argentinian drunkards. Judging in a "human way," we contract the divine image to our own. But in describing the imageless face concealed in silence and darkness, Nicholas describes a way to break the hold of our ordinary ego-mind. The practice with which he began his essay first showed to the monks how intimately the loving gaze of Christ remained on them. But the second step of the practice showed this intimacy present to every person, every being—we might add, and every tradition. For Nicholas silent, imageless awareness and awareness of the radical universality of Christ's mercy are utterly interdependent. "For with you having mercy is no different than seeing. Your mercy follows after every person as long as one lives and wherever one may go, just as your gaze never abandons anyone."[44] Facial vision is a way of describing the radical interconnectedness of all things. When we recognize that we share a common humanity and a common divinity, suffering anywhere becomes our own suffering. "It is not just a 'logical consequence' that I become involved in the suffering of others, but an *unavoidable inner exigency*; it is my own pain!"[45] By cherishing the uniqueness of one's own Christ-face we are compelled to cherish the Christ-face of every being: it is our own face.

SPIRITUALITY OF VISION AND OF JUSTICE

The interpenetration of divinity and humanity in human faces is both metaphysics and practice. It is metaphysics in the sense that it has to do with real or authentic nature: the presence of Christ in human faces is the deep truth of human being. It is the ultimate truth, disguised in ordinary persons and events and in the ugliness of persecution and affliction. Yet this ultimate truth is existentially obscure. We do not see divinity in one another. We often do not even recognize one another's humanity. It is a miracle of awakening to perceive the uncreated

43. Mechthild of Magdeburg, *Flowing Light of the Godhead* 6.4 (p. 231).
44. Nicholas of Cusa, "On the Vision of God" 5.15 (*Selected Spiritual Writings*, 242).
45. Habito, *Living Zen, Loving God*, 98–99.

light of Christ in human faces. This vision is therefore a practice as well as a metaphysics. The contemplative movement from visible to invisible light is a practice that deepens the capacity to perceive the invisible in the visible. Seeking the "face of faces" breaks up the attachments of the ego. The blaze of Divinity burns away the ego-mind and frees us for truer vision. In this way response to suffering becomes an "*unavoidable inner exigency.*"

This "facial vision" suggests a practice through which this exigency can be deepened. By soldering together human and divine faces, the poignancy and obscenity of suffering and oppression might become more existentially obvious. Our fantasies about other people are mitigated. The disgust aroused by white people or gay people or drunkards is eroded. It is natural when the veil begins to lift that we not only see the truth of one another but that we become more concerned about the conditions that produce suffering. This is where contemplative practice intersects with a spirituality of social justice.

Emilie Townes points out the way in which spirituality too centered on love can ignore justice. "Justice is that notion that each of us has worth, that each of us has the right to have that worth recognized and respected. In short, justice lets us know that we owe one another respect and the right to our dignity as children of God. If we deny justice, we are telling those who go without that they are worthless. Perhaps that is one of the reasons that the Rodney King and Malice Green beatings cut so deep into our souls. For it didn't seem to matter to some folks that no one in creation deserves to [be] beaten like that."[46] Townes's "spirituality of social witness" reminds us how necessary it is to link these dimensions of reality. This face, fairest in heaven, is displayed in brown faces and female faces, in gay bars and dance halls, in crucifixions and celebrations. If we cannot recognize this fairest face, we will also find it difficult to recognize that no one in creation deserves to be beaten the way Rodney King was.

Mindfulness of this face calls us to attend to the social structures that produce racism and poverty, which obscure the beauty of same-sex desire and disenchant the natural world. Nicholas of Cusa describes the link between practice and theology that helps to soften the ego boundaries that sustain our indifference and hostility. Emilie Townes, Monica Coleman, Marcella Althaus-Reid, and Robert Goss tie our consciousness down to the concrete social, political, and religious realms where suffering is produced and justified.

TRUE GOD FROM TRUE GOD

The ancient creeds of the church attempted to preserve the life-giving truth at the center of the experience of salvation: in a way that must infinitely befuddle conceptual awareness, apophatic mystery embodies itself as Wisdom, creates a

---

46. Townes, *In a Blaze of Glory*, 143.

world, and becomes incarnate as a human being. This saving truth displays the enchantment of nature and the beauty of humanity: "All things came into being through him" (John 1:3). Because of this proximity of the Divine to creation only one thing is required of us, that we love one another (John 15:12). Although they have not always been used in this way, the creeds invite us to the practice of radical compassion because absolutely everything and everyone that exists is created through Wisdom and beloved of the Beloved. This truth is a perennial invitation to lay down our egocentric fears and loathing, anger and cravings and become naked to the Divinity constantly playing around us and within us. If we were raised in a conservative and homophobic church, we are invited to see Christ's face in the radical fairies and the Sisters of Perpetual Indulgence. If we are consumed with a passion for social justice, we might begin to appreciate centering prayer groups that had seemed hopelessly irrelevant. In gratitude for and devotion to the incarnation, we are carried outside Christianity itself to delight in the puzzling wisdom of other traditions and the glorious, amoral beauty of the natural world.

We tend to split up the gospel so it becomes only a message of social liberation, a call to moral purity, or a pathway to contemplative union. We constrain it to whatever patch of time and space in which we find ourselves. When we feel bound by these attachments, we might return to Nicholas's practice and witness the gaze of Christ moving in opposite directions even while remaining unfailingly on us. "And while the brother observes how this gaze deserts no one, he will see that it takes diligent care of each, just as if it cared only for the one on whom its gaze seems to rest and for no other, and to such an extent that the one whom it regards cannot conceive that it should care for another. He will also see that it has the same very diligent concern for the least creature as for the greatest, and for the whole universe."[47] The love songs we sing to Christ, to Christa, to the Absolut Christ, and to the black Christ become a harmony. Jesus, the man with the long chain on, is also God from God. She can "mother you, comfort you, and get you through" because she is Light from Light. Through whatever door we enter, we find ourselves over the wall of reason to the garden where opposites coincide. This is paradise—where unitive contemplation perfumes justice, where a womanist passion for justice is a spirituality of compassion and endurance, where the marred and tortured face of Christ is "the fairest of heaven."[48]

47. Nicholas of Cusa, "On the Vision of God" Preface 4 (Selected Spiritual Writings, 236–37).
48. This image of the coincidence of opposites is drawn from Nicholas of Cusa: "This is the wall of paradise, and it is there in paradise you reside. The wall's gate is guarded by the highest spirit of reason, and unless it is overpowered, the way in will not lie open. Thus, it is on the other side of the coincidence of contradictories that you will be able to be seen and nowhere on this side. If, therefore, impossibility is necessity in your sight, O Lord, there is nothing which your sight does not see" ("On the Vision of God" 9.37 [Selected Spiritual Writings, 252]).

Chapter 9

"This Will Be a Sign"
Gospel Christianity

This will be a sign for you: you will find a child wrapped in bands of cloth and lying in a manger.

Luke 2:12

If Jesus of Nazareth, the Christ of God, cannot be an option for gays and lesbians, then he cannot be an option. . . . *If the risen Christ cannot identify with gay and lesbian people, then the gospel announces no good news and the reign of God presents no real alternative to the "reign of sin." Only an* ekklesia *that follows Jesus of Nazareth in (re)marking its flesh as "queer" as his own may set a welcome table in the household of God.*[1]

The Queer God may then show us God's excluded face, which is the face of a non-docile God, a God who is a stranger at the gates of our loving and economic order.[2]

The Divine Eros incarnates as Wisdom, bodying forth in cosmos, earth, and humanity. Christians know small pieces of this story from our root story: the gospel of Jesus Christ. We have looked at the incarnation in Wisdom, in creation, in a Savior, in humanity. In this chapter we spend time with the gospel narratives. If Scripture arises in any sense out of the inspiration of the Holy Spirit, it is not by providing us with accurate facts. What use are facts to salvation—correct or otherwise? Confusing correct information with the

1. Copeland, *Enfleshing Freedom,* 78.
2. Althaus-Reid, *Queer God,* 153.

power of salvation is an odd conflation of scientific method and religious ideals. Scripture breathes with the Holy Spirit by continuing to speak to humanity across time and space in ways that are healing and wise. Reading Scripture is divine reading, *lectio divina*. It is closer to reading poetry than a textbook. It continually feeds us by the sheer beauty of its images, which continually open out onto new meanings.

Historians labor to get nearer to the tantalizing presence of Jesus in the early decades of the first century. They learn more about the details of life under Roman rule, about the economic impact of empire, about the use of violence to pacify a restless colony. I find the general argument made by a number of recent New Testament scholars that Jesus lived in solidarity with those who were particularly harmed by Roman rule compelling. But it is difficult to know where history and theology part ways. That Jesus was a real person seems evident. But the Gospels were all written not only decades after his death but after the utter devastation of the Jewish war against Rome. This disastrous war saw the Temple reduced to rubble, Jerusalem necklaced by thousands of crosses, women and children dragged to slavery. Temple Judaism as it had survived for hundreds of years was destroyed forever. It was left to Pharisaic Jews and early Christians to create from these ashes twin religions that would survive in Diaspora. That these two faiths continue to survive is astonishing testimony to their wisdom and courage in the midst of horrific suffering. This trauma reverberates through all of the Gospels and gives decisive, if retroactive, shape to the way the story of Jesus was finally told. It imports back into the narratives about Jesus a split between Jewish and Christian communities that was not even really foreshadowed during his lifetime.

I have no way of knowing much about the "historical Jesus" or the communities that produced the narratives of his life. It is perhaps a modern obsession to wish for such information. I do find in the four Gospels an almost unearthly beauty. Unearthly, but entirely of this world: a vision of how to live in this world, in the midst of difficulty and injustice, on the edge of despair and impotent to challenge the kingdom of might. Part of what is so compelling about the Gospels is that they view their story to be one of good news. Considering the conditions under which Jesus lived and the stories told, that seems hard to credit. But it is good news to glimpse something of Jesus' strange, crazy, wild idea of a divine kingdom that is right here in our midst. It is a kingdom that rivals "the world" for our allegiance but does not propose we leave one kingdom for another. Here, now, in the midst of economic injustice and war and oppression, in the midst of whatever work we do and families we raise, we are asked to live as if insane—as if love rather than patronage governed our lives, as if people were not rich, poor, slave, master, patriarch, wife, adulteress, or tax collector but simply bearers of the divine image: beautiful, suffering perhaps, but beautiful and wonderful. This chapter is a meditation on the strange vision Wisdom's Messiah left behind.

LAID IN A MANGER

When Constantine gained his military victory under the sign of the cross, the conflation of the kingdom of God and the empire of Caesar became an essential part of Christian history and theology. But it is possible to retrieve a contrary meaning to this image of a divine kingdom. In particular, the Gospels seem to offer an alternative reality in which power, community, authority, law, and morality are all reconstituted.

Much recent scholarship has unearthed the Roman context behind the Christian symbols. We are familiar with the messianic images: Son of God, Son of the Most High, Savior, Lord, bringer of peace, whose kingdom was to have no end, and whose coming was *euangelion* (good news, gospel). But these are all bizarre riffs on the original possessor of these attributes, Caesar Augustus.[3] The early Christians took up these names that adorned the Roman emperor and applied them to a shabby victim of the Empire's justice. The appropriation of these particular titles to interpret Jesus' ministry is an outrageous mockery of the glory and might of Rome.

According to early Christians who told the story, when Wisdom chose to incarnate herself, she arrayed herself in clothing that befitted her own glory and might. And so we find her born to an unwed mother amid the most destitute of a brutalized and impoverished community, denuded of beauty and comfort. Incarnate Wisdom retains the titles of a glorious emperor but gives them an astonishing and even horrifying meaning. The Savior of the world is not the military victor whose legions bring peace through victory and terror but a baby wrapped in swaddling clothes. The Prince of Peace does not come with a sword but with healing hands. The very term *basileia tou theou* is ironic: an empire of God in which beggars, peasants, and women are the dignitaries. Patronage, the lifeblood of privilege, is dismantled by table fellowship indifferent to social and religious boundaries. The symbol of kingly birth is a manger; of royal entrance, an ass; of enthronement, a cross and thorns. The wealth of this kingdom lies not in gold or land but in the beauty of flowers and birds. Witnesses to its victory are terrified women. A weeping woman is its first apostle. These symbols announce a ludicrous empire in which every expression of power is turned upside down.

A particularly absurd symbol of power in this divine empire is a manger. The initial appearance of the incarnation in a manger is so troubling that, except for children's Christmas pageants, it is relegated to theological oblivion. We do not wear tiny mangers around our necks or set them on our walls. We do not walk, consoled, under a manger as it radiates its message from the top of church towers: image of feeding, of natality, novelty, the joy of a birth, the proximity of a nursing woman; image, too, of vulnerability, poverty, exile. The great revelation

---

3. Crossan, *God and Empire*, 28; Richard Horsley, *Liberation of Christmas*.

of Christianity, the ever-fresh and astonishing good news, is that the Divine Eros has set her tent up among our tents: Emmanuel, dwelling with us. But in casting around for the right set pieces to symbolize this yoking of Divinity to humanity, we find a backwater country and a backwater town. Bethlehem, "who are one of the little clans of Judah" (Micah 5:2), seems like the right place. And in this little shepherds' town outside Jerusalem there is still no place for incarnate Wisdom. There is no habitation among humans that can receive incarnate Wisdom, and so Mary delivers in a barn. A barn, a shelter for animals; it has no furniture, no place to put a baby. So the baby is swaddled, as babies are, and placed there in a manger: a place for food. This entrance of Wisdom into our world in human form reminds us that her power and glory are outside every human place, not only the glorious palaces of Rome and Herod but outside even the relative protection of a peasant's home.

The family into which Wisdom is born is not one we would honor as upholding traditional family values. A presumably very young woman (women were betrothed around puberty, perhaps twelve or thirteen) has become pregnant. It is crucial to Christian theology that this anomaly be cast in the grandest and most miraculous terms: it is neither her betrothed nor an unnamed, possibly violent man who is the father of Jesus, but the Holy Spirit, the Most High. However fabulous Mary later became, spread across acres of cathedrals as Theotokos, the narrative of Jesus' birth gives us a story of a young teenager who is unmarried and pregnant, taken under the protection of her divinely guided fiancée. Wisdom is born outside the fragile safety of a happily married mother and father. She has entered this world in the precarious and curious form of an apparently illegitimate child, driven by Roman tax collectors from a native village and rushed out of Judea altogether to escape the savagery of Herod.

The birth narratives are certainly not historical, but they are symbols of an alternative universe of power. They also witness to the precariousness of Jesus' birth and the violence that surrounded it. Recent scholarship emphasizes the desolate context into which Jesus was born. Sepphoris, a few miles from Nazareth, was captured, burned, and its inhabitants massacred, raped, or enslaved. Emmaus, to which many fled, was likewise burned to the ground. Romans scoured the countryside for rebels and crucified some two thousand who were caught.[4] Some scholars speculate that the fatherless birth of Jesus was a result of this massive violence. "The archaeological evidence of the siege of Sepphoris confirms at least one event during which Roman soldiers combed through Mary's neighborhood and, following their standard procedure, raped whomever they could catch."[5]

That Jesus was born seems clear, but beyond that nothing certain can be known about his birth. Locating Jesus' birth in the context of Roman violence

---

4. Horsley, *Liberation of Christmas*, 31.
5. Marianne Sawicki, *Crossing Galilee: Architectures of Contact in the Occupied Land of Jesus*, 192.

is not historical but theological. It shows that the "preferential option for the poor" is extended not only to the economically destitute but to those who are particularly helpless to male violence and to the violent moral codes that make their sexuality so dangerous to them. Jane Schaberg spells out the range of possibilities available to a young girl who had been seduced or raped before marriage. That such a girl could be subject to death or humiliation or permanent notoriety reminds us of the high cost of sexual deviance to women—whether chosen or forced upon them.[6] The story of the incarnation continues in Galilee's hill country as its inhabitants suffer the ravages of history. The infancy stories allow us to see that the same logic that chooses little Bethlehem as a royal city and a manger for a crib also chooses an unwed young woman as Theotokos, God-bearer. Wisdom reaches out to "the outcast, endangered woman and child. God 'acts' in a radically new way, outside the patriarchal norm but within the natural event of a human conception. God 'acts' here not as a *deus ex machina* interrupting or bringing to an end the history of human betrayal and violence and subjugation, but as one who reaches into that history to name the messiah."[7]

The birth stories are guidelines for entering into the mystery of incarnation. They open the gospel with good news for women who drop their babies in refugee camps, by the side of the road, in strange towns, in public hospitals with or without insurance. These birth narratives are good news for women who hold their babies to their breasts, knowing that the world beyond the circle of their arms is indifferent to them. It is good news for outcasts from respectability and decency. Women are not stoned in the United States for adultery or rape, but they may join the statistics that make Georgia one of the worst states for low birth rate babies (and attendant death and disability) among African American women and the United States among the worst of developed nations for caring for young pregnant women.[8] Their story is woven into Mary's story, into Wisdom's story.[9]

The story of incarnation begins with Mary's youth and indecency, even if covered by an angel's announcement and the support of her betrothed. It should prepare us for a story that dislocates our spiritual and ethical moorings—as much now as two thousand years ago. The medieval contemplative Hadewijch identifies Mary's story as the decisive moment of salvation. Not prophets or kings, but the aperture of love that Mary opened created the possibility of incarnation:

---

6. Jane Schaberg, *The Illegitimacy of Jesus: A Feminist Theological Interpretation of the Infancy Narratives*, 42–62.

7. Ibid., 74.

8. Various sources provide these statistics and analysis, including Med Guru, February 3, 2010.

9. Horsley points out that Mary, like Deborah and Jael, is described as the most blessed of women. Her plight represents the plight of many women in Galilee, and yet she is commissioned as a deliverer, a prophet of the reversal of power that announces the empire of God (*Liberation of Christmas*, 89).

No matter what benefits God ever conferred on us,
There was no one who could
Understand veritable Love
Until Mary, in her flawlessness,
With deep humility,
Had received Love.
Love first was wild and then was tame;
Mary gave us for the Lion a Lamb.
She illuminated the darkness
That had been somber for long ages.[10]

Wisdom enters history, homeless and bereft of a traditional family and yet held by a young woman of enormous love and courage: Theotokos. In this way Wisdom is woven into history and humanity, beloved and yet an outsider whose arrival is heralded by angels and massacres. The confidence we enjoy knowing that God is in his heaven and all is right with the world is shattered. This birth does not seem to be good news for those who find comfort in kings and crowns as signs of divine approval. It portends badly for the consolations of a theodicy that perceives poverty, suffering, and shame as evidence of divine disfavor. Divine humanity, incarnate outside every human habitation, enthroned in an animal's feeding stall or at his mother's breast—what parable is this for power?

BLESSED ARE THE POOR

Contemporary scholars depict the Palestine in which Jesus wandered as one roiled by economic displacement: workers driven from land, kinship networks shattered by violence, fishermen who could no longer freely fish in the Sea of Galilee, communities crushed by taxes to Herod and Rome. He is presumed to be a peasant or a sort of wandering charismatic. But even by the modest standards of his community his entourage is unimpressive: bleeding women, the sick, the lame, lepers, sexually deviant women, half-crazed women, working women, fishing men, tax collectors. He wanders, not staying in one place long enough to sink in roots or build a community. He is impoverished but not ascetic.[11] He eats. He drinks. He is found dining comfortably in widows' huts and Pharisees' homes. Something of the distinctiveness of his divine kingdom emerges when we look at its citizenship.

Palestinian society, like most societies, was structured by social location, economic stratification, and dynamics of power. Some people commanded, oth-

---

10. Hadewijch, "To Learn Mary's Humility," in *Complete Works*, 208–9.
11. A picture of Jesus' context can be built up from many sources. The ones I have consulted include: Borg and Crossan, *First Christmas*; Rieger, *Christ and Empire*; Crossan, *God and Empire*; Horsley, *Liberation of Christmas*; Sawicki, *Crossing Galilee*; Schaberg, *Illegitimacy of Jesus*; Elizabeth Schüssler Fiorenza, *In Memory of Her*; Goss and West, eds., *Take Back the Word*; Mary Ann Tolbert, *Sowing the Gospel*; E. P. Sanders, *Historical Figure of Jesus*.

ers obeyed. Social, religious, and ethnic expectations governed who dined with whom. In any society, normal people have an immediate, preconscious grasp of how to respond to the various categories of people they encounter.[12] But these markers crucial to ordinary social interaction were apparently invisible to the incarnate Wisdom. This gave to his interactions a disturbing quality: he did not understand how he was supposed to treat people. He appeared to be wandering through an entirely different social world than the one he shared with other Galileans. His way of life seemed oblivious to social and religious assumptions. This was evident, for example, in the way he responded to "the poor."

Recent historical research locates Jesus' ministry among the poor, even the destitute, of Galilee. His rhetoric and his actions did not compete with Rome or Herod for political and economic control of Galilee, but they did challenge the obviousness or inevitability of imperial values.[13] John Dominic Crossan is among those who point out that Jesus' parables expressed this concern for the poor: he used images of weeds, children, impurity, women. In short, a kingdom of nobodies: "not of the Peasant or Artisan classes but of the Unclean, Degraded, Expendable classes."[14] Mary Ann Tolbert also notes that wealth is understood in the Gospel of Mark as an obstacle to participation in the kingdom. The "thorny ground" upon which the sower sows seeds is ground that could produce good fruit but that is too overgrown to do so. Mark identifies "the cares of the world, and the lure of wealth, and the desire for other things" (4:19) as obstacles to the kingdom.[15] It is painful for those of us who are not poor to realize how dedicated the Gospels, especially Luke, are to displaying the divine adoration of those who are ground down by socially constructed destitution.

Shawn Copeland identifies the message of Christianity as one opposed to the logic of domination: Jesus' "solidarity with the outcast and poor revealed God's preferential love."[16] Crossan echoes this point: "Jesus spent his time on and beside the lake because it was precisely and specifically by the shores of the Sea of Galilee that the radicality of Israel's God confronted the normalcy of Rome's civilization under Herod Antipas in the twenties of the first century."[17] Juan Luis Segundo interprets this preferential option for the poor to be the fundamental meaning of the gospel: "The kingdom itself cannot be preached indiscriminately as good news, as gospel. The kingdom is destined for certain groups. It is theirs. It belongs to them. Only for them will it be a cause for joy. And, according to

---

12. See Mary McClintock Fulkerson, *Places of Redemption: Theology for a Worldly Church,* which provides an unusual and ingenious analysis of the bodily way we respond to markers of race, gender, able-bodiedness, sexuality, class, work, and education.

13. Sawicki, *Crossing Galilee,* 173–74.

14. Crossan, *Historical Jesus,* 273; cf. Segundo, *Historical Jesus of the Synoptics,* 110–11; Sawicki, *Crossing Galilee,* 174.

15. Tolbert, *Sowing the Gospel,* 156.

16. Copeland, *Enfleshing Freedom,* 89.

17. Crossan, *God and Empire,* 122–23.

Jesus, the dividing line between joy and woe produced by the kingdom runs between the poor and the rich."[18]

This emphasis on Jesus' solidarity with the poor and otherwise marginalized persons challenges one of the most basic ways we structure our consciousness and societies. Middle-class people like myself rarely see poor people, unless we go out of our way to do so. We might be vaguely aware they exist, we might believe they deserve health care and decent education, and we perhaps vote in ways, however mediated, that might serve those ends. But even in the absence of any explicit theories that justify economic stratification, the poor tend not to exist for the nonpoor in any significant way. The gnaw of hunger, the anxiety when one's child is sick or injured, the desperation when lack of insurance or citizen papers make it impossible to seek a doctor, the ugliness of public housing, the uniqueness of each person's face and story are all vague shadows. The creative use of fashion, the importance of music, the threads of friendship and love that are present in impoverished communities are less real than a dream.

Jesus' presence among the poor is not a social program. It is in a sense more radical than that. For Jesus, the poor were persons who mattered. A woman with debilitating menstrual flow mattered to him. A hungry clutch of women with babies and children, men young and old, mattered to him. He saw them. They came into focus for him. When he could he healed them or fed them or told them stories. Simone Weil may have had this kind of attention in mind when she wrote: "The love of our neighbor in all its fullness simply means being able to say to him [or her]: 'What are you going through?' It is a recognition that the sufferer exists, not only as a unit in a collection, or a specimen from the social category labeled 'unfortunate,' but as a man [or woman], exactly like us, who was one day stamped with a special mark by affliction. For this reason it is enough, but it is indispensable, to know how to look at him [or her] in a certain way."[19] A passion for social justice may be built on this awareness, but Jesus does not give us a particular social program. His ethics is an optics. He sees persons, not social types. He sees in society's throwaways beings to cherish, enjoy, befriend.

It seems incontrovertible that Jesus' ministry included those who had been savaged by political, military, and economic upheaval. His good news was for those who had no other source of good news. Yet the effort to produce from Jesus' ministry a simple opposition between rich and poor misses the still more radical point: what is most obvious to us is invisible to him. He does not see social distinction. What is mostly invisible to us is what is most visible to him: we are all bearers of the divine image. But precisely in seeing this he manages to offend virtually everyone. Segundo and other liberation theologians can find a great deal to exemplify Jesus' preferential option for the poor. But would they not share the Galilean crowd's disgust when he goes home to dine with Zacchaeus

18. Segundo, *Historical Jesus of the Synoptics*, 90.
19. Simone Weil, "Reflections on the Right Use of School Studies with a View to the Love of God," in *Waiting for God*, 115.

(Luke 19:7)? Collecting taxes meant carrying out the rapacious, crushing policies of Rome and Herod through which their empires were built up, their outsized building projects were funded, the machinery of war was maintained, the legions fed, criminals punished, and the wealthy amused.[20] Debt and displacement decimated families during the first century. Jesus throws his lot in with those for whom taxes are a constant terror and yet he is friends of publicans (toll collectors) and tax collectors. He dines with them. There is at least one tax collector in his inner circle. He claims that tax collectors and prostitutes (not "the poor") will lead the way into the kingdom (Matthew 21:31–32).

The Pharisee is shocked that Jesus cannot "see" that the woman who touched him was a sinner (Luke 7:39). But lest we find ourselves pleased at his rejection of Pharisees and with them all Jews, we should notice that he is, after all, eating with them—he is friends with them. His disciples are shocked that he brazenly talks to a woman, also a sinner, at a public well (John 4:27). When he heals the madman in the country of the Gerasenes (or Gadarenes or Gergesenes), whose demons were legion, the neighbors beg him to leave (Mark 5:1–17). He tells stories that must be calculated to offend. In the verbal swordplay with a legal expert about how far love of neighbor should extend, he makes a hero of a despised Samaritan while religious leaders turn their backs—a troubling image for ministers and professors of religion. In a scene cited by Segundo, after exciting his audience with an inspired reading of Isaiah 61, Jesus enrages them with biblical stories that tell of foreigners who are the preferred recipients of divine favor (Luke 4:18–30). The Gospel of Mark concludes with the failure of every single disciple to understand or follow Jesus. Reading the newspapers most days, we can conclude that this failure has not diminished.

These things cannot help but outrage the sensibilities of people closest to him. People get so mad they want to throw him over a cliff or at least ask him to leave the neighborhood. Others want to create social and political strategies that would install the kingdom of God on earth. But it may be that simply remaining attentive to each being that crosses our path is more difficult than either. "The soul empties itself of all its own contents in order to receive into itself the being it is looking at, just as he is, in all his truth. . . . Should the occasion arise, [such a person] can one day make us better able to give someone in affliction exactly the help required to save him, at the supreme moment of his need."[21]

In trying to take in Jesus' "option for the poor," we might notice that it is not itself a social program. This does not mean that it would not affect how we inhabit our social and political systems. But being present to one another, including those whom might be tempted to ignore, is not only an economic policy. It is a kind of joyousness. Encountering someone, seeing their face, evokes

---

20. Palestine paid Rome about 12.5 percent of their crops. Rome responded to the failure or even delay in paying taxes with the same collective brutality with which it would respond to a rebellion. See Horsley, *Liberation of Christmas*, 35.

21. Weil, *Waiting for God*, 115.

compassion for their suffering. It generates an anguished and energetic desire to contribute to economic and social policies that are just and humane. But it is most immediately the joy of being fully present in the world with one another: sharing food, casually picking wheat as we walk through a field, noticing the beauty of flowers as we pass by.

IN MEMORY OF HER

Jesus' obtuseness about basic social mores is if anything more pronounced in his relationship with women. It is somewhat astonishing to realize that Jesus' entourage includes so many unattached women. In a patriarchal society like that of first-century Palestine, women were generally attached to husbands or fathers. But we find Jesus escorted and supported by women who are described as wives (Joanna, wife of Herod Antipas's chief of staff) and mothers (the mother of James and Joseph and the mother of the Zebedee boys) as well as women who do not belong to any man, such as Mary Magdalene and the sisters, Mary and Martha. These are not counted as among "the Twelve," but they seem to constitute an inner circle of friends.

It is an oddity that the male disciples are often portrayed as failing to understand Jesus. But this inner circle of women, named and unnamed, seem to understand Jesus quite well and to enjoy a particular intimacy with him. In extracanonical texts such as the *Gospel of Mary*, Jesus is shown giving teachings to Mary Magdalene to share with the other disciples. She is presented as someone who not only understands him but has the spiritual maturity to comfort the other disciples in their grief and encourage them to go out and preach the gospel of peace.[22] In Matthew 16 Jesus gives the keys of the kingdom to Peter, but according to John 4 it is an unnamed, promiscuous Samaritan woman who recognized him and gathered many to him based on her testimony. In Mark it was not Peter or any other male disciple who understood the significance of his death but another unnamed woman who anointed him for burial, over the protests of the disciples (14:8).

The women around Jesus seem not only to understand him, they enjoy an intimacy that is typical of only close friends. He defends them and revises his actions or ideas in conversation with them. Jesus supports Mary when she chooses to study with him among the men. He encourages Martha to lay down her caretaking role and join her. He bows to Mary and Martha's double-barreled scolding when he fails to come in time to save their brother. He accepts the rebuke of the Gentile woman whose daughter he hesitated to heal.

Jesus is not portrayed as a particularly good spokesperson for family values.

---

22. See Karen King's introduction to *Gospel of Mary* in *Nag Hammadi Library*, ed. Robinson, 523–24; as well as her translation and analysis of the text in *The Gospel of Mary of Magdala*.

For example, fathers exercised enormous power in this period. Peter Brown describes the right of a Roman father to decide whether a baby born in his house lived or was simply taken out with the refuse.[23] Nicola Denzey evokes the pervasiveness of patriarchal privilege less violently and yet with chilling succinctness: "a harmonious marriage . . . was one in which the husband was pleased."[24] By contrast, followers of the Way were to leave "the dead to bury their own dead." For Jesus it is not one's place in a patriarchal web but citizenship in the empire of God that creates relationship. His own mother, sisters, and brothers are those who do the will of God (Mark 3:35). Jesus defines "the kind of family suitable to this new age . . . Traditional roles, customary relationships, established laws no longer obtain; the sole criterion of the new age is to do the will of God."[25] This completely rearranges dynamics of power, relating people who have no natural connection while qualifying the patriarchal family's authority. New family values, a new way of life, a new community released women from subjection to men.

This liberation from patriarchal control allows women to follow Jesus, sit at his feet, and provide for him out of their own resources (Luke 8:1–3). Perhaps, paradoxically, his rejection of divorce is also a defense of women. In a culture where women could not initiate divorce, it was a legal fiction that allowed a man to leave his wife and children. In attacking the legitimacy of divorce, Jesus is protecting women from the "hardness of heart" that permitted them to be abandoned without cause. He underlines his sympathies by noting that such a divorce is an act of adultery against the wife. "It is for this reason that Jesus uses the dramatic term 'adultery' in so surprising a way. He thus brought sharply into focus the wife's honor. It is as much to be protected and respected as the husband's."[26]

Women, like "the poor," appear to be real people to Jesus. He seems indifferent to the sexual ethics that endanger them and resistant to domestic systems that oppress them. They are not ciphers of a patriarchal social system; they are not sexual temptations or threats. They are beloved fellow travelers. But he goes further: he grants to them not only friendship but authority. Each Gospel has a version of the women being commissioned to be apostles to the apostles. Thomas Hanks points out that the commissioning of the eleven at the end of Matthew's Gospel is often deployed as an excuse not to ordain women. But it might be read

---

23. Brown, *Body and Society*, 28. A chilling quotation indicating the cheapness of life and its dependence on the whims of men and their laws: my youngest daughter was left in just this way, but did manage to be collected and, eventually, find her way from a Chinese orphanage to our home.

24. Nicola Denzey, *The Bone Gatherers: The Lost Worlds of Early Christian Women*, 66.

25. Mary Ann Tolbert, *Sowing the Gospel*, 148. Cf. Horsley: "The true family is now constituted not by physical kinship or blood relationships but 'whoever does the will of God is my brother, and sister, and mother' (Mark 3:35). . . . Within the new, egalitarian familial community, moreover the followers of Jesus were to 'call no one father, for you have one father (and you are all siblings)' (Matt. 23:9)" (*Liberation of Christmas*, 87).

26. Crossan, *Historical Jesus*, 301.

to show that "Jesus is graciously inviting the cowardly 'losers' (the 'eleven') to join up with the courageous women, led by Mary of Magdala, who had already begun to proclaim the good news of his triumph over death."[27]

Matthew's narrative places the commissioning of the eleven after their reception of the news of the resurrection. Women had just joyously brought them the good news, having stood by Jesus through execution and death. After those harrowing days, they are the first to see Jesus, to hear him, embrace him, and receive from him instructions to go and tell the brothers in Galilee what has happened. To the ecclesiastically unsophisticated, that may sound like a commission to discipleship, apostleship, and leadership. It exemplifies the craziness of a kingdom in which wisdom and leadership are not restricted by social or religious codes. In his reconfiguration of family, in his dismissal of the right of leaders to dominate followers, the Jesus of the Gospels "will tear the hierarchical or patriarchal family in two along the axis of domination and subordination."[28] If this were ever taken seriously it would enact an entirely novel social world.

TAX COLLECTORS AND SINNERS

A more inclusive social world sounds attractive to many of us. But what of one where not only social but moral standards become virtually invisible? This may be more disorienting than it first appears.

In a number of scenes Jesus upholds and protects women who have a bad reputation: the woman at the well, the woman about to be stoned, the woman who washes his feet with her tears. He accepts a tax collector to be among his closest disciples. He consorts with Romans enough to heal the centurion's slave. He violates conventions dictating appropriate eating companions. He allows women, even unclean, bleeding women, to touch him. Some of these codes are ones we may not share and so they do not shock us. But they represent a rather appalling indifference to the structuring of social relationships by reasonable moral codes.

Queer readings of Scripture point out that Jesus is as indifferent to sexual deviance as he is to economic morality. Thomas Hanks speculates that the beloved slave of the centurion was his lover. Because Matthew links this story with a story in which someone unclean is healed, his "emphasis on the greatness and adequacy of the centurion's faith (8:10–13) reminds readers that Jesus came, not to break up loving consensual same-sex relations . . . but to heal and empower them. Sexual minorities, like everyone else, can experience authentic freedom through their faith in the Liberator God of the Exodus, incarnate in the

---

27. Hanks, "Matthew and Mary: Good News for Sex Workers," in *Take Back the Word*, ed. Goss and West, 188.
28. Crossan, *Historical Jesus*, 300.

poor carpenter from Nazareth."[29] Hanks also raises the question whether Matthew became a despised publican, "a notoriously dishonest profession in service of a hated empire and thus a traitor to the Jewish people," because he was kicked out of his home "for being an 'abomination' (gay) and thus had to enter the only profession open to him."[30] Without pinning too much on the historical accuracy of such speculation, these reconstructions are riffs on Jesus' indifference to sexual morality and his openness and love for all the transgressive people who crossed his path. Imagining Jesus' love for sexual minorities is not merely anachronistic fantasy; it is an extension of the logic of the kingdom into our own context.

The figure of Mary Magdalene participates in this work of opening the kingdom to those whom society despises. Feminists have, appropriately, decried her demotion from someone who received special teachings and authorization from Jesus to a prostitute. As my eldest daughter pointed out to me, when men want to disempower women, they immediately assail their sexuality. But queer hermeneutics recovers the tradition's characterization of Mary Magdalene as a sex worker, allowing her story to witness to Jesus' particular tenderness for sexually marginalized peoples.

Martín Hugo Córdova Quero is among those who point out the importance of Mary Magdalene for sexually persecuted persons. He describes the shock and gratitude of prostitutes when he defended the use of condoms to protect them from HIV/AIDS. Prostitutes did not imagine anyone in the church would care what happened to them. When the situation of "prostitutes, single mothers, GLBTTIQ folks, non-machista males" is interpreted in light of meditation with Mary Magdalene it is easier to refuse the hetero-patriarchal morality that condemns and degrades everyone on the wrong side of the right/wrong, good/bad divide.[31] The Argentinian church colludes with, even demands, the silencing and condemnation of people with nonconformist sexual preferences and of married women suffering from cruel husbands. It refuses to baptize children of single mothers or prostitutes. Quero insists that we need "a theology that stands up when people feel like outcasts not only from society but from Christianity. We need a theology not afraid of indecencies."[32] From Quero's point of view, Mary Magdalene symbolizes this compassionate impulse.

Mary Magdalene offers a reminder of the solidarity of Christ with every outcast, every person battered by oppressive religious morality. A queer reading of Mary Magdalene is oddly in tension with the feminist repatriation of her as a good, decent, female leader. Yet it can also be a "counter-icon" that helps disrupt assumptions about sexuality. She is a figure of liberation for outcasts and those "excluded by their gender or performances of sexuality." In these ways she opens

---

29. Hanks, "Matthew and Mary," 191–92.
30. Ibid., 186, 187.
31. Martín Hugo Córdova Quero, "The Prostitutes Also Go into the Kingdom of God: A Queer Reading of Mary of Magdala," in *Liberation Theology and Sexuality*, ed. Althaus-Reid, 98.
32. Ibid., 97, 98.

up an "encounter with the new life fully manifested in the risen Christ."[33] It is to be hoped that the spirit of this favorite friend of Jesus is wide enough to speak to this variety of experiences.

People who live out unconventional sexual identities can find in Mary of Magdala a sympathetic image: a person famous for her particular friendship and intimacy with Jesus who has been vilified for her presumed sexual deviance. But all women have bodies that make them particularly vulnerable, not only to sexual violence but to dangers associated with the natural consequences of heterosexual activities. The church's sexual ethics, which overemphasizes chastity at the expense of access to birth control and demonizes the tragic decision for abortion, only exacerbates this vulnerability. Elina Vuola highlights consequences of this religious morality in a battery of statistics. In part because of the Catholic Church's rejection of birth control, 529,000 women died in 2000 from pregnancy-related causes, 99 percent in developing countries, most of whom already had other children who were left motherless. Globally 78,000 women die from unsafe abortions, though many more go unreported. In Nicaragua 30 percent of maternal mortality is among adolescent girls, many of whom are victims of violence.[34] We could add to these statistics ones that highlight the consequences of "abstinence only" response to the spread of HIV/AIDS. The refusal to support the use of condoms to slow down the spread of HIV/AIDS is implicated in the terrible death toll that also leaves so many children orphans. Christian sexual morality can be deadly.

Mario Ribas is another Latin American theologian who recovers the spirit of Mary, mother of Jesus as a figure that challenges the violence of Christian sexual ethics. Countering her role as an upholder of female piety, Ribas finds Mary among women, sex workers, single mothers. Mary is discovered in "bars, cabarets, and brothels as well as in garages, displayed alongside naked women."[35] Women who gathered around Jesus enable us to consider sexual vulnerability outside the harsh morality too often associated with the church. People caught in impossible cross-currents of homophobic and domestic violence, poverty, dangerous births, abortion, and motherhood turn to these women. Mary, mother of God, does not come in the guise of an oppressive, submissive daughter of the church but as "a divine female figure, which sustains them, listens to them, is like them, but which also is able to transcend human experiences."[36] Like Jesus, the Marys burst out of the confines church authorities set for them and walk with power and love among those who need them most.

Jesus' amorality cherishes those on the wrong side of Christian sexual ethics. His own indifference to morality as a marker of humanity translates in our own

---

33. Ibid., 99, 100.

34. Elina Vuola, "Seriously Harmful for Your Health? Religion, Feminism, and Sexuality in Latin America," in *Liberation Theology and Sexuality*, ed. Althaus-Reid, 138.

35. Mario Ribas, "Liberating Mary, Liberating the Poor," in *Liberation Theology and Sexuality*, ed. Althaus-Reid, 126.

36. Vuola, "Seriously Harmful for Your Health?" 154.

time into an opportunity to extend compassion for victims of sexual denigration and to celebrate sexual differences as essential components of the gospel. But it does little to guide people toward the creation of healthy relationships. We can be harmed by oppressive morality but we can also be harmed by mutual objectification. It is all the more difficult to find our feet when sexuality has been vitiated by trauma or violence, objectification or shame. These experiences may make us accept bad treatment as if it were natural. For sexual minorities, desire is already off of the map of moral behavior. Desire is synonymous with perversity. In this situation, there remain few markers for healthy and life-giving sexual activity. Gratitude for the experiences of sexual freedom may make it difficult to identify what is emotionally harmful. The gospel does not seem to help us with this much. Jesus seems simply to encounter the person before him, unmoved by class or gender or decency. The only thing that seems to really irritate him is religious self-righteousness. We do not get guidelines for a sexual ethic any more than we get an economic program. But the ability to be present to ourselves and one another compassionately and nonjudgmentally may provide a context in which life-giving interpersonal, social, and political relationships would be more likely to emerge.

SERVANTS OF ALL

Jesus' teachings do not give us much direct guidance for constructing particular moral systems. He is neither Karl Marx nor the inspiration for *Humanae Vitae*. This glaring hole in Christian ethics is only made worse by his reconstruction of authority. His own band of followers seems disorganized, lacking clear hierarchies or divisions of power. When pressed to identify leaders and valorize its most important members, he gently chides them, contrasting the authority of Gentiles with this strange kingdom in which the greatest is the youngest, or the one who serves at the table, not the one who sits and eats (Luke 22:24–27). This itself is an odd way of putting it. It is not an image of powerful persons interpreting their authority as a service to others. It says that the ones who are now servants and slaves, the ones handing out dishes at a meal, are already the greatest of all. "Whoever wants to be first must be last of all and servant of all" (Mark 9:35).

One visual image of what this might look like is Jesus kneeling on the floor, washing his friends' feet. This is an incredible image for the *kenosis* of the logic of domination. But it has not prevented churches from using the language of servanthood to keep inferiors in their place. Shawn Copeland points out that Jesus' ministry is a judgment on oppressive regimes, but it also "exposes the way in which we all have betrayed the very meaning of humanity—our own, the humanity of exploited, despised poor women of color, and the humanity of our God."[37] The ideal of servanthood has not prevented power from accumulating in

37. Copeland, *Enfleshing Freedom*, 90.

the church. It has not prevented Christians from re-creating structures of domination and coercion in their homes, communities, and countries. It has perhaps only reinforced resignation to thankless hard work, passivity, and silence in those who are handing out food but not eating it at the table.

But if we linger over Jesus' enactment of servanthood, we do not seem to be provided with a good exemplar of a passive and downtrodden servant. He is a "servant" that blazes with energy and power; he heals, he feeds, he speaks with authority. He is constantly innovating, unafraid to challenge the values and authorities of his time and place. If he is any guide, a servant of the kingdom renounces her inferiority as much as the privilege to command. Just as images of imperial rule are applied to a crucified and impoverished Galilean, the language of slavery symbolizes the unique qualifications of women, slaves, the poor, workers—anyone who does the will of God—to disseminate good news. Far from being a demand for subservience, servanthood calls us to engage the full vitality of our unique authority and beauty. A servant in this kingdom leaves the dead behind to go out in the world, acting with compassion, courage, and vitality in the family of humanity. Such a servant embodies the joyousness of a kingdom that is within and among us whenever we abandon the deadly patterns of subjugation and domination. This is a kingdom in which women and sexual minorities are servants precisely by embracing their identity as richly as possible. As servants in the divine empire, we are commanded to speak with authority the truths we have learned from our place on the margins of the church and at the breast of our divine Lover.

A NEW TEACHING

The images of power that accompany the birth of Jesus and the impossible community that springs up around him are signs of an even deeper anomaly of his kingdom. In an outrage against any possible way of organizing a family, let alone a society, he permits love to do the work of law. I do not mean that families should not love one another. But even a very indulgent mother knows that more than a steady rain of love is required to raise children.

The great power of law is to hold chaos at bay. The importance of this power is reinforced by the image of God as a divine lawgiver, commanding obedience. Many Christians understand evil to be symbolized by disobedience in the otherwise idyllic garden of Eden. Law and its violation fundamentally structure reality. This does not mean that religion is narrowly legalistic, but these myths affirm law as a gift of a good God. Violating this order brings suffering, even disaster. After rehearsing a spectacular devolution of violence from rape to war, the author of Judges laments simply: "In those days there was no king in Israel; every man did what was right in his own eyes" (Judges 21:25 RSV).

But the gospel deliberately attacks the mythology of law. Jesus does this in part by flagrantly, even flippantly, transgressing Sabbath law. On one occasion the Gospel of Mark depicts Jesus and his disciples wandering through a field of grain, idly plucking its ears (Mark 2:23). On another occasion a man with a withered hand approaches him on the Sabbath in the synagogue. Jesus could not wait until the next day? He could not wait until the service was over? He could not heal the hand in someone's house? It had to be in the middle of a Sabbath service? Sabbath observance permits observant Jews to care for someone who is sick or injured. "Pharisees might have returned to their studies with the conclusion that Jesus was not a good legal debater, since he stretched 'save life' to cover a minor cure. But, in view of the general level of Sabbath disputes in the first century, nothing in the gospel account would have led them to seek Jesus' life."[38] These conflicts seem to be generated on purpose. Christians expose their ignorance of Torah by finding in these conflicts a condemnation of Rabbinic Judaism. But for a heartless defense of Sabbath legalism we will be ill served if we seek it among our Jewish friends. We might do better to reread Laura Ingles Wilder or John Muir for memories of excruciating and violent Sabbath observance.

Jesus' toying with the Sabbath should not be understood as an assault on Jewish Torah, so humane in its defense of rest not only for the privileged classes but for maidservants and even cattle. His own life and that of his closest followers remained committed to Jewish religion and culture. But by playfully plucking grain while wandering through a field or speaking wholeness into a withered hand in the synagogue, Jesus allows another order to gleam through. The immediacy of healing, compassionate power, unstructured by law or religious observance, glimmers for a moment. It seems to mean not that we are forbidden the concreteness of religious observance but that these observances have no ultimate reality. They are like the clothes we wear after the fall to hide our nakedness. God gave Adam and Eve garments to clothe them on their way out of Eden. God gave Israel means to worship. But these things are to aid us in our weakness; they have no ultimate significance and do nothing to reveal the divine image within us. To the extent that clothes—and religious observance— reinforce hierarchies and exclusions, they are worse than nothing. Attachment to them only obscures our Beloved from our eyes. We are invited to inhabit religious observance without self-righteousness and without insisting it provides exclusive access to divine mercy.

Jesus' parables also provide little windows on an alternative universe. Vagrants who were gathered from a marketplace just before sundown are paid the same as—and before—workers who worked all day. Shepherds abandon ninety-nine sheep to look for one wayward one. A carousing, irresponsible son gets rings and shoes and a fatted calf while the good, responsible son just has to suck it up and accept his father's crazy wisdom. The blessed ones on this earth are the poor, the hungry, weeping ones, persecuted ones, peacemakers. The great banquet is filled

---

38. Sanders, *Historical Figure of Jesus*, 215. This point is echoed by Mary Ann Tolbert, though she emphasizes that Jesus is deliberately stretching the point to reinforce the point that "human welfare, to do good, always takes priority over ritual observance or custom" (*Sowing the Gospel*, 134).

up, indiscriminately, with "the poor and maimed, and blind and lame" (Luke 14:21). Our social divisions are nothing. Our hard work and good moral respectability are nothing. His yoke is easy and his burden light. This is all good news for lost sheep, vagrants, and badly behaved sons, but it does not seem to make much sense for normal, everyday, responsible, law-abiding, genuinely pious and God-loving earnest Christians.

But as we try to adjust to this assault on ordinary consciousness and try to make our way in a kingdom that seems to have no moral or social structures, we run into a demand for perfection that excludes everyone, possibly even the most devoted saints. After welcoming the halt and lame with no recommendation beyond their being poor or maimed, Jesus tells the multitudes that whoever does not hate their mother and father, wife, children, brothers, sisters, and even their own life cannot be a disciple. Whoever does not recognize prisoners, the sick, and the naked as Christ himself is doomed to the eternal fire. At least we will have lots of company.

Love is a country without boundary or condition, in which the destitute and despised are raised up for special affection. But love also accepts centurions, Rome's tax-collecting lackeys, rich people like Jairus, the wife of Herod's steward, Gentile dogs. In this empire neither victims nor perpetrators find the door slammed in their faces. Jesus' immorality repairs the damage done by domination, by religious intolerance, by madness and destitution.[39] This counter-empire "challenge[s] contemporary morality to its depths."[40] If we accept its healing we are asked to accept that everyone else in the entire world is a citizen in this kingdom. Terrorists? Sex traffickers? Practice loving your enemies. Pray for them. Fast for them. Anyone can love the ones who love them. This small and simple thing is all we are asked. Knock and the door will be opened. Ask and you shall receive. Yet there is great anguish in walking through this invisible portal into the blazing Eroticism of Christ.

The yoke is easy and burden light, but it is also more excruciating than the most exacting morality. It demands nothing but perfection: be perfect as Abba, who sends rain on the just and the unjust, is perfect (Matthew 5:45, 48). It reflects a divine kingdom not awaiting us "in the sky, Lord, in the sky," but here and now. It is no wonder that Jesus' friends and family think he is crazy (Mark 3:21–22). He lives as if in a world governed by love—a world infinitely more generous and more exacting than the one with which we are familiar.

---

39. Some of this language is a loose paraphrase from Sawicki's *Crossing Galilee*, 196.
40. Crossan, *Historical Jesus*, 292.

Chapter 10

"They Disbelieved for Joy"

Incarnating and Practicing the Gospel

As they were saying this, Jesus himself stood among them. But they were startled and frightened, and supposed that they saw a spirit. And he said to them, "Why are you troubled, and why does questioning rise in your hearts? See my hands and my feet, that it is I myself; handle me, and see; for a spirit has not flesh and bones as you see that I have." And while they still disbelieved for joy and wondered he said to them, "Have you anything to eat?"

Luke 24:36–41

There is a spirit abroad in life of which the Judaeo-Christian ethic is but one expression. It is a spirit that makes for wholeness and for community. . . . It broods over the demonstrators for justice and brings comfort to the desolate and forgotten who have no memory of what it is to feel the rhythm of belonging. . . . It knows no country and its allies are to be found wherever the heart is kind and the collective will and the private endeavor seek to make justice where injustice abounds.[1]

All the previous chapters of this book conspire to make a single point: the Abyss of Divinity beyond all names and all negations is disclosed to us as love. As Christians we experience this disclosure through the incarnation of Wisdom in the cosmos, in the Savior, in Jesus of Nazareth, and in one another. That the apophatic depths of divine love can be embodied in the particularity of a human body is a truth not only about the Trinity; it is our own truth as well. Christ saves us from

---

1. Howard Thurman, quoted in Barbara Holmes, *Joy Unspeakable: Contemplative Practices of the Black Church*, 164.

the tyranny of suffering as well as for the illumination of our being by the divine light. This gospel is good news for anyone subject to the human condition, but it is particularly good news for those drowning in the wreckage of church teachings that defraud us of our spiritual beauty: the lame, the orphaned, the foreigner, the queer, the feminine, the afflicted—those driven away. The incarnation tells us our true name and it shows us a path to walk to claim our name.

Christianity shares with the other religions of the world the wisdom that this healing is difficult to obtain, not because it is not freely given but because it is so difficult to take in. In the old language of the Reformation, we are always already justified. That is, we are always already perfect and beloved, cherished from before time, carried in the womb of the Divine Eros. The process of sanctification is the path we walk to integrate this eternal truth into our conscious, embodied, communal experience. The incarnation is continually realized as a way of life embodied in concrete practices. One practice might be going to church, but practice is also all of the things we do in the course of every day. The way of life is not different or separate from ordinary, everyday life. "The fact that we prefer stained glass windows, pomp and circumstance, and the pastor's appreciation celebrations has nothing to do with the sacred. It may seem as if the mysteries of divine-human reunion erupt in our lives, when in fact . . . it was always there."[2] Since the practice of incarnation is everything we do, there is not a separate set of practices that are "religious." This concluding chapter meditates on examples of practices through which we learn to embody our own incarnation. In particular, this chapter reflects on truth, compassion, and joy as practices of a kingdom in which we wander: immigrants and refugees just learning how to live in a land of freedom.

YOU SHALL KNOW THE TRUTH: DEVOTION TO TRUTH AS SPIRITUAL PRACTICE

In the incarnation two realities are melded into one. Divinity and humanity become one taste. In the kingdom of God, likewise, two dimensions of our earthly life are melded into one. We live in the world structured by economic, social, religious, political realities. We eat, we work, we make love, we play, we raise families. But as Christians we live in this world as witnesses to the Incarnate One. Being committed and dedicated to a love of truth is an important practice that attempts to weave together the different dimensions of our lives.

This love, as a form of Christian love, has distinctive qualities. It attempts the paradoxical and difficult interweaving of a genuine devotion to truth with nonattachment. As devotion, love of truth requires a kind of fearlessness that is able to accept unpleasant aspects of truth. Sigmund Freud and Stephen Colbert

2. Holmes, *Joy Unspeakable*, 169.

describe illusion or "truthiness" (respectively) as the confusion between what is true and what one wants to be true. This conflation of truth with wishes is a spiritual problem; its antidote is to struggle for the courage to love the truth regardless of whether it accords with our wishes or not.

A Christian adoration of truth also reflects an acknowledgment that we humans do not enjoy the privilege of an unmediated possession of truth. Our understanding of a situation and the values through which we assess it cannot be ultimate or unchanging. More information may require that we change our point of view. Even those with different points of view have their story and may, like us, be struggling to discern factual and ethical issues in a difficult and muddy context. Devotion to truth does not require inflexibility. That we seek the truth as Christians does not mean that our search is guaranteed to be successful. Possession of truth may be something for God; we must dwell in a desire for truth. Desire for truth pushes beyond every penultimate assertion, requiring not dogmatism but openness and courage.

Our devotion to truth should not be at the expense of our compassion for other people. Love of truth as a spiritual practice should attempt to overcome hostility to other people, though it is admittedly an advanced spiritual practice to resist frustration with people whose point of view seems to us very destructive. But even in these cases we need not hate people who oppose us, even as we work with energy and passion in the opposite direction. The desire for truth is a practice, not an accomplishment. We can love the truth and seek it and desire it but refrain from being too attached to the scraps we unearth. In the play of time and deepening understanding, they may be more partial than we realized.

CONSUMERISM AND TRUTH

These dispositions of courage and openness support a desire for truth but can be undermined by the conditions of our life, which tend to support illusions and the desire for illusions. Consumer culture, for example, is its own pervasive ideology. It infiltrates our actions and our social worlds with the assumption that our happiness and our identity come from objects of consumption.[3] Even if we do not consciously hold this belief, we act on it and our world is molded by it so deeply we cannot escape it. Many forms of entertainment numb us to violence but they also numb us to beauty by their sheer banality. These are simple examples of ways in which culture delivers meaning to us before we even have a chance to reject it. It comes to us not as an idea to be evaluated, a truth claim to be investigated, but by images and opportunities that construct our minds as

---

3. Many books analyze consumer culture and its relationship to religion; one very fine one is Vincent Miller's, *Consuming Religion.* Joerg Rieger's *No Rising Tide: Theology, Economics, and the Future* also deserves mention in this context. Two films that make this point more accessibly are *Advertising and the End of the World* and *Affluenza.*

well as our world. The tension between these values and those of our faith is difficult to surface. The values of a consumer economy insert themselves into our
interpretations of faith itself.

I often show the film *Advertising and the End of the World* to my undergradu-
ate classes. It describes the worldview that underlies the seductions of consumerism as well as its environmental cost. My students are usually offended and angry,
denying that they believe things you buy make you happy or that consumerism
is as costly to the environment as the film suggests. But as they think about it
over the course of the semester they often come to other conclusions. Having the
chance to reflect on the effect of the media on their conscious and, even more,
unconscious awareness undermines their sense that they are totally free agents
and that their view of the world and of their identity is arrived at through clear
and unconstrained deliberation. They begin to realize how deeply formed they
are before they even have a chance to make any choices at all. Our minds are
shaped for us by all kinds of images and assumptions that we passively receive
simply by living in the world: riding the subway, turning on the radio or television, driving down the interstate. This means our devotion to truth is severely
challenged, not only by conflicting political points of view or contradictory factual accounts but by the blandishments of a market economy that inflects every
aspect of our social life.

There are various responses to this by religious people: simplicity movements, fair trade, "more fun, less stuff." But getting some purchase on ways we
are absorbed into consumer values requires a commitment to truth as well as a
degree of self-education. There is a real sense in which reading books and articles
on the inner workings of capitalism is a spiritual practice requiring discipline
and courage.

TRUTH AND IDEOLOGY

Social worlds are constructed in part by ideological structures that make political
and economic habits natural, necessary, reasonable, virtuous. Control of ideology is perhaps the most important form of power there is. It is a set of language
rules that shapes reality by redescribing it. When Virgil advised the Romans to
pursue wars of brutal imperialist conquest, he described it as a high political calling, a manifest destiny of sorts: "You O Roman, remember to rule the nations
with might. This will be your genius—to impose the way of peace, to spare the
conquered and crush the proud."[4] But a Caledonian chief was suspicious of this
"way of peace." Speaking to fellow victims of Roman conquest, he pierced the
language of ideology by describing the material reality it attempted to conceal:
"You have sought in vain to escape [the Romans'] oppression by obedience and

---

4. Virgil, *Aeneid* 6.850–53, quoted by Horsley, *Liberation of Christmas*, 28.

submissiveness. . . . They rob, butcher, plunder and call it 'empire'; and where they make a desolation, they call it 'peace.'"[5]

The control of ideology allows the violent conquest of Celtic Britain to be a work of peacemaking. The crosses that lined the roads of Galilee are a beneficent empire's way of crushing the proud. Control of ideology transforms torture ("enhanced interrogation techniques") into a necessary tactic in the defense of democracy. It makes same-sex love the primary threat to American families. In ancient Rome and the contemporary United States, the desire for truth is confronted with ideology's powerful machinery. The new commandment incarnate Wisdom imposes does not replace one religion, Judaism or paganism, with a new religion, Christianity. But it does try to give clearer eyes to practitioners of love so that the ideology of power and wealth becomes less compelling, less self-evident. Christianity's love of truth might be understood to be less about believing true things about God or Jesus or sin and more about the effort to challenge ideological constructions.

Notwithstanding the omnipresent message of consumer happiness, we Christians find ourselves choking with frustration as we survey the massive injustices that tangle the planet. Like the Hebrew prophets of ancient Israel, we smother on lies that call evil good. It is difficult to sustain a devotion to truth when much of the public discourse is more or less overtly dedicated to ideological shaping of information. This affects such basic things as factual information: are there weapons of mass destruction in Iraq or not? This question quickly became factually irrelevant, and those who insisted it was important found themselves punished for it.[6] Not just facts but webs of meaning and value are put together in mendacious ways in order to uphold particular systems of power. Facts emerge or are repressed as they benefit a point of view. Images and confused emotions stand in for deliberation. The omnipresent machinery of ideology creates great difficulty for the desire to distinguish truth from deception.

Political regimes are committed to shaping our interpretation of events to obfuscate some of the hidden ways policies benefit those behind the scenes. Public policy is shaped by the deployment of rhetoric that conceals both its aim and its means. How many noticed the recent Supreme Court ruling that corporations can donate virtually unlimited funds to election campaigns? Yet, hidden in the rhetoric of democracy, this ruling granted corporate entities supremacy in shaping the flow of images and information. This supremacy is evident not only in political campaigns but in advertisements that are allowed to appear on television and radio or in magazines. The effect of this control of ideology is difficult to overestimate. It does not control but deeply shapes the symbols and information

---

5. Quoted by Horsley, *Liberation of Christmas*, 29–30.

6. As an example, one thinks of the revenge that was sought against Ambassador Joseph Wilson when he publicized information contradicting White House claims to have found proof of Iraq's exploration of weapons of mass destruction. On the recommendation of the president and vice president, his wife was outed as a CIA agent and her career ended.

through which Americans decide the fate of their nation and, to some extent, the world. The interpretation of corporations as primary participants in political decisions comes close to trading democracy—the ideal that government would be by the people, for the people, and of the people—for oligarchy.

These are political questions, of course; but they are also spiritual ones. Christians, in their devotion to truth, are invited to care about factual truth and to acquire intellectual and spiritual disciplines that would enable them to be more suspicious of ideologically manufactured facts and worldviews.

TRUTH AS DISCERNMENT

Canonical and noncanonical writings provide models for how early Christians struggled in the midst of their own culture wars. From a Christian perspective this is a world in which "discerning between the seemingly good and what is authentically good has become impossibly obscured and confused. Only revelation can provide hope and the possibility of salvation in a society and a cosmos gone seriously awry."[7] Christians then and now try to envision an ethical and spiritual universe that is in many ways at odds with the dominant culture.

Ancient scriptures provide opportunities to retrain our vision and reignite a desire for a different kind of truth. The symbols of the gospel are themselves a type of training that contrasts the kind of peace Caesar brings and the kind of peace symbolized by Jesus. Karen King describes the way in which the Savior enables us to orient to the confusions of our world more humanely: "Arguably, the most explicit aim of the *Secret Revelation of John* is found in its liberating spiritual agenda in which the Savior's revelation forms and transforms people through instruction, moral purification, and ritual empowerment. Through this process, they come to take up a socially critical orientation to the world expressed in utopian commitments to God and in resistance to the evils of injustice, ignorance, violence, arrogance, and malice."[8] Scripture does not offer us strange or impossible facts to be believed but retrains our vision. It is an optics that inspires and shapes our desire for truth in all of its forms. The wild mythology of the *Secret Revelation* as well as the gospel narratives are eyeglasses that help us read our life and times.

The images of mother and child, of a manger and shepherds, form our imagination so a different kind of truth can find purchase in our heart and mind. If we train ourselves to understand peace through the symbolism of the gospel, the peace of Caesar becomes less compelling. The violence that upholds it might come into focus; the entertainments that distract us may seem less titillating. The gospel pierces the illusions of the world. It tears the mask off oppression

---

7. King, *Secret Revelation of John*, 162.
8. Ibid., 262.

and domination and shows them to be not the natural order of things but an obscenity, a heartbreaking outrage. But it also reminds us of the simple pleasures of companionship, of quiet and solitude, of nonutilitarian creativity. The symbols of the gospel are an optics, a way to penetrate befuddling lies so we can see reality more as it is: the evil masquerading as good and goodness wandering incognito.

If the kingdom of God is not going to decisively overcome Rome—or any of its historical imitators—the question becomes, how does one live in the midst of lies, how does one bear the impossibility of a total transformation of society? In a world created by and for love but dominated by treacherous powers and principalities, a first order of business is to unmask deception. Early Christian writings expose political power and the theology that maintains it as false and illegitimate. Violence becomes less natural and regimes no longer rule by divine right. Clarity in the face of ideology empowers Christ's followers to resist "seductions and false claims . . . In conceiving salvation in this way, the *Secret Revelation of John* inseparably links spiritual formation, social criticism, and resistance to evil."[9] In their vigorous portrayal of a nonimperial counterculture, canonical and noncanonical writings can be treasured as training manuals that help us unite spiritual formation with more clear-eyed—or at least more self-critical—participation in our political and ethical systems.

AND THE TRUTH SHALL SET YOU FREE: THE DESIRE FOR THEOLOGICAL TRUTH

In telling the truth about power, these writings also tell the truth about ultimate reality. Again, this does not mean that any particular document is in possession of a final, objective truth that can be possessed the way one retains the multiplication tables. Scripture provides narratives, symbols, and ideals that challenge not only political and economic values but religious ones as well.

Several of the canonical and noncanonical Gospels understand the "ruler of this world" to be Satan or an evil demiurge. It is his power we see displayed in the brutality of Rome. We see his rule also in religious and political justifications of violence. We see his gospel in the "good news" of the emperor cult. Then as now religion and politics were closely aligned.

In reflecting on this symbolism, we are not asked to affirm a mythological worldview inhabited by a supernatural cast of characters. When Mark or John refers to Satan as the ruler of this world, we are alerted to be more suspicious of the power and prestige we see glorified in the convergence of religious and political symbols. Religious affirmations of a just world where the good are rewarded and the bad are punished align the vagaries of economic and political success

9. Ibid., 156.

with the divine will. Challenge of the social status quo is a challenge to the all-seeing wisdom of Providence. A new story dominates: God is angry, as angry as Nero or Caligula, and demands blood to satisfy his righteous rage. But if we are loyal to him and his earthly viceroys we can enjoy a heaven in which streets are paved in gold and the endless suffering of our enemies is constantly before our eyes. Limitless wealth and the titillating pleasure of tortured enemies: the Pax Romana forever.

Christians turn to the writings of our ancient brothers and sisters for clues about another vision of reality. These writings persistently describe the primary effect or quality of divine power as compassion.[10] The primacy of compassion is a secret (gnostic) teaching in the sense that it defies the public truths of empire. The Savior has come to make these truths available to suffering humanity. "According to Christ, suffering never comes at the hand of the true Deity, but only from the false gods—and even that suffering will end when humans receive true understanding. . . . Christ instead exposes violence and deception as strategies of the ignorant and the proud. These strategies expose the character of all worldly power."[11] Remembering this truth is hard when religions themselves uphold wealth as a sign of divine favor and warfare as a sacred obligation. But the countercultural theology of these ancient texts points to an alternative. Rather than the justice of an all-powerful Providence, suffering is arbitrary. It comes at the hands of tyranny and accident, indifferent to the moral worth of its victims. The suffering of the Galileans whose blood Pilate mixed with sacrifices were not worse sinners than others (Luke 13:1–4).

The gospel depicts a different relationship between world history and divine Providence. This is why Christians were killed as atheists. Their countercultural theology remains an important guide for contemporary Christians. We recognize the intimacy of Divinity in all unjustified and afflictive suffering as we meditate on the Eternal Goodness subjected to death on a cross. Images of divine compassion offer the miracle of returning sight to the blind. Reshaped by the gospel, we try to interpret our own time in ways that honor the theological truths to which it witnesses.

---

10. For example, "the Mother-Father whose mercy is great, the Spirit who is holy in every respect, the compassionate, who troubles herself for you" (*Secret Revelation of John* 24.2). Later the feminine personification tells John: "Arise and remember that you are the one who has heard, and follow your root, which is I, the compassionate" (26.28–29). This is the revelation that Christ, the Savior, gives to John, who in turn shares it with the other disciples (King, *Secret Revelation of John*, 75, 79). In the *Dialogue of the Savior* Mary expresses the desire to understand all things. She and the other disciples are told that wealth is misleading and that they must be prepared in the face of everything. The beginning of this path is "love and goodness. For if one of these existed among the governors, wickedness would never have come into existence" (142.74, *Nag Hammadi Library*, ed. Robinson, 253). The *Gospel of Truth* also conjoins qualities of transcendence—incorruptibility, invisibility, unspeakability, unengendered—with qualities of mercy and compassion (*Nag Hammadi Library*, 48–50).

11. King, *Secret Revelation of John*, 171.

TRUTH AND ETHICS

We do not live in ancient Rome, but we do live in a global capitalist context that does much of its business through exploitation and war. Ethics and aesthetics are often reduced to entertainment. One need not be a fundamentalist to feel uneasy about the usurpation of humane family and communal practices. It is difficult to instill in children a sense of compassion, serenity, healthy discipline, and enjoyment when the primary cultural messages celebrate unrestrained wealth accumulation and ever more violent games, shows, films, sports.

Early Christians were not always completely successful in resisting the social values of their time, as we see in the defense of slavery and patriarchy in the pseudonymous epistles (1 and 2 Timothy, Ephesians, 1 and 2 Peter, etc.). It is easy for us to be horrified by early Christians' assimilation into a slave culture, but perhaps for them slaves functioned the way ecological degradation does for us. We can operate inside destructive economic and ideological systems slightly more humanely (be kind to our slaves), but getting out of the system altogether is virtually impossible—only the desert ascetics attempted that bold move.

Drawing an analogy between our own economic system and slavery is not intended to trivialize the horrors of ancient slavery. It is perhaps the ethical constructions of consumer capitalism that make us think maiming and destroying animals, plants, and ecosystems is of no real importance. It is easy to be sensitive to evil that no longer benefits us.

Analogies between Christians' relationships to slavery and to a market economy alert us to the fact that we also find ourselves accommodating to oppressive systems we seem unable to overthrow. Plastic toys grow like mold in my house, probably made by a factory worker who may be treated little better than a slave, sold by a person working for minimum wage, only to end up in a landfill without ever generating any real pleasure. As I immerse myself in the truth of climate change, my family acquires ever more environmentally unsound paraphernalia. Yet I am not prepared to move to the desert. Is there a desert sufficiently removed from these practices?

Our devotion to truth is enacted in all of our daily tasks and decisions. In our domestic lives we renounce hopes of total victory as well as the enticement to despair. Or rather, in the midst of these riptides we find the joyousness of gospel living. As citizens we sort out the claims of various parties, candidates, and issues. As consumers we try to be more responsible in what we buy and how we amuse ourselves, the companies we support and the policies we advocate. As mothers we are entangled in hopelessly complex and contradictory demands for time, emotional vitality, and practical wisdom. The practice of telling the truth is unlikely to provide easy answers to any of the conundrums of daily life, but it might help peel away the ideologies, guilt, self-sacrifice, and self-aggrandizement that sabotage patience and insight. As lovers we counter lies about our sexuality. We explore more carefully the moral no-man's-land of heterosexual or same-sex freedom. Instead of ignoring the ways in which our sexual practices fail to ignite the spiritual beauty between sexual partners, we might find ways to integrate sexuality into our practices of the gospel's erotic empire.

Living toward truth about our domestic practices certainly engages us more deeply and responsibly in our economic, religious, and political institutions. But something is wrong if it does not also free up energy to enjoy our children, our partners, our friends. Truth frees us to turn toward delight in everyday moments when we laugh together at a meal or take a walk as the new moon splinters into the sky. We might sometimes trade a moment of obligation for the simple enjoyment of a garden or rest or music.

Attempting the practice of truth about ourselves and our world should not be a guilt-filled horror at all of our personal and collective failings. The truth should set us free for fuller and more humane ways to be with ourselves and with one another. It should explore prophetic but also joyous ways to live in this world, which is not perfect, whose laws are often unjust, in which jobs and family life can be difficult. But the truth about our life would also acknowledge the beauty all around us. Seeking the truth might also allow us to tolerate the ambiguities of truth, to find ways to inhabit this world in which wheat and tares grow up together, even interdependently.

Some of the noncanonical texts have been accused of hating this world and imagining only the desire to get out of here. This could equally be said about the apocalyptic texts that cannot imagine anything good here worth saving. Both of these kinds of writing reflect the deep pain arising from seeing too well how omnipresent and apparently omnipotent injustice is. Early Christian writings are important antidotes to the normalization of domination. But they should not be allowed to tell us another untruth: that there is only darkness here. Sharon Welch, an inveterate activist herself, provides a picture of how to endure histories that permit only partial change but also forbid us the luxury of indifference:

> Love provides the resiliency of commitment, vision, and hope when efforts for change either are defeated repeatedly or are shown to be insufficient . . . the recognition that we cannot imagine how we will change society is the beginning point, not the end of an ethic founded on love for oneself and others. Resistance to injustice and the creation of intrinsically temporal and limited social structures are acts of love, affirmations of the delightfulness and profundity of life. Such acts declare the tragedy of what is lost because of injustice, and they celebrate the satisfaction of life lived under conditions of injustice. A deep joy accompanies the cycle of providing shelter and food, nurturing the young, and celebrating the beauty of life in art, music, and poetry.[12]

The deepest truth of the divine empire is joy; followers of the Way need to keep their eyes open to see that, too.

---

12. Welch, *Feminist Ethic of Risk*, 165.

"AND WHEN HE SAW HIM, HE HAD COMPASSION": TRAINING IN CHRISTIANITY

The desire for truth is always a pursuit for what cannot be unambiguously possessed. The same is true for another central Christian practice: loving-kindness. The "good news" strips away the consolations of religion and society alike, opening our hearts wider, onto a world of pain. Like the Samaritan, our gut will burn in us and force us to the side of those who suffer. But we do not enter into this deep compassion simply by assenting to it. We are reformed by the gospel, which becomes a lifelong training in Christianity. But even if we remain imperfectly attentive to human suffering, we can remember the attractiveness of the ideal of compassion.

Elaine Pagels points out that early Christians were identified by their shocking and countercultural expressions of loving-kindness. They supported abandoned orphans, they brought food and medicine to prisoners condemned to mines, they provided burial for criminals and the poor, they took no money for their healing offices. Like Jews, they envisioned Divinity as one who loved humanity and who evoked love in return.[13] She uses Justin, nicknamed Martyr in light of the manner of his death, as a witness to the odd desirability of this outlaw faith. An educated pagan, he was attracted to Christianity by its moral beauty. He contrasted Christianity with the personal and interpersonal violence normalized by Roman society, even as it is in our own: "We, out of every tribe of people . . . who used to take pleasure in promiscuity, now embrace chastity alone; we, who once had recourse to magic, dedicate ourselves to the good God; we, who valued above everything else acquiring wealth and possessions, now bring what we have into a common fund, and share with everyone in need; we who hated and killed other people, and refused to live with people of another tribe because of their different customs, now live intimately with them."[14] Even bad-tempered, misogynistic Tertullian characterized the draw of Christianity as a human intimacy that transformed strangers into brothers and sisters: "What marks us in the eyes of our enemies is our practice of loving-kindness."[15] For these Christians, love was not only the most distinctive but the most beguiling name of Divinity.

Love names God's attitude toward humanity but it also describes the way mind is transformed when it is aligned with ultimate reality. The sublimely beautiful writings of Plato and Plotinus made service to humanity a central effect of contemplation of the Good, but a vision of love that recognizes the Divine in the faces of prisoners, sick and impoverished people, and strangers and outcasts awaited the revelation of the Incarnate One. We are overfamiliar with Christian love rhetoric, numbed to it by misuse and trivialization. Ancient texts can help us reconnect to the visceral outrageousness of the twin love commandment.

13. Pagels, *Beyond Belief*, 6–7.
14. Ibid., 13.
15. Ibid., 10.

Christian love required a rejection of the patriarchal family in favor of the universal family, composed of all those who bear the divine image. Roman citizens gathered with slaves as siblings. Communities entered into solidarity with the afflicted not as patrons but as friends. Such love is always difficult, joyous, and offensive. Love is an intolerable social practice now, as it was then. But perhaps another reason love and compassion have become somewhat trivialized as Christian practices is that we do not think of love as requiring training. We do not think of Christianity as a spiritual analogue to athletic discipline. When we conceive of Christianity as beliefs, love fades into the background and the challenge of Matthew 25 loses its edge. Early Christians tended to be more realistic about this challenge. Rather than allow the seeming impossibility of it to deflate them, they interpreted Christianity as a path in which love is practiced the way one practices the piano or rock climbing. Because human beings are capable of many forms of excellence, we *can* train in them. Because excellence is difficult we *must* train.

DIDACHE: APPRENTICES OF LOVE

This ancient vision of the human being as capable of divinity has been all but extinguished in the modern world. The emphasis on belief characteristic of the Reformation and the flattening out of the capacities of mind by science conspire to erase this older sense of possibility that made the Christian path so inviting. The recent popularity of Buddhism may relate to the hunger to expand the human spirit to full reach. There is still an unquenched thirst for human excellence not only as art or athletics but as joy and compassion. But Christianity contained this wisdom too. The *Didache* is an example of a first-century text intended for ordinary followers of Christ. *Didache* means "training" in the sense of "the systematic training that a mentor (or a master craftsworker) would give to an understudy (apprentice)."[16]

This text is thought to be written in the last half of the first century, a rough contemporary of the Synoptic Gospels. A number of sayings familiar from these Gospels are found in it. In this community, to follow Christ meant undertaking a training that is both ordinary, in the sense that anyone who is a Christian would undertake it, and extraordinary, in the sense that it envisions a dramatic reformation of human life and community. Recovering texts like this one may be a way to reinvigorate that aspect of Christian practice that "little by little . . . make[s] possible the indispensable metamorphosis of the inner self."[17]

The *Didache* does not does not invite the reader into a particular religion but rather into *the Way of Life*. This way is extremely simple: "love the God

---

16. Milavec, *Didache*, x. In what follows I quote from Milavec's translation.
17. Pierre Hadot, *Philosophy as a Way of Life: Spiritual Exercises from Socrates to Foucault*, 83.

who made you" and love your neighbor as yourself. This latter love is specified negatively: "as many [things] as you might wish not to happen to you, likewise, do not do to another" (1.2). That is it. Do not do things to other people that you would not like being done to you. But the text recognizes that this simplicity belies its difficulty. After this extremely succinct summary of the Way of Life, the author provides something less than twenty pages to outline training for this Way. This simple Way of Life is embodied in the rituals of baptism and Communion through which community is constituted. But it requires the transformation of mind, and this transformation is accomplished by concrete practices of mindfulness.

The first training mentioned in the *Didache* is the renunciation of "bodily desires," by which the writer means (somewhat counterintuitively) fear, anger, and attachment.[18] Readers are instructed to pray for enemies and to fast for those who persecute them. In an echo of the canonical Gospels, we are reminded that even Gentiles love those who love them. But "you, on the other hand, love the ones hating you, and you will not have an enemy" (1.3). It is natural—even a kind of spontaneous "bodily desire"—to hate enemies, to fear those who hurt us, and to wish them harm. But since we would not want harm to come to us we must practice in such a way that we do not even *wish* harm to come to those who persecute us.

We cannot and should not simply repress the natural fear and anger that arise when we are endangered or mistreated. But the *Didache* understands bodily desires to be malleable and subject to change. Like athletes, we are able to rise above fear or lethargy and achieve greatness. But, like athleticism, this requires specific training. Without repressing or condemning these emotions, we can, imaginatively, wish someone who harmed us well and even engage in a spiritual practice for their well-being. They still might anger or frighten us, but we visualize their well-being, which includes their freedom from the impulse to harm us. We are bound together, and in practicing for our own well-being we practice for theirs. We do not do this because Christians are nice to people who hurt them. We do it to ignite our own ferocious power: we are not merely victims but athletes who have a freedom to respond with spiritual power to those who harm us. We have the power to heal the deep hurts of violence and to draw the one who harms us into a path of transformation. We participate in the work of salvation in which my fate and that of the world are interdependent. Mind transformation uses concrete mental and physical practices that acknowledge pain and then works with it in creative and healing ways.

When we turn the other cheek or walk two miles instead of one (*Didache* 1.4), the apprentice of love exaggerates the assault, turning defeat into victory. What was intended as humiliation provides an occasion to manifest the divine

---

18. Core teachings of Tibetan Buddhism parallel this teaching: the capacity for meditation on emptiness is dialectically related to the purification of attachments and aversions. See, for example, the Dalai Lama's book, *How to Practice: The Way to a Meaningful Life*.

nature that smolders in each of us. Instead of being long-suffering or forgiving, the practitioner erupts with the luminosity and power of compassion. It is spiritual tai chi.[19] The would-be enemy attempts to erase one's humanity, but the practitioner calls out another power. She rides the river of divine-human unity that manifests a power much deeper than the one deployed against her.

This kind of practice is reminiscent of Gandhi's *satyagraha* or the nonviolent practices of the civil rights movement. Far from being "passive resistance," it is the force of truth. John Newman uses the analogy of a bullfighter to describe a similar spiritual training. "Under everyday conditions a bull charging at me across an open space will result in the emotion of fear. *I am a body* which can be gored, hence killed, and hence something whose power of action can be radically reduced by charging bulls. But if I am a professional bull-fighter facing the same bull across a ring, I may feel something we might call exhilaration. Since *I am a bull-fighter*, the charge of the bull can be an occasion of the highest exercise of my powers."[20] Training in Christianity calls us to an exhilarating excellence.

Training requires vigilant attention to socially normalized violence and to dispositions that seem harmless. It may seem an exaggeration to say that envy or unkind speech lead to murder. But actions are rooted in prior dispositions, and these dispositions represent obstacles to the spontaneous flow of gentleness, mercy, and calm (*Didache* 3.7–8). The point of these exercises is to practice in such a way that the impulse to love the neighbor takes ever more radical and spontaneous form. The entire psyche and spirit, the conscious and unconscious, are transformed so that courage, generosity, and love infiltrate the wellspring of one's heart. Because society and religion sometimes mediate values at odds with the Way of Life, and because our minds are complex and much is hidden from direct consciousness, there are no perfectly reliable guides. We simply continue to practice so that our minds become gradually more relaxed and open to others.

Apprenticeship requires vigilance regarding our interior life and concrete practices that reflect a new form of community, a new way to relate to enemies and strangers. The difficulty of practice should not become the cause for self-condemnation or judgment. Attachment to imperfections is yet another bit of mental detritus that interferes with a peaceful and compassionate disposition. Notice them, but do not attach to them. "For, on the one hand, if you are able to bear the whole yoke of the Lord, you will be perfect; but if, on the other hand, you are not able, that which you are able, do this" (*Didache* 6.2).[21]

---

19. A gentle and wise contemporary (Buddhist) version of this practice is Sharon Salzburg's book and CD, *Lovingkindness Meditation*. My eldest daughter discovered her own spiritual tai chi. When her brother was mercilessly teasing and tormenting her she happened to be reading *The Golden Compass*. A yogini-like witch provided her with a model for resistance. With perfect dignity and equanimity, the witch said: "How could you insult a witch? What would it matter if you did?" My daughter took on this sense of dignity and self-worth. How could you insult me? It proved extremely efficacious.

20. Newman, *Disciplines of Attention*, 66.

21. John Cassian, for example, quotes his own master as saying: "But in order that I may observe

These straightforward and simple trainings describe acts, intentions, and emotional dispositions that contribute to or inhibit our ability to love God and neighbor. Training is not heroic renunciation of sex and food; it is not living in the desert or preparing for torture and death. It is just not doing to someone else what you would not have done to you. This simple, moralistic little phrase with which we are all familiar was recognized as both the definitive way of life and also as requiring a serious apprenticeship. If we are to renounce harm to one another, we have to practice by praying for enemies and turning back no one in need. We are apprentices of love: completely ordinary and yet extraordinary.

PELAGIUS: LOVE IN ACTION

The *Didache*'s emphasis on concrete and active kindness is echoed in Pelagius's writings. Vilified by Augustine for his supposed works righteousness, Pelagius was a Celt who took with perfect seriousness the commandment that love of God and neighbor is the foundation and primary content of Christian identity. Like the *Didache*, he expressed this negatively: "Those people love their neighbor as themselves therefore who do no evil to them since this is not what they would wish for themselves. But they gladly share the good things which they themselves wish to receive from everyone else, since a Christian is expected not only to refrain from doing evil but also actively to do good."[22]

Pelagius's description of the Christian life is striking not so much for its theological sophistication but for his heartfelt pain in the face of cruelty. He laments the behavior of those who, believing "that all things are allowed them which it is in their power to do," killed men and left women and children orphaned, with too little food, "forced now to beg and to suffer a lack of clothing . . . What a terrible sin! What a grievous outrage! This is cruelty too great to bear!"[23] Cruelty upsets him and he is shocked that people find no connection between violence and Christian faith: "Such a person boldly enters the church, brashly and without a thought stretching out hands which are dishonored with illicit gains and with the blood of the innocent."[24]

By contrast, a true Christian is one "who cannot endure the oppression of the poor before their very eyes, who comes to the aid of the wretched, who helps the

---

more clearly your thirst for the doctrine of the life of perfection, I want to say a few things to you about the particular excellence and beauty of discernment. Among all the virtues it holds the scepter and the rule" (Conference 1.23 [p. 58]). Conference 2 is entirely dedicated to a discussion of discernment but the general thesis is: "Without [discernment] there are many who despite the intensity of their struggle have been quite unable to arrive at the summit of perfection. For discernment is the mother, the guardian, and the guide of all the virtues" (Conference 2.4 [p. 64]).

22. Pelagius, "On the Christian Life" 10 (*Celtic Spirituality*, 392–93). Dwight Hopkins is one who phrases this as a positive rather than negative ideal: "enjoy another's self as each of us would have our self enjoyed" (*Being Human: Race, Culture, and Religion*, 105).

23. Pelagius, "On the Christian Life" 3 (*Celtic Spirituality*, 384).

24. Ibid., 11 (p. 396).

needy, who mourns with those who mourn, who feels the suffering of others as if it were their own."[25] She or he is "incapable of hurting or wounding anyone, but can only come to the aid of everyone. That person is a Christian who, with Christ as an example, cannot even hate their enemies but does good to those who oppose them, praying for their persecutors and enemies. For if anyone is ready to wound or harm another, then they falsely call themselves Christians. They are Christians who can truly say: I have harmed no one and have lived in righteousness with all."[26] Recognizing the profundity of much of Augustine's thought, I have to confess I miss in him this spontaneous compassion for those who suffer violence or injustice. I am sorry that his vehemence on the subject of the bondage of the will confined Pelagius's defense of the practice of love to the history of heresy.

COMPASSION AND JUSTICE

As contemporary Christians struggle, as all Christians have, to practice our faith in a confusing world, it is helpful to be reminded of the countercultural practices of the "Way of Life" or of the outraged love that scalded Pelagius's tender heart. Like the Dalai Lama's description of compassion as an inability to bear the suffering of another person, they speak of the radical compassion that enlivens religious practice. The unbearable quality of other people's suffering takes on a particular quality through the transformation of mind. It calls out for justice but not hostility toward enemies. Loving-kindness integrates social justice, communal care, and contemplative practices, revealing their interdependence.

Radical compassion moves in several directions that are important to consider. It provides a critical edge to culture. From this perspective a thirst for justice is as obvious as washing hands when they are dirty. Christians have been at the forefront of struggles against slavery, for women's rights, for civil rights, for health care, for peace, for economic justice, and against the death penalty, against torture, against environmental degradation. But great compassion not only calls us to practices of social justice, it also challenges us to inhabit this quest through practices that help us recognize the humanity of those we identify as opponents.

Paul Knitter reminds Christianity of its own deep truth, one he relearned through his dialogue with Buddhism. The judgment on oppressive systems arises from great compassion. But the interconnection of all things makes the temptation to divide the world up into oppressors and the oppressed, victims and murderers, a false path. Not only are we hopelessly enmeshed in the very systems we criticize, we are "oned" with all of humanity. Knitter quotes Roshi Bernie Glassman's gentle scolding: "'You will be able to stop the death squads only if

---

25. Ibid., 14 (p. 402).
26. Ibid., 6 (p. 387).

you realize your oneness with them.' Only if I feel my actual connectedness with them. Only if I feel genuine love for them. Only then is there any hope for having peace with them."[27] The admonition to love our enemies is a difficult spiritual practice that Christians might reemphasize as we continue to labor for justice. It should not dilute desires for political transformation but it makes of social justice a spiritual practice not reducible to social ethics.

Loving-kindness is expressed in large political and social movements and in the intimacy of our daily interactions with strangers, family members, and members of our community. From this point of view, Christianity is a practice that is manifest in an observable way of life characterized in particular by compassion and justice. Such compassion is both ordinary and extraordinary. It is the normal, expected practice of anyone claiming the name of Christian, and it is a heroic practice empowered by union with the Divine Eros and inspired by fellowship with incarnate Wisdom. "Where indeed would compassion find a name except with the Father [Mother]?"[28] Loving-kindness is not a moral code or commitment to certain political policies but a reconstitution of persons and communities through practices that secure the dignity of every creature, not least by securing basic goods that beings need to flourish.

Practices of radical compassion deepen our capacities to live as if the earth were the garment of Wisdom, diaphanous with beauty; and to live as if each person was Christ, precious and lovely. Meditation on the passion is a meditation on the human condition that makes response to suffering and its social causes intrinsic to the way of life. Meditation on the symbols of the kingdom opens on the inbreaking of the divine-human union that we adore in Christ and aspire to as our own truth. The practice of great compassion makes every ordinary action prayer. Every act is an opportunity to transform mind: mothering, shopping, sex, food, music, driving the car, work, friendship, amusement, discipline. Every moment offers a chance to recognize that all things are already dwelling in the eternity of the incarnation. The practice of loving-kindness is not a religion but a way of life. It is the intersection between the Nameless Good, the Divine Eros into which our best thoughts disappear as nothing, and the Beloved, the Wisdom that became incarnate and becomes incarnate in us. In it our suffering is blessed and our pleasure is divine.

"THE BEGINNING OF THE GOSPEL OF JESUS CHRIST"

That Jesus lived in solidarity and compassion with history's losers seems beyond doubt. Rome apparently considered him to be a sufficiently annoying threat to dispense with him with particular cruelty. He was not able to change the

---

27. Knitter, *Without Buddha*, 188.
28. *Gospel of Truth* 39.25.

economic policies that drove people from landed poverty to destitution. In that sense he disappointed hopes for a world-changing messiah. In our own time we are also trapped in a global, multinational world system that is largely impervious to elections and social protest. Like the people of Galilee we are enmeshed in a system we cannot wish away. What does the gospel say about life in this world? It is far from indifferent to the sufferings caused by oppression. Yet it gives little hope that the roots of injustice will be decisively transformed. We face irreversible environmental disasters, foreshadowed by Hurricane Katrina and the latest earthquake in Haiti. Yet the spiritual and political challenge to act with responsibility toward the environment seems to be beyond us. Despairing that there is hope for the earth, we push redemption outside the earth, realized only beyond death and beyond history.

Theologians, womanist and feminist thinkers, and New Testament scholars underscore the liberating message of the gospel. The canonical and extracanonical writings alike situate the message of Jesus in a precarious and frustrating political system estranged from the ideals of an empire of God that is within and among us. We walk a razor's edge between accommodation to political and religious institutions that govern world history and world-denying disengagement that projects liberation outside history. Christianity has tended to fall off this edge in both directions at once. But how does one live on this knife-edge? Perhaps the secret of the gospel lies deeper than devotion to truth, deeper than our labor for justice, deeper even than the flame of compassion. Perhaps the good news whispered by our Savior is joy.

Jesus wandered among the despised of his time and his presence to them was sweet. The incarnation inflects humanity with the fullest blast of Divinity that this form of life can bear. A word that is often overlooked to describe this blaze of glory is joy. There is nothing more joyous than the divine presence. The Divine Eros is a kind of intoxicating overabundance of life, a radiant delight in the interdependence of existence and the random beauty of being. If this is the power that is flowing through Jesus of Nazareth, a foundational practice of the erotic kingdom is joy.

Jesus walks past some wildflowers and insists they are more beautiful than Solomon in his glory. This is how God clothes grass in the field, weeds that live today and tomorrow are thrown in the oven (Matthew 6:28–30): random, irrelevant, useless beauty. They serve no purpose. People pass by every day without noticing or caring. This beauty does not feed them when they are starving or save them when the soldiers come pillaging. But because they are naked to the inflowing energy of the Divine Eros, the flowers are radiant with an intensity of beauty that no human wealth can manufacture. When Jesus says the divine empire is within and all around us, perhaps he is saying that this influx of beauty is constantly available to us, is always raining down on us, purposeless and perfect.

In Matthew 6 Jesus advises against building up treasures on earth where moth and rust consume and thieves can break in. He tells his listeners not to be anxious about drink or food or clothing. How can the poor not be anxious about their hunger? Admonition to shun anxiety must have sounded insane then, as it does now. Even if one is not desperate with poverty, illness stalks us, jobs are precarious, children and lovers are constantly vulnerable to danger. The earth itself moans when it is ravaged and trembles in the face of mass extinctions. The gospel shows itself to be particularly tender toward those who are weeping and mourning, and yet Jesus is as blithely indifferent to anxiety as he is to social hierarchies. We are challenged to evaluate our attachment to material goods. We would not be remiss to consider the way our own well-being is costly to others. This release from anxiety does not obviate ordinary needs or justice's call that we concern ourselves with others' needs. It invites us to inhabit these concerns differently, interweaving them with a practice of useless joy. Like Martha we "are anxious and troubled about many things" (Luke 10:41 RSV). But Mary has everything needful.

The news of incarnation announces the intimate nearness of the Divine Eros. This truth does not propel us outside history or even outside our domestic concerns. Incarnation places us right in the middle of the present, seeing that nirvana and samsara coincide, that heaven and earth are one taste. This simultaneity is not a place to go where there is no suffering. It is not another world, a place in the sky where all will be well. It is simply the way things are all the time. This is the fall: to be asleep and unaware of the beauty of the present moment. Jesus talks to people facing difficulty, frustration, unbearable compromises, and an implacable political structure. He talks to them about the beauty of birds in the air and flowers in the fields. Be like them: exist in the impermanence and precariousness of life radiant with beauty. Be a light to the world. Be light. Be Christ. Be the intersection of Divinity and humanity and see Christ in one another. Be like Christ with one another—eating and drinking, gluttons and drunkards (Matthew 11:29; Luke 7:37). As Bob Marley puts it: "Then we cook corn meal porridge, of which I'll share with you."[29] The emblem of our chief duty is a joyous meal in which our blind eyes have opened to one another's beauty.

The Incarnate One, upon returning from the harrowing of hell, does not make a lot of moral demands or give another inspiring speech or tell confusing parables. When Jesus wanders again among his friends after the upheaval of crucifixion, he asks: "Is there anything to eat?" No great moralism here, no miraculous pyrotechnics, just the pleasure of food and friends, pleasure, admittedly, in the midst of terror and grief. Eating and drinking is just the ordinary pleasure we take in one another. Eating and drinking together, we look directly at Christ. We see Christ in ordinary pleasures, in everything we do. The incarnation blesses ordinary sensual existence. The bodying forth of the Divine is ordinary life. When we hold our children, sweet smelling in our arms, we witness a beauty like that of the lilies. When we make love to our lover we have a taste of the ecstasy of nonduality, when ego-consciousness dissolves in union with

---

29. Bob Marley, "No Woman, No Cry."

another. The pleasure we take in a cup of tea, in whatever music moves us, in the delicious gift of not setting the alarm clock one morning are all prayers. When we abandon abuse and unkindness our bodies are instruments of joy: this is the ongoing incarnation of Erotic Divinity.

Our bodies are instruments of transformation and prayer whether we are doing yoga or trance dance or benefiting from a massage; whether we march in protest or tutor homeless gay youth. Christ moves through the cells of our bodies, unlocking the painful things we hold. When we find ways to pray with the body, we train ourselves for openness and bliss. On the cross, the incarnation shows us that no suffering can separate from the love of the Beloved. In Wisdom's eating and drinking, she shows us that pleasure too is prayer. The joy of healthy sensuality has a beauty to it that nothing in Solomon's temple can match. In this strange and hard world, joy is the most countercultural practice of the kingdom. From this joy the other practices grow naturally and spontaneously. Joy is a great, bushy, weedy mustard plant in which the birds of the air find a home. Compassion and truth and justice nest in our joy; they are protected and nourished there.

Barbara Holmes emphasizes the contemplative power of music, dance, and art to defy suffering and to move into a journey that overintellectualism can "reduce to ashes. The restoration of wonder is the beginning of the inward journey toward a God who people of faith aver is always waiting in the seeker's heart. For some the call to worship comes as joy spurts from jazz riffs, wonder thunders from tappers' feet, each riff and blues note is just slightly beyond our understanding. What a gift it is, this lack of understanding. Perhaps we are confounded so that we might always have much to contemplate."[30] To demand joy may seem insane, more insane even than wasting time by the road giving wildflowers a shout-out. But the upside-down world of the gospel is not only the reversal of symbols of power and social hierarchies. It is a kind of delirious, divine madness. To be fingered by joy in this world is to be a fool for Christ.

The practice of the gospel is to tell the truth: the truth about power, about suffering, the truth about the Bible and Christianity, and perhaps even more the truth about ourselves and our luminous lovemaking with the Divine Eros. We may not be privy to the unvarnished or total truth, but the practice of bearing the truth is a practice of the kingdom. When Divinity pours out on humanity it illuminates the world in a different way. The holy eroticism that delights in beauty flows toward a world that seems to do everything possible to mangle us. Gospel joy invites us into the truth of our beauty: our specific and individual beauty as well as the beauty emerging out of the interdependence of every living being. From this truth emerges the judgment against those institutions that defraud us of these beauties: patriarchy, racism, homophobia, socially generated poverty, totalizing consumer culture. But the gospel invites us to judge these

---

30. Holmes, *Joy Unspeakable*, 183.

things from its own, idiosyncratic, countercultural, illogical point of view. If we want justice we must become inflated by universal compassion. This compassion itself has as its deeper root joy.

Julian of Norwich saw the whole cosmos as a tiny hazelnut ready to fall into nothingness. It seemed too small to exist, but: "It lasts and always will, because God loves it."[31] Our sense of division is illusory: we are held in life as one inter-dependent whole, as infinitely various as the cosmos yet from another perspective as tiny as a hazelnut, held in existence by infinite and amoral divine love. Each of us is necessary to the full display of the beauty that vapors off the Divine Eros. Without the carnival of humanity, Christ's body is incomplete. We ourselves and the entire, unthinkably vast cosmos are less than a hazelnut, a breath. Our joy is to be a feather on the breath of this amoral, useless love.

The gospel is an easy yoke and a light burden (Matthew 11:30). It has no requirements, no conditions. It is as free and universal as sunshine. It is also impossibly difficult, more outrageously demanding than the most exacting asceticism: a joyous, compassionate delight in this world and all its difficult inhabitants. But our Beloved "does not use violent means to obtain what he desires."[32] We should not use violence against ourselves as we dance to the Beloved's piping on our poor, crippled legs or mourn with Mother Christ over all of her exiled children (Luke 7:32). The divine empire is entirely present, entirely perfect. Our mourning is blessed. Our despair is prayer. In these practices the extraordinary and ordinary are woven together. If we find ourselves confronted with disaster, personal, local, or worldwide, let us burn with compassion for every soul, for every burnt blade of grass. But let us even in hell remember the joy of loving Christ.

The disciples "disbelieved for joy." The "idle tale" of the women turned out to be true after all. Let joy be our practice, and from this priceless, worthless treasure may beauty and friendship flow.

31. Julian of Norwich, *Showings*, 183.
32. Irenaeus, *Against Heresies* 6.1.1.

Bibliography

Adams, Marilyn McCord. *Christ and Horrors: The Coherence of Christology*. Cambridge: Cambridge University Press, 2006.

Althaus-Reid, Marcella. *From Feminist Theology to Indecent Theology*. London: SCM Press, 1994.

————. *The Queer God*. London: Routledge, 2003.

————, ed. *Liberation Theology and Sexuality*. Hampshire, Eng.: Ashgate, 2006.

Armour, Ellen T., and Susan M. St. Ville, eds. *Bodily Citations: Religion and Judith Butler*. New York: Columbia University Press, 2006.

Athanasius. *The Life of Anthony and the Letter to Marcellinus*. Translated and introduced by Robert C. Gregg. Classics of Western Spirituality. New York: Paulist Press, 1980.

————. *On the Incarnation*. Translated and edited by a religious at CSMV. Cambridge: Cambridge University Press, 1944.

Barnes, Timothy D. *Athanasius and Constantius: Theology and Politics in the Constantinian Empire*. Cambridge, MA: Harvard University Press, 1993.

Barth, Karl. *The Epistle to the Romans*. Translated by Edwyn C. Hoskyns. Oxford: Oxford University Press, 1968.

Bonhoeffer, Dietrich. *Letters and Papers from Prison*. Edited by Eberhard Bethge. New edition. New York: Macmillan, 1971.

Borg, Marcus J., and John Dominic Crossan. *The First Christmas: What the Gospels Really Teach about Jesus's Birth*. New York: Harper One, 2007.

Bourgeault, Cynthia. *Centering Prayer and Inner Awakening*. Cambridge, MA: Cowley, 2004.

————. *Chanting the Psalms*. Boston: Shambhala, 2006.

————. *The Wisdom Jesus: Transforming Heart and Mind—A New Perspective on Christ and His Message*. Boston: Shambhala, 2008.

Brakke, David. *Athanasius and the Politics of Asceticism*. Oxford: Clarendon Press, 1995.

Brock, Rita Nakashima. *Journeys by Heart: A Christology of Erotic Power*. New York: Crossroad, 1988.

————, and Rebecca Ann Parker. *Saving Paradise: How Christianity Traded Love of This World for Crucifixion and Empire*. Boston: Beacon Press, 2008.

Brooten, Bernadette J. *Love between Women: Early Christian Responses to Female Homo-eroticism.* Chicago: University of Chicago Press, 1996.

Brother Lawrence. *The Practice of the Presence of God with Spiritual Maxims.* Grand Rapids: Baker Book House, 1967.

Brown, Peter. *The Body and Society: Men, Women, and Sexual Renunciation in Early Christianity.* New York: Columbia University Press, 1988.

———. *Power and Persuasion in Late Antiquity: Towards a Christian Empire.* Madison: University of Wisconsin Press, 1992.

Cameron, Averil. *Christianity and the Rhetoric of Empire: The Development of Christian Discourse.* Berkeley: University of California Press, 1991.

Cassian, John. *Conferences.* Translated by Colm Luibheid. Classics of Western Spirituality. New York: Paulist Press, 1985.

Chittister, Joan. *The Ten Commandments: Laws of the Heart.* Maryknoll, NY: Orbis, 2006.

Chu-Cong, Joseph. *The Contemplative Experience: Erotic Love and Spiritual Union.* New York: Crossroad, 1999.

Cleaver, Richard. *Know My Name: A Gay Liberation Theology.* Louisville: Westminster John Knox, 1995.

Cloke, Gillian. *This Female Man of God: Women and Spiritual Power in the Patristic Age, AD 350–450.* New York: Routledge, 1995.

Cobb, Michael. *God Hates Fags: The Rhetorics of Religious Violence.* New York: New York University Press, 2006.

Coleman, Monica A. *Making a Way Out of No Way.* Minneapolis: Fortress Press, 2008.

Copeland, M. Shawn. *Enfleshing Freedom: Body, Race, and Being.* Minneapolis: Fortress Press, 2010.

———"Theology at the Crossroads." Pages 97–107 in *Uncommon Faithfulness: The Black Catholic Experience.* Edited by M. Shawn Copeland. Maryknoll, NY: Orbis, 2009.

Crossan, John Dominic. *God and Empire: Jesus Against Rome, Then and Now.* San Francisco: HarperSanFrancisco, 2007.

———. *The Historical Jesus: The Life of a Mediterranean Jewish Peasant.* San Francisco: HarperSanFrancisco, 1991.

Dalai Lama. *How to Practice: The Way to a Meaningful Life.* Translated and edited by Jeffrey Hopkins. New York: Pocket Books, 2002.

Daniélou, Jean. *From Glory to Glory: Excerpts from Gregory of Nyssa's Mystical Writings.* Edited and translated by Herbert Musurillo. London: John Murray, 1961.

Denzey, Nicola. *The Bone Gatherers: The Lost Worlds of Early Christian Women.* Boston: Beacon, 2007.

Desikachar, T. K. V. *Health, Healing and Beyond: Yoga and the Living Tradition of Krishnamacharya.* New York: Aperture, 1998.

Devi, Indra. *Yoga for You.* Translated by Fundacion Indra Devi and David Lifszyc. Salt Lake City: Gibbs Smith, 2002.

Donne, John. *Complete English Poems of John Donne.* Edited by C. A. Patrides. London: Dent, 1985.

Douglas, Kelly Brown. *The Black Christ.* Maryknoll, NY: Orbis, 1994.

———. *Sexuality and the Black Church.* Maryknoll, NY: Orbis, 1999.

Drake, H. A. *Constantine and the Bishops: The Politics of Intolerance.* Baltimore: Johns Hopkins University Press, 2000.

Eck, Diana L. *Encountering God: A Spiritual Journey from Bozeman to Banaras.* Boston: Beacon, 1993.

Eckhart, Meister. *Meister Eckhart, from Whom God Hid Nothing: Sermons, Writings, and Sayings.* Edited by David O'Neal. Boston: Shambhala, 1996.

Ehrman, Bart D. *The Orthodox Corruption of Scripture: The Effect of Early Christological Controversies on the Text of the New Testament.* Oxford: Oxford University Press, 1993.

Ellison, Marvin M. *Erotic Justice: A Liberating Ethic of Sexuality.* Louisville: Westminster John Knox, 1996.

Elm, Susanna. *"Virgins of God": The Making of Asceticism in Late Antiquity.* Oxford: Clarendon Press. 1994.

Eriugena, John Scotus. *The Voice of the Eagle: The Heart of Celtic Christianity: John Scotus Eriugena's Homily on the Prologue to the Gospel of St. John.* Translated by Christopher Bamford. Great Barrington, MA: Lindisfarne Books, 2000.

Evagrius Ponticus. *The Praktikos; Chapters on Prayer.* Translated by John Eudes Bamberger. Kalamazoo, MI: Cistercian Publications, 1981.

Farley, Edward. *Divine Empathy: A Theology of God.* Minneapolis: Fortress Press, 1996.

———. *Ecclesial Reflection: An Anatomy of Theological Method.* Philadelphia: Fortress Press, 1982.

Finley, James. *Christian Meditation: Experiencing the Presence of God: A Guide to Contemplation.* San Francisco: HarperSanFrancisco, 2004.

Floyd-Thomas, Stacey M., ed. *Deeper Shades of Purple: Womanism in Religion and Society.* New York: New York University Press, 2006.

Forstman, Jack. *Christian Faith in Dark Times: Theological Conflicts in the Shadow of Hitler.* Louisville: Westminster/John Knox, 1992.

Frantz, Nadine Pence, and Mary T. Stimming. *Hope Deferred: Heart-healing Reflections on Reproductive Loss.* Cleveland: Pilgrim Press, 2005.

Fulkerson, Mary McClintock. *Places of Redemption: Theology for a Worldly Church.* Oxford: Oxford University Press, 2007.

Gaddis, Michael. *There Is No Crime for Those Who Have Christ: Religious Violence in the Christian Roman Empire.* Berkeley: University of California Press, 2005.

Goatley, David Emmanuel. *Were You There? Godforsakenness in Slave Religion.* Maryknoll, NY: Orbis, 1996.

Goss, Robert E. *Queering Christ: Beyond Jesus Acted Up.* Cleveland: Pilgrim Press, 2002.

———, and Mona West, eds. *Take Back the Word: A Queer Reading of the Bible.* Cleveland: Pilgrim Press, 2000.

Greene-McCreight, Kathryn. *Feminist Reconstructions of Christian Doctrine: Narrative Analysis and Appraisal.* New York: Oxford University Press, 2000.

Gregory of Nyssa. *The Great Catechism.* Pages 471–509 in *The Nicene and Post-Nicene Fathers,* Series 2. Vol. 5: *Gregory of Nyssa: Dogmatic Treatises, Etc.* Translated and edited by Philip Schaff and Henry Wace. Grand Rapids: Eerdmans, 1954.

———. *The Life of Moses.* Translated by Abraham J. Malherbe and Everett Ferguson. Classics of Western Spirituality. New York: Paulist Press, 1978.

Gregory Palamas. *The Triads.* Edited by John Meyendorff. Translated by Nicholas Gendle. Classics of Western Spirituality. New York: Paulist Press, 1983.

Griffin, Horace L. *Their Own Receive Them Not: African American Lesbians and Gays in Black Churches.* Cleveland: Pilgrim Press, 2006.

Habito, Ruben L. F., and John Keenan. *Living Zen, Loving God.* Boston: Wisdom Publications, 2004.

Hadewijch. *The Complete Works.* Translated by Mother Columba Hart, OSB. Classics of Western Spirituality. New York: Paulist Press, 1980.

Hadot, Pierre. *Philosophy as a Way of Life.* Edited with an introduction by Arnold I. Davidson. Translated by Michael Chase. Oxford: Blackwell, 1995.

Hafiz. *The Gift: Poems by Hafiz.* Translated by Daniel Ladinsky. London: Penguin Books, 1999.

Haight, Roger, S.J. *The Future of Christology.* New York: Continuum, 2007.

Hallie, Philip P. *Lest Innocent Blood Be Shed.* New York: Harper & Row, 1979.
Harrelson, Walter. J. *The Ten Commandments and Human Rights.* Macon, GA: Mercer University Press, 1997.
————. *The Ten Commandments for Today.* Louisville: Westminster John Knox, 2006.
Heschel, Abraham Joshua. *The Prophets.* New York: Harper & Row, 1962.
Heyward, Carter. *Speaking of Christ: A Lesbian Feminist Voice.* Cleveland: Pilgrim Press, 1989.
————. *Touching Our Strength: The Erotic as Power and the Love of God.* San Francisco: Harper & Row, 1989.
Hodgson, Peter C. *Liberal Theology: A Radical Vision.* Minneapolis: Fortress Press, 2007.
Hollywood, Amy. *The Soul as Virgin Wife: Mechthild of Magdeberg, Marguerite Porete, and Meister Eckhart.* Notre Dame: University of Notre Dame Press, 1995.
Holmes, Barbara Ann. *Joy Unspeakable: Contemplative Practices of the Black Church.* Minneapolis: Fortress Press, 2004.
Hopkins, Dwight. *Down, Up, and Over: Slave Religion and Black Theology.* Minneapolis: Fortress Press, 2000.
————. *Heart and Head: Black Theology—Past, Present, and Future.* New York: Palgrave, 2002.
————, and George C. L. Cummings. *Cut Loose Your Stammering Tongue: Black Theology in the Slave Narratives.* Louisville: Westminster John Knox, 2003.
Horsley, Richard A. *The Liberation of Christmas: The Infancy Narratives in Social Context.* New York: Crossroad, 1989.
Irenaeus. *Against Heresies.* Pages 309–567 in *The Ante-Nicene Fathers.* Vol. 1: *The Apostolic Fathers—Justin Martyr—Irenaeus.* Edited by Alexander Roberts and James Donaldson. 1885. Reprint, Grand Rapids: Eerdmans, 1973.
Irigaray, Luce. *Sexes and Genealogies.* Translated by Gillian C. Gill. New York: Columbia University Press, 1993.
Isaac of Nineveh. *On Ascetical Life.* Translated by Mary Hansbury. Crestwood, NY: St. Vladimir's Seminary Press, 1989.
Isasi-Díaz, Ada María. *Mujerista Theology: A Theology for the Twenty-first Century.* Maryknoll, NY: Orbis, 1996.
Jantzen, Grace. *Becoming Divine: Towards a Feminist Philosophy of Religion.* Bloomington: Indiana University Press, 1999.
————. *God's World, God's Body.* Philadelphia: Westminster, 1984.
Jensen, David H. *Responsive Labor: A Theology of Work.* Louisville: Westminster John Knox, 2006.
Johnson, Elizabeth A. *Quest for the Living God: Mapping Frontiers in the Theology of God.* New York: Continuum, 2007.
————. *She Who Is: The Mystery of God in Feminist Theological Discourse.* 10th anniversary edition. New York: Crossroad, 2002.
Jones, Serene. *Feminist Theory and Christian Theology: Cartographies of Grace.* Minneapolis: Fortress Press, 2000.
————. "Rupture." Pages 47–65 in *Hope Deferred: Heart-Healing Reflections on Reproductive Loss.* Edited by Nadine Pence Frantz and Mary T. Stimming. Cleveland: Pilgrim Press, 2005.
Jones, William R. *Is God a White Racist? A Preamble to Black Theology.* Garden City, NY: Anchor Press, 1973.
Jordan, Mark. *The Ethics of Sex.* Oxford: Blackwell, 2002.
Julian of Norwich. *Showings.* Translated by Edmund Colledge, OSA, and James Walsh, SJ. Classics of Western Spirituality. New York: Paulist Press, 1978.
Keating, Thomas. *Invitation to Love: The Way of Christian Contemplation.* Rockport, MA: Element, 1992.

———. *Open Mind, Open Heart: The Contemplative Dimension of the Gospel.* New York: Continuum, 2001.

Keller, Catherine. *Face of the Deep: A Theology of Becoming.* New York: Routledge, 2003.

King, Karen. *The Gospel of Mary of Magdala: Jesus and the First Woman Apostle.* Santa Rosa, CA: Polebridge Press, 2003.

———. *The Secret Revelation of John.* Cambridge, MA: Harvard University Press, 2006.

Knitter, Paul. *Without Buddha I Could Not Be a Christian.* New York: Oneworld Publications, 2009.

Lanzetta, Beverly. *Radical Wisdom: A Feminist Mystical Theology.* Minneapolis: Fortress Press, 2005.

Lewis, Thomas, Fari Amini, and Richard Lannon. *A General Theory of Love.* New York: Random House, 2000.

Loughlin, Gerard. *Alien Sex: The Body and Desire in Cinema and Theology.* Oxford: Blackwell, 2004.

———, ed. *Queer Theology: Rethinking the Western Body.* Oxford: Blackwell, 2007.

Lüdemann, Gerd. *Heretics: The Other Side of Early Christianity.* Louisville: Westminster John Knox, 1996.

Lyman, Rebecca. "Athanasius of Alexandria." Pages 63–78 in *Empire and the Christian Tradition: New Readings of Classical Theologians.* Edited by Kwok Pui-lan, Don H. Compier, and Joerg Rieger. Minneapolis: Fortress Press, 2007.

McDougal, Joy Ann. *Pilgrimage of Love: Moltmann on the Trinity and Christian Life.* Oxford: Oxford University Press, 2005.

McFague, Sallie. *Metaphorical Theology: Models of God in Religious Language.* Philadelphia: Fortress Press, 1982.

———. *A New Climate for Theology: God, the World, and Global Warming.* Minneapolis: Fortress Press, 2008.

McFarland, Ian A. *The Divine Image: Envisioning the Invisible God.* Minneapolis: Fortress Press, 2005.

McKim, Donald K., ed. *Calvin's Institutes: Abridged Edition.* Louisville: Westminster John Knox, 2001.

Meadow, Mary Jo, Kevin Culligan, and Daniel Chowning. *Christian Insight Meditation: Following in the Footsteps of John of the Cross.* Edited by Mary Jo Meadow. Boston: Wisdom Publications, 2007.

Mechthild of Magdeburg. *The Flowing Light of the Godhead.* Translated by Frank Tobin. Classics of Western Spirituality. New York: Paulist Press, 1998.

Merrill, Nan C. *Lumen Christi—Holy Wisdom: Journey to Awakening.* New York: Continuum, 2002.

———. *Psalms for Praying: An Invitation to Wholeness.* New York: Continuum, 2005.

Milavec, Aaron. *The Didache: Text, Translation, Analysis, and Commentary.* Collegeville, MN: Liturgical Press, 2003.

Miller, Vincent J. *Consuming Religion: Christian Faith and Practice in a Consumer Culture.* New York: Continuum, 2005.

Mollenkott, Virginia. *Divine Feminine: The Biblical Imagery of God as Female.* New York: Crossroad, 1983.

Moore, Mary Elizabeth. *Ministering with the Earth.* St. Louis: Chalice Press, 1998.

Mount Shoop, Marcia W. *Let the Bones Dance: Embodiment and the Body of Christ.* Louisville: Westminster John Knox, 2010.

Nelson-Pallmeyer, Jack. *Is Religion Killing Us? Violence in the Bible and the Quran.* Harrisburg: Trinity Press International, 2003.

Newell, J. Philip. *Christ of the Celts: The Healing of Creation.* San Francisco: Jossey-Bass, 2008.

Newman, John W. *Disciplines of Attention: Buddhist Insight Meditation, the Ignatian Spiritual Exercises, and Classical Psychoanalysis.* New York: P. Lang, 1996.

Nicholas of Cusa. *Selected Spiritual Writings.* Translated by H. Lawrence Bond. Classics of Western Spirituality. New York: Paulist Press, 1997.

Niebuhr, H. Richard. *Radical Monotheism and Western Culture, with Supplementary Essays.* New York: Harper, 1960.

Nomura, Yushi, trans. *Desert Wisdom: Sayings from the Desert Fathers.* Revised edition. Maryknoll, NY: Orbis, 2001.

Nugent, Robert, ed. *A Challenge to Love: Gay and Lesbian Catholics in the Church.* New York: Crossroad, 1984.

O'Connor, Flannery. *The Complete Stories.* New York: Farrar, Straus, and Giroux, 1971.

Oduyoye, Mercy Amba. *Introducing African Women's Theology.* Cleveland: Pilgrim Press, 2001.

Origen. *On First Principles.* Introduced by Henri de Lubac. Translated by G. W. Butterworth. Gloucester, MA: Peter Smith, 1973.

———. *The Song of Songs: Commentary and Homilies.* Translated and annotated by R. P. Lawson. Ancient Christian Writers 26. Westminster, MD: Newman Press, 1957.

Pagels, Elaine. *Beyond Belief: The Secret Gospel of Thomas.* New York: Random House, 2003.

———. *The Origin of Satan.* New York: Random House, 1995.

Paulsell, Stephanie. *Honoring the Body: Meditations on a Christian Practice.* San Francisco: Jossey-Bass, 2002.

Pelagius. "On the Christian Life." Pages 379–404 in *Celtic Spirituality.* Translated by Oliver Davies. Classics of Western Spirituality. New York: Paulist Press, 1999.

Pennington, M. Basil. *Centering Prayer: Renewing an Ancient Christian Prayer Form.* Garden City, NY: Doubleday, 1980.

Plantinga Pauw, Amy, ed. *Feminist and Womanist Essays in Reformed Dogmatics.* Louisville: Westminster John Knox, 2006.

Plotinus. *Enneads.* Translated by A. H. Armstrong. Loeb Classical Library. 7 vols. Cambridge, MA: Harvard University Press, 1966–1988.

Porete, Marguerite. *The Mirror of Simple Souls.* Translated by Ellen L. Babinsky. Classics of Western Spirituality. Mahwah, NJ: Paulist Press, 1993.

Pseudo-Dionysius. *The Complete Works.* Translated by Colm Luibheid. Classics of Western Spirituality. Mahway, NJ: Paulist Press, 1987.

Pui-lan, Kwok, Don H. Compier, and Joerg Rieger, eds. *Empire and the Christian Tradition: New Readings of Classical Theologians.* Minneapolis: Fortress Press, 2007.

Raguin, Yves. *Paths to Contemplation.* St. Meinrad, IN: Abbey, 1974.

Rahner, Karl. *Foundations of Christian Faith: An Introduction to the Idea of Christianity.* Translated by William V. Dych. New York: Seabury, 1978.

Ray, Darby Kathleen. *Deceiving the Devil: Atonement, Abuse, and Ransom.* Cleveland: Pilgrim Press, 1998.

———. *Incarnation and Imagination: A Christian Ethic of Ingenuity.* Minneapolis: Fortress Press, 2008.

Reid, Barbara E. *Taking Up the Cross: New Testament Interpretations through Latina and Feminist Eyes.* Minneapolis: Fortress Press, 2007.

Rieger, Joerg. *Christ and Empire: From Paul to Postcolonial Times.* Minneapolis: Fortress Press, 2007.

———. *No Rising Tide: Theology, Economics, and the Future.* Minneapolis: Fortress Press, 2009.

Rivera, Mayra. *The Touch of Transcendence: A Postcolonial Theology of God.* Louisville: Westminster John Knox, 2007.

Robinson, James M. *Nag Hammadi: The First Fifty Years*. Claremont, CA: Institute for Antiquity and Christianity, 1995.

———, ed. *The Nag Hammadi Library in English*. 3rd ed. San Francisco: HarperSan-Francisco, 1988.

Rogers, Eugene F., Jr. *Sexuality and the Christian Body*. Oxford: Blackwell, 1999.

Rubenstein, Richard L. *After Auschwitz*. Indianapolis: Bobbs-Merrill, 1966.

Sanders, E. P. *The Historical Figure of Jesus*. London: Allen Lane, 1993.

Sawicki, Marianne. *Crossing Galilee: Architectures of Contact in the Occupied Land of Jesus*. Harrisburg: Trinity Press International, 2000.

Schaberg, Jane. *The Illegitimacy of Jesus: A Feminist Theological Interpretation of the Infancy Narratives*. San Francisco: Harper & Row, 1987.

Schleiermacher, Friedrich. *Christian Faith*. Edited by H. R. Mackintosh and J. S. Stewart. Reprint, Philadelphia: Fortress Press, 1978.

———. *Christmas Eve: Dialogue on the Incarnation*. Translated by Terrence N. Tice. Reprint, San Francisco: Edwin Mellen Press, 1990.

———. *On Religion: Speeches to Its Cultured Despisers*. Translated by John Oman. Louisville: Westminster John Knox, 1994.

Schneider, Laurel C. *Beyond Monotheism: A Theology of Multiplicity*. New York: Routledge, 2008.

Segundo, Juan Luis. *The Historical Jesus of the Synoptics*. Translated by J. Drury. Maryknoll, NY: Orbis, 1985.

Soelle, Dorothee. *Suffering*. Translated by Everett R. Kalin. Philadelphia: Fortress Press, 1975.

Spencer, Daniel T. *Gay and Gaia: Ethics, Ecology, and the Erotic*. Cleveland: Pilgrim Press, 1996.

Spong, John Shelby. *The Living Commandments*. Haworth, NJ: Christianity for the Third Millennium and St. Johann Press, 2000.

———, and Denise G. Haines. *Beyond Moralism: A Contemporary View of the Ten Commandments*. 1986. Reprint, Haworth, NJ: Christianity for the Third Millennium and St. Johann Press, 2000.

Stalnaker, Aaron. *Overcoming Our Evil: Human Nature and Spiritual Exercises in Xunzi and Augustine*. Washington, DC: Georgetown University Press, 2006.

Stone, Ken. *Practicing Safer Texts: Food, Sex, and Bible in Queer Perspective*. New York: T & T Clark International, 2005.

Stuart, Elizabeth. *Daring to Speak Love's Name: A Gay and Lesbian Prayer Book*. London: Hamish Hamilton, 1992.

———. *Gay and Lesbian Theologies*. Hampshire, Eng.: Ashgate, 2003.

———. *Spitting at Dragons: Towards a Feminist Theology of Sainthood*. London: Mowbray, 1997.

Sullivan, Nikki. *A Critical Introduction to Queer Theory*. New York: New York University Press, 2003.

Teilhard de Chardin, Pierre. *The Heart of Matter*. Translated by René Hague. New York: Harcourt Brace Jovanovich, 1978.

———. *Letters from a Traveller*. Translated by René Hague, Violet Hammersley, Barbara Wall, and Noel Lindsay. Edited by Bernard Wall. New York: Harper & Row, 1962.

Terrell, JoAnne Marie. *Power in the Blood? The Cross in African American Experience*. Maryknoll, NY: Orbis, 1998.

Tillich, Paul. *The Essential Tillich: An Anthology of the Writings of Paul Tillich*. Edited by F. Forrester Church. New York: Collier, 1988.

———. *A History of Christian Thought*. Edited by Carl E. Braaten. New York: Harper & Row, 1968.

————. *Systematic Theology.* Volume 3: *Life and the Spirit: History and the Kingdom of God.* Chicago: University of Chicago Press, 1963.

Tolbert, Mary Ann. *Sowing the Gospel: Mark's World in Literary-Historical Perspective.* Minneapolis: Fortress Press, 1989.

Torjesen, Karen Jo. *When Women Were Priests: Women's Leadership in the Early Church and the Scandal of Their Subordination in the Rise of Christianity.* San Francisco: HarperSanFrancisco, 1993.

Townes, Emilie M. *In a Blaze of Glory: Womanist Spirituality as Social Witness.* Nashville: Abingdon, 1995.

Valantasis, Richard. *The Making of the Self: Ancient and Modern Asceticism.* Eugene, OR: Cascade Books, 2008.

Wallace, B. Alan. *Mind in the Balance: Meditation in Science, Buddhism, and Christianity.* New York: Columbia University Press, 2009.

Weil, Simone. *Waiting for God.* New York: Harper & Row, 1973.

Welch, Sharon D. *A Feminist Ethic of Risk.* Minneapolis: Fortress Press, 1990.

Whitehead, Alfred North. *Modes of Thought.* New York: Free Press, 1968.

————. *Process and Reality: An Essay in Cosmology.* New York: Macmillan, 1929.

Williams, Delores S. *Sisters in the Wilderness: The Challenge of Womanist God-talk.* Maryknoll, NY: Orbis, 1993.

Williams, Rowan. *Arius: Heresy and Tradition.* Revised edition. Grand Rapids: Eerdmans, 2001.

Yeats, William Butler. *The Poems of W. B. Yeats: A Sourcebook.* Edited by Michael O'Neill. London: Routledge, 2004.

Index

Adams, Marilyn McCord, 58, 132, 158n10, 164
affliction, 156–8, 162, 164, 183, 194–5, 206
Alexander, Bishop of Alexandria, 21–23
Alison, James, 98
Alliaume, Karen Trimble, 100–101
Althaus-Reid, Marcella, 8, 38, 55, 139, 151, 182, 187
apophasis, 39, 78, 83, 90–1, 112, 115, 123, 148, 162, 169, 180, 205
Apostles' Creed, 149
Arianism, 12, 27
Arius, 21–24, 26–28, 34
asceticism, 173–5
Athanasius, 18, 19, 21–34, 165, 170, 172
Atonement, 12, 156–9
Augustine, 46, 51, 61, 68

Barnes, Timothy, 23n18, 27n38, 30n50 and 51
Barth, Karl, 42, 69, 84n60, 131n35
Blandina, 153
Body of Christ, 1, 5, 6, 10, 13, 16, 38, 225
Borg, Marcus, 192n11
Bourgeault, Cynthia, 28, 96–7, 103, 105, 106n49
Brakke, David, 21n12, 2n14 and 15, 23n21, 24n27, 25n29 and 31, 29n45 and 47, 30n48, 32n58, 172
Brock, Rita Nakashima, 158n10
Brown, Peter, 21n11, 25n29 and 31, 27n36, 30n51, 172, 174n17, 197

Buddha, 154
Buddhism, 104–6, 216, 217n18, 220
Burrus, Virginia, 105n49
Butler, Judith, 101, 12n65

Calvin, John, 38, 41
Canon, Katie, 141n22
Chalcedonian Creed, 115, 146
Chillemi, Nicole, 104n47
Chittister, Joan, 53n36
Cho, Min-Ah 15
Chodron, Pema, 106n49
Christa, 182, 185
Chu-Cong, Joseph, 106n49
Cleaver, Richard, 38n4, 55, 140
Clement of Alexandria, 172
Cobb, Michael, 4, 45n11
Colbert, Stephen, 206
Coleman, Monica, 8, 140–1, 182
Compier, Don, 20n7
consumerism, 207–8
contemplation, 116, 89–114, 124, 156, 172–5, 177, 224
Constantine, 19, 20, 23–27, 53, 189
Cooder, Ry, 137n10
Copeland, Shawn, 1, 153, 187, 193, 201
Council of Nicaea, 19, 20, 27, 135, 148
Council of Chalcedon, 148 (*see also* Chalcedonian Creed)
Creation, 7, 12, 53, 74, 83, 85, 117, 123–9, 173, 177, 184–5, 187, 222
cross, 154–6, 159, 163–6, 224

235